Beginning literary animal studies

Manchester University Press

Beginnings
Series editor: William Hughes

'Beginnings' is a series of books designed to give practical help to students beginning to tackle recent developments in English, Literary Studies and Cultural Studies. The books in the series

- demonstrate and encourage a questioning engagement with the new;
- give essential information about the context and history of each topic covered;
- show how to develop a practice which is up-to-date and informed by theory.

Each book focuses uncompromisingly upon the needs of its readers, who have the right to expect clarity to be the distinctive feature of a book which includes the word 'beginning' in its title.

Each aims to lay a firm foundation of well understood initial principles as a basis for further study and is committed to explaining new aspects of the discipline without over-simplification, but in a manner appropriate to the needs of beginners.

Each book, finally, aims to be both an introduction and a contribution to the topic area it discusses.

To buy or to find out more about the books currently available in this series, please go to: https://manchesteruniversitypress.co.uk/series/beginnings/

Beginning literary animal studies

William Welstead

MANCHESTER UNIVERSITY PRESS

Published by Manchester University Press
Oxford Road, Manchester, M13 9PL

www.manchesteruniversitypress.co.uk

British Library Cataloguing-in-Publication Data
A catalogue record for this book is available from the British Library

ISBN 978 1 8070 7227 8 hardback
ISBN 978 1 8070 7228 5 paperback

First published 2026

Typeset
by New Best-set Typesetters Ltd

Contents

Acknowledgements

I am very grateful for the help I have received as I wrote this book and prepared it for publication. I owe a particular debt to Peter Barry for encouraging me to develop my first idea into a proposal and for his continuing advice, and to Matthew Frost for picking up the formal proposal. The two anonymous readers of that proposal gave me valuable advice about the scope of the book. I would like to thank Michelle Houston and Bill Hughes for progressing the book once a draft was completed. The two anonymous readers of the complete draft, who were meticulous in their task, provided me with many detailed and very helpful suggestions for improvement. I would like to thank them for their diligence, and for sharing my view that literary animal studies is an important topic. I am particularly grateful to Rachel Evans for her careful editing. I have found 'animals good to think with'. Much of that thinking has been in the company of our Labrador retrievers, Barley and Taran, who have completely different ideas about what they want out of a walk. Finally I thank my wife Moira for her support and for joining me in paying attention to the nonhuman world.

Introduction

Literary human–animal studies is a relatively new discipline that has many different points of entry, theoretical viewpoints, academic principles and end applications. This book lays the foundations for the critical study of creative literature that brings nonhuman animals into focus. The scope of this book covers the different names that have been given to the 'animal turn' in the humanities: animal studies, human–animal studies, studies of humans and other animals, and animals and society. All have shortcomings, and in naming these literary studies of creative works that concern both human and other animals, I adopt the shorthand 'literary animal studies' or sometimes just 'animal studies'. Humans are included as animals in this terminology, but it is other animals or nonhuman animals that are the focus of this work. I have adopted the shorthand 'nonhuman' rather than 'other than human' as being more convenient. Broadly speaking, the turn to animals reflects the move away from liberal humanism, which has dominated literary criticism, towards a more posthuman framework. It is important to stress that posthumanism, in 'drawing attention to the primacy of nonhuman influences in formative processes [should not be seen as] expressing a lack of concern or care for humans' (Braidotti and Bignall, 2019: 2). The posthuman paradigm introduces new values and ways of relating across the species boundary that are outside the human sphere of influence, but do not discount it (Braidotti and Bignall, 2019: 2).

The discipline of literary animal studies is closely related to ecocriticism, which became established in the humanities following the 1992 UN Earth Summit in Rio de Janeiro. The three conventions that followed – on biological diversity, climate change, and environment and development – inform the background texts in ecocriticism that are read with and against works in the humanities. Human–animal studies became established in the social sciences following the debate around the legal rights of animals and humans' moral responsibility towards them. The animal turn in the humanities came later. While ecocriticism engages with the systems thinking that is the basis for ecology, literary animal studies has its focus on the subjectivity of the individual animal, with agency and sentience. It is this difference that makes literary animal studies a separate discipline. This book explores the overlap and interaction between literary animal studies and ecocriticism. It also draws on this wider field of animal studies in the humanities and the social sciences, and engages with direct conversations between literary studies and the natural sciences. The spread of disciplines consulted by literary animal studies is very wide. It includes discourses in biology, genetics, taxonomy, ecology, ethology, neuroscience, psychology, ethnography, sociology, philosophy, anthropology, economics and political studies. For McFarland, the intersections between these disciplines are investigated 'in order to articulate how notions of species operate and how nonhuman animals signify and are signified in human lives and cultures' (McFarland, 2010). No one person can be an expert in this wide range of disciplines. Literary animal studies owes a particular debt to thinking about humans and other animals in the social sciences and philosophy.

Allowing animals to have subject status in the critical analysis of literary texts is a political statement; but where possible I have tried to avoid taking an ideological position at the exclusion of other standpoints. It should be recognised that political pressures are also at work in knowledge production, including in some of the disciplines that must be consulted in an animal studies reading of literary works. In this book I use the term 'animal studies reading' for a critical reading of texts from an animal studies viewpoint. The very complexity of these issues, and the exposure it brings to unfamiliar ideas, is a challenge for students of literary animal studies, but will be welcomed by those who enjoy the stimulation that flows from engaging with other ways of thinking.

The structure of this book reflects the different starting and end points for animal studies. It is not necessary to read chapters in sequence. They should be seen as a repository of the ideas that have provoked the 'animal turn' and that sustain its discussion across the humanities. The first two chapters summarise the ideas that inform literary animal studies, flowing from initial thinking in classical times to various points of inflexion where a change of emphasis took place. There is no single method or discipline in literary animal studies, rather there is a bundle of ways of looking at nonhuman animals in literary texts, some parts of which will be useful and others irrelevant. The last seven chapters each take a theme from this bundle and use it to develop ideas that are useful in literary animal studies. Each chapter also focuses on a particular literary genre across a range from creative non-fiction, poetry and fiction. There is some progression of ideas through the chapters, but each can be read in isolation; previous introduction of ideas is signposted or can be referred to using the index. Each chapter includes suggestions for further reading.

In the first chapter, the development of ideas about humans and their relationship with nonhuman animals is explored. This very brief history of the body of knowledge that literary animal studies engages with begins with classical writers such as Aristotle, Pliny the Elder and Virgil, but accepts that these writers were building on a rich oral culture that is lost to the record. The chapter follows a historical framework with the emphasis on points of inflexion where there was a shift in thinking about animals, from St Thomas Aquinas to René Descartes, showing how advances in theoretical rigour sometimes brought dogmatism around the exceptional qualities of humans. Confronting such dogmatism is an essential precondition for a posthuman reading of literary texts. The contributions of evolutionary biologists in understanding what a species is, and of ethologists in exposing how animals have capabilities that were thought exclusive to *Homo sapiens*, has helped to challenge the human claim to exceptionalism. Further research in neuroscience has shown that even animals with a distributed nervous system can be sentient, and should be accorded subject status in discourse about humans and other animals. This field is developing all the time, which opens the possibility of new insights that will inform an animal studies reading of literary texts.

In chapter 2 the various strands that contribute to literary animal studies are unpicked and the contribution that each theme can make is discussed. The chapter introduces the concept of posthumanism, which rejects the idea that it is only humans that have subjectivity and agency. The early move towards animal welfare was mainly directed at domesticated animals for which humans have a duty of care. It was later extended to include those wild animals that we interact with, take for eating, kill as pests or pursue for sport. The species that are deserving of this care has widened considerably, as insights from neuroscience have shown that even the most unlikely species may have sentience and be able to experience pain. The chapter introduces arguments based on the material reality of animals determined solely by their biology and a social science model in which the meaning of animals is socially constructed. Claimed by some as the pivotal moment in the animal turn, the extension of arguments based on the rights of marginalised humans to animals, brings with it an obligation to listen to what animals want, rather than assume that it is some subset of what humans would want. Moving from rights to relations, the concept of kinship between species and the acceptance that there will always be complexity in a multispecies world, introduces yet another way of reading animals in literary texts. All of these are examples of posthumanism, but to make progress they need to confront the human exceptionalism that is embedded in the liberal humanism that has until now played a major part in literary criticism. Some texts, particularly in speculative and science fiction, look to a world in which humans themselves are threatened with extinction. The chapter concludes with a list of tenets that should inform an animal studies reading of literary texts. These are offered as a way to get started in literary animal studies.

Chapter 3 introduces the concept of posthumanism developed by Cary Wolfe and others. Taking as examples texts in literary non-fiction, the chapter considers Wolfe's departure from the dominant liberal humanism of literary studies. His stress on the importance of understanding the biopolitical context of writing is applied to an examination of J. A. Baker's *The Peregrine*, claimed as the gold standard in nature writing. Nature writing is a popular but rather vague term. Many of the texts gathered under this term, including Baker's *The Peregrine*, could be described as animal writing and therefore within the scope of literary animal studies. Wolfe suggests that we should take account of the context of a literary work. Baker's book came at a time of rapid expansion in amateur and professional ornithology after the Second World War. This expansion in fact started before the war, with some ornithologists diverted to war work and others held as prisoners of war. The latter continued their watching from within the confines of the camp and all were to play a major role in ornithology's growth after the war. Critical reception of *The Peregrine* has focused on whether or not Baker was able to overcome the subject/object gap. This discussion exposes how difficult it is to achieve this move towards a truly posthuman approach. The process is also explored by which *The Peregrine* has been admitted to the nature writing canon.

Chapter 4 raises the issue of the intersection between feminism and animal studies, drawing in particular on writing by the Australian philosopher Val Plumwood. She finds that discourse about the natural world is dominated by a phallocentric 'master narrative'. She also warns that the supposed closeness of women to nonhuman animals brings with it yet another opportunity to marginalise female writers. Women such as Jane Goodall, Biruté Galdikas and Dian Fossey have made outstanding contributions to our understanding of the capability of animals, which falsify any assumption that they are machines whose behaviour is determined by instinct. Len Howard was one writer who went out of her way to break down the subject/object gap by allowing wild birds to come and go freely into her home, to work with them as collaborators in her research on individual personality and learning behaviour. The tendency of men to dismiss such research and to explain nature to women is examined in the context of Jasmine Donahaye's concept of 'birdsplaining'. The chapter also considers how intersectionality can invoke other oppressed groups, and how that could link academic enquiry with activism. Such a research paradigm is termed 'critical animal studies'. As each new theme is introduced, so is the complexity of the analysis in which the different interests have conflicting objectives. Haraway suggests this complexity should be approached through tentacular thinking using string figures.

Chapter 5 considers the contribution to literary animal studies from Bruno Latour's concept of actor–network theory (ANT). Developed as a way of reimagining the social by admitting nonhuman and even inanimate actants, ANT offers a way to move forward in a posthuman reading of literary texts. Taking its cue from an anecdote by Latour, in which he was interrupted from repairing at the end of the day to the Beaver pub in the London School of Economics, the first example considered is a chapter of nature writing on the reintroduction of the beaver to British rivers. The beaver is a celebrity in ecological circles for its ability to rewild the landscape. It was selected as the emblem for LSE for being social, hardworking and good at problem-solving, all qualities that were aimed for in the college's students. ANT works well alongside ecology, but it also admits all the networks needed to make things happen, from the sourcing of beavers, to the collaboration between scientists, landowners and government bodies. The part that affect has in gaining public acceptance would be overlooked in purely science-based ecology. The second case study is the writing by a farmer in Cumbria as he struggles to farm sustainably using traditional breeds and methods. He came to understand the importance of the soil if he was to avoid high inputs of artificial fertiliser and pesticides. Soil, together with its worms and other organisms, become actants in ANT. Above all, this chapter discusses the constantly changing relationship between actants, some whose effect is only fleeting.

Allowing animals to speak demands that we play close attention to the nuances and context of their behaviour in a multispecies world. Chapter 6 introduces the concept of attentiveness in animal studies in order to read it alongside the poetic imagination in the creative process. Close attention allows the individual animal to express its subjectivity, not all of which would register in a data-driven scientific method. The human experience of another species' subjectivity opens the way for the poet to develop new insights and meanings. Further changes occur as the reader brings their own creativity to find new meaning in the text. A case study considers two well-known poems: Yeats's 'Wild Swans at Coole' and Heaney's 'Postscript'. Both were assigned to a particular species in an anthology of bird poems. It seems this attribution to a species might be wrong; allowing for uncertainty about the taxonomy gives the reader scope to explore how meanings might change over time. From Coleridge onwards, there was a nervousness that close attention could result in mimesis. The chapter addresses whether there are circumstances where mimesis can help in a posthuman reading to close the subject/object gap. Not all people see things in the same way. The same is true of individuals in a nonhuman species. Neuroscience is directing attention to the way imagination works in creative processes and how it differs between neurotypical and neurodivergent people. Turning attention to physical processes introduces the embodiment that some people feel as they allow their body to respond when fully attentive to nonhuman others.

Chapter 7 turns its attention to the role of affect and empathy in literary fiction. In defining the terms, it notes that 'affect' had been claimed as one of invisible behaviours in behaviourist psychology. The chapter also defines empathy and sympathy as feelings that a human can have for a nonhuman other. It discusses examples of empathy in fiction and shows how this term has been applied in literary animal studies, taking the example of Sewell's *Black Beauty* and Stevenson's treatment of his donkey in his *Travels in the Cévennes with a Donkey*. The way that Hardy deployed empathy in his rural novels is used to compare how he constructs his human characters and their animal charges. For domestic animals, the chapter raises the dissonance between showing empathy for individual animals during their life, when at their end they will be sent to slaughter. It questions the feasibility and moral acceptability of using the power of literature to develop empathy.

In chapter 8, priority is given to listening closely to Indigenous voices, particularly where they might be better able to recognise the animal subject in its environment, with sentience and agency. The chapter looks at the intersections between postcolonial narratives and literary animal studies. It asks whether it is helpful to consider the two forms of othering as being related, or does it introduce new ways to avoid allowing animals to become the subject in a narrative. The chapter introduces the two-way transfer of species after Columbus, which introduced domesticated species to the Americas, along with diseases against which the Indigenous people had no immunity. The Africans taken enslaved during colonisation were bought with animals, and treated as livestock. The distinctive African American thinking about animals is introduced. Taking case studies from the Diné and Chickasaw people, the chapter discusses how sheep and horses, which the colonisers had expected to act as a civilising influence, were integrated into these peoples' ways of seeing and living with animals. A further example shows how the reintroduction of locally extinct species can serve as proxies for settler colonialism to marginalise pastoralists and take over their land. Given its debt to western thought and nature conservation regimes, literary animal studies must also be cross-examined to ensure that it is itself decolonised, before it is brought into intersection with postcolonial and decolonial studies.

Chapter 9 examines the new field of extinction studies, to assess its relevance for animal studies. There is widespread support for the proposition that we are facing a sixth mass extinction event but, unlike the other five this one is caused, or at least accelerated, by human activities. It is species that become extinct, but it is individual animals that die during the extinction process. It is claimed that extinction studies can bridge the divide between ecocriticism's concern for biodiversity loss and animal studies' concern for the individual animal. Even rapid extinction can be happening without it being evident in the short term. The concept of shifting baseline syndrome is used to understand how each generation sets its baseline for biodiversity from their own early experience of the natural world. The application of animal studies is examined for texts that address extinction, and for speculative fiction, that imagines a world where humans have lost their dominance. Shifting baseline syndrome is used to address the loss of cultural diversity where the everyday imagery of, and local cultural referents to, a species is lost.

References

Braidotti, Rosi and Bignall, Simone (2019) *Posthuman Ecologies: Complexity and Process after Deleuze*. London: Rowman & Littlefield.

McFarland, Sarah E. (2010) '"The animal" is a verb: liberating the subject of animal studies', *JAC* 30:3–4, pp. 813–23.

1 Animal studies, a brief history

The animal turn in the humanities is based on two important claims of truth: *Homo sapiens* is an animal that shares many common features with nonhuman animals, and while each species of animal is different, there are no grounds for raising the moral standing of any one species over any other. Some might qualify this claim, for example, by suggesting that only those animals with sentience and the ability to feel pain are worthy of moral standing. Such qualities are important, but all animals have the capacity to surprise us and stir our imagination. This chapter gives a historical overview of how thinking has changed over time, about the animality of humans, their relationship with other animals and why thinking about animals has become important. Any introductory text in animal studies should carry the warning, 'this will get complicated'. The challenge is to find ways of understanding this complexity without denying that our relationship with all other living things is too complex for any one theory or way of thinking to tell the whole story. This chapter is a brief historical overview of the changing relationship that *Homo sapiens* has had with other animals, in a material sense, as expressed in narrative and as explored through academic enquiry.

Since the evolution of our own species, we have lived in close proximity with other animals, some threatening, others a potential meal. In between these extremes are many other species that might have symbolic importance. Narrative story-telling has its origins in prehistory, but in this historical overview we also see the development of specialised ways of looking at animals in philosophy, biology, ethology, ethnology and cultural studies.

Animal narratives in prehistory

The history of art is outside the scope of this book; however, the evidence that artistic representation extends well into pre-history is an indication that animals were central to the culture of *Homo sapiens* at least 40,000 years before the present day. The skill of early humans in representing animals is impressive; further, at least some of this very early art has a clear narrative form. The earliest dated representational images made by anatomically modern humans have been found in Sulawesi. These images, dated from 45,500 years ago, are recognisable as portraying a hunt of a species of warty pigs (*Sus celebensis*) that are still endemic to this island. Brumm et al. (2021) suggest that these images form a single narrative composition. If this can be substantiated, it would be a much earlier example of narrative than other authors suggest. For example, Robb (2020) departs from the art history model of looking at prehistoric art, in favour of a visual culture approach to compare art from the Neolithic Age (6000–2500 BCE) with that from the Bronze Age (2500–800 BCE). Robb contends that while Neolithic art used heavily coded imagery, often with geometrical motifs, art from the Bronze Age was narrative in form with clearly identifiable people and animals. Archeologists are making new discoveries and interpretations all the time – the point here is that while written narrative is comparatively recent, story-telling, both orally and through visual art, is ancient and it frequently featured animals.

When the images of a hunt were being drawn in Sulawesi, our European ancestors were coexisting and interbreeding with Neanderthals (*Homo neanderthalensis*). One explanation for why this species of human became extinct is that they were inferior across a wide range of capabilities, including their use of weapons and their subsistence strategies. Archaeologist Steve Mithen (2001) argues that it was the capacity for imagination that distinguished *H. sapiens* from *H. neanderthalis.* He cites in evidence the lack of variety in the design of hand tools and that there are no persuasive examples of the use of imagination in Neanderthal art. He develops the idea that humans evolved with an extended mind with a capacity for analogy and metaphor. We cannot know what our ancestors thought about sharing their existence with Neanderthals and, until recently, our own conviction that we are in some way special has hindered research into other hominid species (Villa and Roebroeks, 2014). This mistaken belief has biased scholarship through the ages.

Domestication of animals

It seems likely that dogs were the first animals to be domesticated, about 15,000 years ago. Cattle, sheep and horses were to follow when agriculture became established in the fertile crescent of the Middle East, about 11,000 years ago. These events have great significance in animal studies, with a contrast being made between the hunting of a supposedly compliant prey and the domination of all aspects of life, which characterises the human relationship with domesticated animals (Ingold, 2000: 72). There are various definitions of domestication, but all involve a relationship between humans and animal populations. Some definitions rely on humans taking control of an animal's movement, feeding, protection and breeding. In this definition the human is the lead partner. Other definitions see domestication as a mutualistic relationship between the species (Zeder, 2012). It is the quality of these relationships, the degree to which they are mutual and the quality of life of the domesticated species that are of special interest in animal studies.

Until recently, archaeologists have had to base their conclusions on skeletal fossils and other material evidence of animals from human settlements, with a particular interest in the burial of animals together with humans. Armstrong Oma (2018) draws on material evidence from Bronze Age buildings to suggest that families lived in close contact with their domesticated animals, particularly sheep, which were housed in the same building as the family home. Armstrong Oma's study is an example of how a discipline changes when it is approached from an animal studies viewpoint. She compares the layout of Bronze Age homes with the practices of modern shepherds who have small enough flocks to house them over winter and take them to the mountain in the spring.

It is now possible from genetic evidence to reconstruct the process of domestication that produced modern breeds. Advances in the twenty-first century in techniques for analysing genetic sequences has enabled new insights in the way that that the genotype (the sum of genetic information) and phenotype (the observable physical form and behaviour) of a domesticated species has changed since it was first domesticated. It seems that for both animals and plants, there have frequently been a number of domestication events. Three pathways for domestication have been suggested:

> **Commensal pathway**, in which species are first habituated to humans, to the point that they do not flee in their presence; they can then form a commensal partnership which benefits both species and may then move to complete control of the animals by humans and intensive breeding. Examples are dog, cat and chicken.
>
> **Prey pathway**, where animals are first hunted, but may then be subjected to active game management followed by extensive breeding and then control of breeding and movement as above. Examples are sheep, goat and cattle.
>
> **Directed pathway**, in which the relationship with other species is one of control and intensive breeding from the start. Examples are horse, donkey and camel. (Zeder, 2012: 171–8)

This process, from the initial stages of domestication to close control, particularly of breeding, is a progressive process. Domestication must always be viewed as a work in progress. The same domesticated species can be managed intensively, as for example cattle in North American feedlots, or can be left to their own devices on extensive mountain and range grazing. It would, however, be necessary to select a breed that is hardy enough to thrive on poor pasture and in exposed conditions. Some can be left untended, while others must be guarded against predators and gathered into a safe enclosure at night. Domestication is not a process that moves only in one direction. Sheep can be developed to be more hardy or to require less attention from their shepherds. Domesticated animals can be turned loose to revert to the wild, for example, as feral pigeons or dogs. Domestication should be regarded as a dynamic process and not an end point.

It is misleading, therefore, to regard the distinction between wild and domestic as binary. Wild has to include animals that never come into contact with a human, as well as those which form a commensal relationship with us. The house sparrows that sit on our windowsill when they want to be fed have clearly learned what it takes to get noticed. Their species name *Passer domesticus* (Linnaeus, 1758) recognises this long-standing relationship with humans, and some authors would regard this species as already domesticated on the commensal pathway. Wild animals include those that are actively managed either for conservation or as 'pest' species. In general our relationship with wild animals differs from those that we have with domesticated animals, and such differences are critical to the way that we approach literary animal studies; they may influence the boundary that is placed around the discipline, the ethical considerations that inform it, and the social, economic and ecological context in which we approach the critical analysis of works in the humanities.

It is evident that the relationships that humans have with other species are varied, complex and full of nuances. Such a rich portfolio of relationships is ill served by imposing a binary category such as wild vs domestic. In pre-history, evidence for the domestication of animals from the wild, such as it is, is very significant in terms of the way that humans conducted their relationships with other species. This issue is discussed further in the next chapter.

Animals in the classical age

The classical age is important for leaving a footprint in texts and artefacts, but the myths and legends documented in these texts would already have had a history in the oral tradition. For example, Ahl has questioned how it could be that narratives about swans came to play an important part in Greek myths and culture, when the birds themselves could only be seen in the extreme north of Greece. He suggests that stories about swans came down the trading routes and were based on Celtic and Norse oral cultures. The myths that came to be recorded may, over time, have been altered and embellished as they were passed by oral exchange. The written record may only be a small part of the oral culture around swans and other animals (Ahl, 1982). These classical myths are still an important source of inspiration for poets, from W. B. Yeats to A. E. Stallings.

The classical age also saw the birth of academic ways of thinking that have laid the ground for future studies in philosophy and science. Aristotle (384–22 BCE) is perhaps the most important of the classical scholars for literary animal studies, and whose influence is still felt across a wide range of disciplines that have changed the way we look at animals. His writing on poetics laid the foundations for literary studies, and his contributions to philosophy and metaphysics identified issues that have concerned scholars to the present day. Further, he carried out original studies in biology, which established the empirical method through direct observation, behavioural study and dissection. Aristotle developed a system for classifying wild animals by species and for some domesticated animals, such as dogs, by breed. Modern taxonomy that developed in the eighteenth century largely rejected his classification, but it remains significant as a way of thinking about differences in the animal world.

Although he did make use of observations of previous writers, Aristotle is held in high regard among biologists for approaching the natural world through a series of questions, for example, why fishes have gills and not lungs, why pigeons have a crop and elephants a trunk (Leroi, 2015: 8). Aristotle saw the organisation of the natural world as following the principles of a household or army composed of a collective of cooperating members. This recognition that one species depends on many others, and that humans are dependent on nonhuman species and vice versa, is central to the animal turn in the study of the humanities. Although using the analogy in a different sense, in 1866 Ernst Haeckel adopted the term *oikologie* from the Greek word *oikos* for a household, for the new science of the economics of nature (Egerton, 2013: 222). Modern ecologists trace the start of their discipline to Haeckel's formulation. Paying close attention to animals is one of the foundations of animal studies. By understanding their biology, we can get a better understanding of key issues such as their ability to experience pain, to have agency as individuals and the degree to which they form social relationships.

Aristotle's philosophy developed from Plato's theory of forms that distinguished between immaterial substances and the objects that we perceive in the world, of which they are mere shadows. For Aristotle the material body is also defined by a metaphysical property of 'what-it-is-to-be' or its essence. This essence defines a species, while qualities such as being musical do not. For Aristotle the intellect is not limited by the capability of any one material organ, and so the mind must therefore be a non-physical entity. He developed a very broad idea of the soul, which in humans was the source of life and intellect. Animals also had souls, but with more limited functions than those of humans. This concept that the body and the mind are separate entities, one material and the other immaterial, is the foundation of western and eastern philosophy. When applied to nonhuman animals the dualism between mind and matter can be a barrier to animal studies, especially if it is held that animals lack intellect and therefore exist as mechanical automata. Dualism of mind and body is an important issue that plays a central part throughout the history of our understanding of nonhuman species. It is discussed further below.

In contrast to the dualism of Aristotle, the Roman philosopher Lucretius, whose didactic poem *The Nature of Things* was written around 50 BCE, was solely focused on the material property of organisms in the natural world. Based on the philosophy of Epicurus, he explored the natural world from observing the material evidence of what could be seen without any reliance on the metaphysical. For species, he noted how each stayed true to type in subsequent generations, therefore 'each also must contain material that stays the same' (Lucretius, 2007: Book I, line 591). For Aristotle's essence, he proposes a material basis for species consistent with Gregor Mendel and Charles Darwin. He observed that each individual, of human or other animal, was unique enough to be known by their mothers: 'animals, like people, recognise each other too' (Book II, line 351). While this work would be in accord with modern science, it has not influenced the development of philosophy, which is mostly based on the model from the Athenian Academy.

Even though sheep had by then been domesticated for eight millennia, the practices of sheep keeping were first documented in the classical period. The Roman poet Virgil (70–19 BCE) gave a detailed, if not complete, description of how sheep keeping worked in the first century BCE. Virgil's *Georgics,* also written in the didactic form, is most concerned with the practicalities of the shepherd's life and gives an insight into how domesticated animals were viewed in classical times. In these verses he describes different forms of shepherding, from small flocks led back to shelter each evening, to large flocks grazing extensive pastures and to true nomadic sheep keeping in which the shepherd wanders through the wilderness with his flock. The presence of predators is always a concern. Although the music and song most associated with pastoral ways of life will have had a social meaning, it was also used to scare away wolves. It is evident from the *Georgics* that dogs were valued for their boldness with wolves. From an animal studies viewpoint, the close relationship that shepherds have with their dogs and the knowledge of individual sheep in their flock is matched by the recognition that all herbivores are at risk from predation by wild species. These predatory species, although living in the wild, also have a commensal relationship with humans as the source of animals on which they can prey.

Pliny the Elder (23/4–79 CE), in his widely read *Naturalis Historia*, made frequent reference to Aristotle, but was also able to draw on his own observations from his travels around the Roman Empire. Not all these observations have a sound basis in fact. For example, he repeats claims of a race of humans with a single eye in the middle of the forehead. In support of giving space to such counterintuitive material, he asks who would believe in Ethiopians without having seen them. Pliny's *Naturalis Historia* is regarded by contemporary naturalists as too much like an encyclopaedia, which included disparate facts, some of which were of doubtful reliability. Pliny is very authoritative about the different types of fleece from different geographical breeds of sheep. Some are only fit for carpets, while others can be used to weave the fine cloth that was the height of Roman fashion. Apart from their utilitarian value as a source of wool, there is little attention to the animals themselves. Pliny places humans apart from the rest of the animal world as only they can experience grief. The idea that humans are unique in the animal kingdom, in intellect, moral worth and ability has been very persistent. The animal turn in the humanities is committed to refuting this assertion. Pliny's influence continued to the Enlightenment. Even in the nineteenth century he was seen as the champion of natural history; Charles Darwin was a member of Edinburgh University's Plinian Society for undergraduates interested in natural history.

Stop and think

Story telling is an ancient practice, some of which was captured in text in Greek and Latin. The classical period established new ways of thinking about all living organisms, including humans, which have persisted in philosophy to the present day. In summary, this period provided ways of thinking about animals that included the formulation of important questions about the natural world and the animals that inhabit it, and the idea that physical and metaphysical properties coexisted in the individual animal. This period also promulgated the idea that the human species is both unique and superior to all other species, and is the only one that can experience grief.

Animal studies is predicated on refuting claims of human exceptionalism. Writers like Aristotle and Pliny are seen as the forefathers of natural history. Think about how close attention to animals and their behaviour can contribute to a deeper understanding of their capabilities and their experience of pain and suffering. How does the presence of myth and fantasy in narrative story-telling get in the way of thinking rationally about animals? Does reading Virgil and other writers as the originators of the pastoral tradition tell us anything about the animals themselves?

Animals in the early middle ages

The fall of the Roman Empire at the end of the fifth century CE, and the closure of the Platonic Academy in the middle of the sixth century CE, brought the classical period to a close. The foundation of the Benedictine abbey at Monte Casino in 529 CE meant that intellectual life did not come to a complete halt. The monasteries became a centre for scholasticism and were largely responsible for the copying of classical texts. Despite this body of scholarship, information about how the medieval world regarded animals is patchy.

An exception is in accounts of the lives of saints, where evidence of their power over nature was seen as a sign of their sanctity. Many of these stories, while subject to the tendency of hagiographies to bias the narrative to show the saint in a good light, have inspired writers and poets to the present day. For example, when St Patrick arrived in Ireland in the fifth century CE, it was believed that he was instrumental in banishing snakes from the island. There is no fossil evidence that snakes ever inhabited Ireland, but there is a powerful allegorical value in the idea that snakes, as symbols of evil since Old Testament times, left as Patrick converted pagan Ireland to Christianity. In Northumberland, St Cuthbert (634–87 CE) has been named as the patron saint of otters, based on a legend of a pair of otters drying his feet after he sang psalms in the sea. He is also associated with the common eider ducks that nested around his hermitage on the Inner Farne island to the south of his monastery on Lindisfarne. The legend is still strong in Northumberland, where eiders are known as cuddy ducks. St Cuthbert is supposed to have enacted a law to protect these ducks, particularly when they are most vulnerable during the breeding season. The narrative that this was the first official conservation law, has particular resonance in the context of the British and European conservation model and is frequently cited by the National Trust, which has responsibility for conserving the Farne Islands.

The complexity of some of these narratives is illustrated by the legend of St Melangell, a seventh-century Irish noblewoman who fled to north Wales to escape an arranged marriage and to live as a hermit. The story is that she was praying silently, on the site of a Bronze Age burial pit from between 1500 and 1000 BCE, when the Prince of Powis and his hounds put up a hare. The hare ran to the stationary figure and sheltered under her cloak, the hounds would not follow and the hare was saved. The latter detail is important as it would have been expected that under command from the prince, his hounds would seize the hare from its refuge. Any hunter will know that when a hare is running towards a person, if they keep quite still, it will run right up to them. This story brings together hunting, the saint's power over the natural world, and the status of the hare in Celtic mythology, as a shapeshifter and link to the otherworld. The myth offers a rich source of material for an animal studies reading. The church that was built on this site is a place of pilgrimage to the present day. St Melangell is the patron saint of hares. Regardless of the authenticity of these stories, contemporary poets are often drawn to the intrinsic interest in such narratives as a point of departure for their own work.

While classical philosophy was at first rejected by the Christian church, Aristotle's body and soul dualism did later provide a foundation for St Thomas Aquinas (1225–74) in his own very influential philosophy based on the immortal soul. Aristotle's works were translated into Arabic and also influenced early Islamic philosophers.

Animals in the Renaissance

The European Renaissance of the sixteenth and seventeenth centuries saw a renewed interest in the classical scholars, including the philosophy of Aristotle. In particular, the natural philosophers looked to Aristotle for his zoological works. While Aristotle's accounts of species that he had seen, and in some cases dissected, was a useful starting point, his inclusion of hearsay about species that he had never seen left the Renaissance scholars with work to do. For Leroi it was Pliny's *Naturalis Historia* that was the authentic voice of ancient natural history: 'gossipy, credulous and insistent that what the author has to tell is marvellous, as indeed it would be if any of it was true' (Leroi, 2015: 99–101). Aristotle remained influential in philosophy, but his ideas about animals, including humans, were largely refuted.

For Leonardo da Vinci (1452–1519) a knowledge of human anatomy was essential if portraits were to be true to their subjects. His drawings of the human body, before and after dissection, reflected a new interest in how the body works and how the underlying structures determined how it could be seen and portrayed in a visual medium. The medical profession also had an interest in such images. In 1543 Vesalius, working with artist Jan van Calcar, published the first comprehensive textbook on human anatomy *De Humani Corporis Fabricus* (the Constitution of the Human Body). Several medically trained scientists studied the circulation of the blood, but it was William Harvey who finally established the role of the heart in pumping blood out through the arteries and back through the veins. Other scientists made advances in reproductive biology and in taxonomy. From an animal studies viewpoint these advances in biology are mainly relevant as preparing the way for the advances that were to be made in the Enlightenment. In parallel with these discoveries, the Renaissance saw a lively body of superstition, folk tales and fables of animals real and imagined.

The invention of printing in the fifteenth century meant that from then on there was a substantial body of printed works for historians and literary scholars to examine. In her introduction to the collection of essays in *Renaissance Beasts: Of Animals, Humans, and Other Wonderful Creatures*, Erica Fudge (2004: 3) discusses how these texts, which make frequent reference to animals, can be read to place 'the animal as a significant figure in early modern cultural and intellectual history'. In looking at this historical period, Fudge stresses that in addition to being good history, it must take account of the modern world in which these new readings are being made (Fudge, 2004: 9). Reading these texts in the light of current concerns about related issues, such as women's history and the history of ethnicity, can contribute to current ethical and socio-environmental debates.

While such readings can be relevant in the current cultural and political context, they can also provide evidence of the start of what was to become a massive assault on the stability of biological systems around the world. In 1610 there was an unusual drop in the carbon dioxide in the atmosphere, around the same time that colonial adventurers were moving large numbers of animals and plants in both directions between the Americas and Europe, Africa and Asia. These movements included domesticated species, traded skins and diseases against which the Indigenous people had no immunity. These were not the first such movements – the Romans introduced rabbits to Britain as a semi-domesticated species, to be kept for meat in warrens, and the Normans brought fallow deer for hunting. Rabbits were later taken to Australia with the first fleet. The scale of the movement between continents in the seventeenth century has been identified as causing sufficient atmospheric disruption in 1610 to be a candidate start date for the Anthropocene: the human epoch in geology in which where human activities began to alter the climate and became dominant in the natural world.

Among the species brought back from colonial expeditions were wild animals to become a spectacle in menageries, including the one built in 1664 at Versailles for Louis XIV. At first the main interest in collecting wild animals in menageries was to amuse the guests of the king. Other aristocrats were customers for the trade in preserved specimens to add to their collections in cabinets of curiosity. After the French Revolution, some of these animals were released and others transferred to the Jardin des Plantes in the centre of Paris. For an account of the development of menageries in Britain, see Jackson (2014).

The rise of science in the Enlightenment

Following the principles of Francis Bacon and René Descartes, the Scientific Revolution led to a great increase in scholars paying close attention to the biology of animals. The animal turn in the late twentieth century was predicated on this growth in the scientific understanding about animals. With the lessening of the role of the church and aristocracy following the French Revolution, arguments based on reason came to prevail. However, at least at first, the advances in science had to be made under the patronage of the church, in England through the Church of England control of Oxford and Cambridge Universities, and in France from Descartes' courting of the Jesuit colleges to promulgate his method.

This method for approaching scientific study was based on intuition; decomposition of the problems into elements that are as simple as possible; organisation of the truths from these two rules in order to arrive at the ultimate consequences, and finally to use deductive reasoning to validate the link between the first principles and the ultimate consequences (Descartes, 1968: 16–17). For animal studies, Descartes' most problematic idea is that all nonhuman animals lack reason and must therefore be machines. For humans, God has given them a rational soul.

> For, examining the functions which could, consequently, be in this body [of nonhuman animals], I found precisely all those which can be in us without our thinking of them, and therefore, without our soul, that is to say, that part distinct from the body about which it has been said above that its nature is only to think. (Descartes, 1968: 65)

A consequence of setting humans apart from other animals, which are mere machines, is that they can be exploited without any concern for their welfare or their subjectivity. The Enlightenment was the age of revolutions, scientific and political. As science advanced, it brought better understanding of the brains and nervous systems of animals. These advances were necessary to refute the dualism between rational humans and mechanistic animals, and to build a sufficient understanding of what animals feel and want. This steady accumulation of knowledge in the field of biology was a precursor to the animal liberation movements of the 1970s.

The collections, amassed in zoological gardens and as specimens in cabinets of curiosity, attracted the attention of scientists, who were keen to explore all the diverse forms of natural organisms. Tim Birkhead, as well as being a distinguished biologist, has explored the development of the science of ornithology in the seventeenth century. For Birkhead two men stand out: John Ray (1627–1705) and Francis Willughby (1635–72). Study of the natural world was seen, at that time, as illustrating the providence of God and the organisation, beauty and intricacy of natural processes as being material proof of His existence. Ray, as a member of the Church of England, had a secure fellowship at Trinity College, Cambridge until the Restoration of the monarchy, when under of Charles II all members of the church had to sign the Act of Uniformity. Unwilling to do this, he lost his fellowship, but was able to join forces with Willughby, who had private means, to carry on with their biological research as private scholars (Birkhead, 2018: 68).

In 1663 Ray and Willughby departed on the first of their grand tours of Europe. They inspected specimens in the cabinets of curiosity in the great houses they visited, procured specimens for dissection and visited fish markets to describe all the species they found there.

> The key to the new science was the organisation of knowledge. Although the scientific revolution sought to overturn much of Aristotle's thinking, it was, at the same time, built on two fundamental Aristotelian assumptions. First, that there was order in nature. Second, the idea of the organism's 'essence' – what made it *it*. (Birkhead, 2018: 45, original emphasis)

In Pliny the Elder, with his encyclopaedic assembly of material of varying provenance, we can see the precedent for the cabinet of curiosity, but it was from Aristotle that these scientists drew the organising principles of their work.

Ray and Willughby followed in the tradition of naturalists since Aristotle and Pliny in describing the species they came across. The Swedish botanist, Carl Linnaeus (1707–78) was to provide a system for organising these species. His *Systema Naturae*, published in 1735, marked a step change in the search for and naming of species. Museums had an insatiable demand for specimens, enabling successful collectors to finance the expeditions that were, in turn, made possible by the empire building of the European nations. The system that Linnaeus established was changing in his own life time with each new edition of *Systema Naturae*. At first he proposed two taxa at his highest level of Kingdom: animals and plants. The Linnaean system is still in use today, but major changes have been found necessary as more organisms have been collected and closely examined. The changes have been at both species level and in the overall hierarchy of higher level taxa in which they have been placed. Assigning specimens to a species depended on the judgement of the taxonomist, who was working in a museum setting on collections sent in from collectors and colonial agents. There were two camps among these taxonomists: those who tended to group differing forms under a single species (the lumpers) and those who tended to identify a new species in each form (the splitters). At these extremes there was a risk that the idea of species might hide evolutionary relationships.

An example from the late nineteenth and early twentieth century is the large collection of insects and butterflies at Lord Walter Rothschild's private museum. For Rothschild it was slight variations that held the key to the evolutionary process. Concentrating on butterflies from South America he was able to collect similar specimens from across the geographical range. If any variations were continuous across this range it was reasonable to assume that these were all the same species. In 1932 Rothschild sold his entire collection to the American Museum of Natural History. Ernst Mayr, whose instincts were to lump varieties together in a single species, found himself in charge of Rothschild's birds. He had been corresponding with Rothschild's entomologist Karl Jordan on the evidence from taxonomy for the biological basis of species. Although he credited Jordan with the development of the biological species concept, it is Mayr's definition that is widely cited, that 'species are groups of interbreeding natural populations that are reproductively isolated from other such groups'. After the Second World War, the network of colonial collectors who had sent specimens in to Rothschild rapidly disappeared. There was no longer the sort of market for specimens that had enabled collectors such as Alfred Russel Wallace and Henry Walter Bates to make a living.

The concept of species is of great importance in animal studies. This is the basic type that can be seen with accuracy by a taxonomist using his judgement, but is also recognisable by Indigenous people, who have in-depth knowledge of the organisms in their immediate environment. The higher orders in Linnaeus's system have also been subject to change. The current hierarchy is: Domain, Kingdom, Phylum, Class, Order, Family, Genus, Species. The three domains are Archaea, Bacteria and Eukarya. Within the Eukarya there are four Kingdoms: Animalia, Plantae, Fungi and Protista (single cell organisms). A question yet to be resolved in animal studies is whether or not its scope includes all organisms in the kingdom Animalia (Linnaeus, 1758), and none from the other three kingdoms. These animals are multicellular eukaryotes (cells with a nucleus), that mostly consume organic material, breathe oxygen and reproduce sexually. Another name for these animals is Metazoa. The degree to which all animals have consciousness is still a matter for debate between philosophers and is discussed below. The advances in science in the seventeenth and eighteenth centuries, lived alongside wide spread superstition and fear of the unknown.

The witches in Macbeth, chanting as they consigned body parts of bats, newts and toads to the cauldron, would have struck a chord with the contemporary audience, and would have made sense to King James VI and I, who had an obsession with witches. Harriet Ritvo in her discussion of animals in the Victorian age, cites the release of animals from 'the burden of guilt for witchcraft, homicide, sodomy, and other crimes [that opened the way for them to be] viewed with affection and even, with scales tipped to the human side, with nostalgia' (Ritvo, 1987: 2–3).

Stop and think

The seventeenth and eighteenth centuries were a time of revolution: scientific and political. It was some time before ideas about witchcraft, and the association of some species with evil, gave way to a more rational mode of thinking. This was a necessary change in progress towards a more enlightened view of nonhuman animals. Animal studies is based on breaking down assumptions about species, in particular the boundary between *Homo sapiens* and other animals. Does the work of taxonomists help to define the problem or does it merely entrench the differences? The collection of specimens from around the world was closely associated with the colonial enterprise. To what extent does the Linnaean practice of assigning names to species in the back rooms of museums deny a voice to the Indigenous people who had already named the species and may well know a lot more about their natural history? Taxonomists mostly work from specimens that are dead. Does this risk losing sight of the individual nature of the living animal?

The question of species in the nineteenth century

The work of the species hunters inspired by Linnaeus, that populated his taxonomy, opened the question as to how each species had come about if not created by God. Geology had challenged the view that the Earth is only a few thousand years old, opening the way for Darwin to develop his theory of evolution, in which new species can result from the accumulation over generations of small changes that contribute to the survival value, or fitness. Darwin saw an important part of his task as the naturalist on HMS Beagle as collecting specimens to be sent back to Britain, where they could be classified under this taxonomy by the experts in each class of organism. He corresponded with many other collectors, including Alfred Russel Wallace, who was collecting in Sulawesi, and the other Indonesian islands separated from the Asian and Australasian continents by deep-water straits. The differences he found from islands on either side of the straits led him to develop his own version of natural selection. When he shared his ideas with Darwin they agreed to publish their findings in a joint paper, presented at the Linnaean Society of London in 1858. This society, a product of the Enlightenment, was founded in 1788 and is the oldest extant biological society in the world.

While Wallace was drawn to the idea of natural selection by the great difference between the fauna of Sulawesi and Australasia, Darwin was also influenced by the way that breeders of domesticated varieties selected the features they wanted. The accumulation of small changes in artificial selection can result in the production of entirely new forms. Selective breeding, for example, by Robert Bakewell, to produce the New Leicester sheep was also a feature of

Enlightenment progress. Although Darwin corresponded with Bakewell, he found more to interest him in the wide variety of forms that pigeon fanciers had produced. His correspondence with fanciers and the observations he made on his own flock of different breeds of pigeons, was formative in the development of his thinking. In *The Variation of Animals and Plants under Domestication* (1868), he devoted two chapters to pigeons. In these chapters you can follow Darwin as he pondered the idea of species. He suggests that if some of the varieties were seen in isolation, under the current rules of taxonomy they would be counted as separate species, but he was unable to find any possible wild ancestor for all these different forms other than the rock dove (*Columba livia*).

Charles Darwin's theory of evolution by natural selection faced many obstacles in a culture that believed that all the species had been created by God, but his most controversial work was his *Descent of Man and Selection in Relation to Sex* (1871). The idea that humans had evolved from another species and shared ancestry with the great apes was too much for many people to stomach. The idea of human exceptionalism from Aristotle's concept of the soul, through the Christian dogma and Descartes' dualism of mind and body, has been difficult to escape. It persists in the academy today. The challenge for animal studies is to set aside this claim to exceptionalism.

The birth of animal protection

Concern for the welfare of animals, especially those that had been domesticated, started to be expressed late in the eighteenth century, but it was not until the nineteenth century that these concerns were given formal recognition. The Society for the Prevention of Cruelty to Animals was founded in 1824, and in 1840 the young Queen Victoria, who had a special interest in animal welfare, granted it a charter to become the Royal Society for the Prevention of Cruelty to Animals (RSPCA). Similar legislation was enacted in the United States, with the state of New York chartering the American Society for the Prevention of Cruelty to Animals in 1866. Eventually these concerns were expressed in statute, for example, when the British Parliament passed the 'Ill-treatment of cattle act 1882'. This act was not immediately enforced, and further pressure in parliament and within the civil sector was required before protection became a reality. The aims of both civil society organisations and legislators was to ensure that individual animals did not suffer at the hands of humans. In this sense they are very much aligned with the animal turn in human–animal relations and its subsequent exploration through critical readings in the humanities.

Towards the end of the nineteenth century, attention became focused on the exploitation of wild birds for the use of their plumage in ladies fashion. In this instance it was not that the taking of these birds was particularly cruel, except during the breeding season, when young could be left to starve in the nest. The concern was that the scale of the trade was threatening birds, in particular egrets, birds of paradise and great crested grebes, with extinction. In 1889 Emily Wilkinson created the Society for the Protection of Birds, which in its early years was led mostly by women. The society received its royal charter in 1904 to become the Royal Society for the Protection of Birds (RSPB). Over the first half of the twentieth century this society acted as a pressure group to protect birds from local and global extinction. Later the emphasis shifted to the acquisition of reserves and the development of international alliances. The passing of the Importation of Plumage Act (1921) was an early success in the society's lobbying in support of its aims. The Protection of Birds Act was passed in 1933. The society did press for prosecution under these and subsequent statutes, but confusion between the names of the RSPCA and RSPB means that the latter still finds cases of cruelty to individual birds being reported to its officers. These two societies have long experience of managing what was to become the boundary between the scope of ecocriticism and animal studies. All cases of cruelty to individual birds are referred to the RSPCA, where animals includes birds, while the RSPB concentrates on 'protection' of species, increasingly including other species in addition to birds, rather than 'prevention of cruelty'.

Stop and think

The nineteenth century was a time when the vast resources of colonial Europe were able to collect and return both living and preserved specimens for display in zoological gardens, and for specialised taxonomists to assign to genus and species. Darwin and Wallace were part of this enterprise, but started to question the immutability of species. The birth of evolutionary science took place in parallel with the development of humane attitudes towards nonhuman species. Consider how these two advances changed the way that we look at nonhuman animals. Was it necessary to understand how species could change over time, to take notice of nonhuman animals? Are organisms assigned to species according to a human construct or is there a material reality that separates one species from another? Would an individual from one species recognise that an individual from another species is different? How necessary is it to go into more and more detail to answer these sorts of question? Does this 'reductionist' approach mean that we stop seeing whole animals?

The 'animal turn' in the 1970s

The online journal *Humanimalia* credits the publication in 1975 of Peter Singer's *Animal Liberation* as the beginning of human–animal studies, in which the relationship between humans and other animals became the focus of enquiry in disciplines as diverse as archaeology, literary studies and postcolonial studies. The commitment to animal rights from philosophers such as Singer and Tom Regan was very influential. For Singer, animal liberation had to be seen as having a common cause with the liberation movements to overcome racism, colonialism and sexism. Liberating animals had to challenge the institutionalist speciesism that mirrored the dualisms driving the other liberation movements. Singer and Regan approached the issue of animal rights from the standpoint of philosophy, but publications from other disciplines in the 1970s provoked discussion that has proved important in giving momentum to the animal turn.

Particularly influential in challenging the concept of human exceptionalism was Jane Goodall's *In the Shadow of Man* (1971), based on her research into chimpanzees in Tanzania. Written in the accessible style of popular science, it became a best seller and is still in print over 50 years later. She was criticised by established zoologists for her 'unscientific' methods and for getting too close to the individuals she was studying. Goodall was one of three women appointed by anthropologist Louis Leakey to investigate *Homo sapiens'* nearest relatives. Her studies of chimpanzees, together with those of Dian Fossey on gorillas and Biruté Galdikas on orangutans, were intended to be read alongside the Leakey family's research into hominid evolution. In social behaviour, their use of tools, and their adaptability, these animals were much closer to humans than previous scholarship thought possible. We will return to this question to discuss the scope of animal studies. The book is a classic in the writing of popular science, but film has also played an important part in the promulgation of ideas about our nearest relations. Goodall's collaboration with Dutch film-maker Hugo von Lawick, later her husband, brought visual evidence of her findings to a wide audience. Since that time, film has been a very important vehicle for progressing the animal turn. Fossey's life and tragic death were brought to light as fiction in the 1988 feature film *Gorillas in the Mist*; David Attenborough's encounter with gorillas in the 1979 film *Life on Earth*, which is one of the most memorable of cinematic moments, was part of the recognition that public support for these threatened species was critical if they were to avoid extinction. Goodall spent her life advocating for the rights of chimpanzees, but this raises a new question: is it only animals that are close to humans that deserve to be liberated? Is it possible to be both a scientist and an activist?

In 1973, three ethologists, Konrad Lorenz, Niko Tinbergen and Karl von Frisch were awarded the Nobel Prize for their discoveries concerning individual and social behaviour patterns. Although much of the work had been completed decades before the award, this was a moment when ethology was recognised as a serious science. The greylag geese studied by Lorenz and his students were 'imprinted' on the researcher by making sure that the first living being that newly hatched chicks saw was their human researcher. Instinct ensured that the chicks would then follow their carer until old enough to manage on their own. The researchers studied the signs that the geese gave to each other and the things that they needed their human step-parent to teach them. The greylag is the species from which domestic geese are descended, which opens the issue of whether

Lorenz's geese can be considered wild or are really on the way to being domesticated.

In contrast, Tinbergen conducted his research into herring gull behaviour in the breeding colony at Walney Island in Cumbria, mostly at a distance. He did supplement this with laboratory experiments in which a herring gull chick was offered sticks of various shapes, each with a red spot on the end. Tinbergen concluded that pecking on a red spot, regardless of the shape of the stick, was instinctual even before they had learned that when they pecked on the adult gull's bill, it would regurgitate food. Von Frisch studied honey bees returning from feeding at a rich source of nectar or pollen. He discovered that the waggle dance that bees performed on their return, differed according to the direction and distance of this source. Are birds and insects within the scope of animal studies in the humanities? It should be noted that Tinbergen, in particular, was very interested in instinct and many of his experiments were designed to prove that some behaviour could not be explained by learning. Could it be that such complex behaviours as migration and predator avoidance were coded in the organism at birth? In this respect Tinbergen is leaning towards the Cartesian view that nonhuman animals are machines. The evolution of behaviour has proved to be one of the problem areas for animal studies.

While von Frisch was studying honey bees, Edward Wilson was looking at the social behaviour and taxonomy of ants. Wilson's extrapolation from the behaviour of the social insects to other vertebrates, and in the last chapter to man, in *Sociobiology: The New Synthesis* (1975) was strongly rejected by Marxist scholars in his own department. Their riposte came in a letter to the *New York Review of Books* 'Against "Sociobiology"' (Allen et al., 1975). The objections of the scientists from Harvard and the Boston area were founded on the concern that arguments drawn from evolutionary theory were overly 'deterministic' and 'reductionist'. It is fair to say that since the discovery by crystallographers of the structure of DNA in 1953, biological research had been focusing increasingly at the molecular level, which might justify the reductionist label attached to any suggestion that a trait was genetically determined. Richard Dawkins's publication of *The Selfish Gene* in the following year seemed to take reductionism to a new level, where the body was merely a vehicle within which genes could replicate themselves. Further, the authors of 'Against Sociobiology' drew attention, in the first paragraph of their letter, to the way that evolutionary theory, from Darwin onwards, was guilty by association with those that have misused it in social policy, to explain social problems such as criminality or alcoholism and to justify eugenics. These objections were from fellow scientists, but philosophers also joined the discussion.

In 1978 the philosopher Mary Midgley entered the field of animal studies when she published *Beast and Man.* Midgley took strong exception to the reductionist approach of the sociobiologists and in particular to Richard Dawkins's claim that organisms were solely there to reproduce molecules that held their genetic code. Writing of Midgley's book 35 years after its publication, Raymond Tallis saw it as a corrective to the 'venerable philosophical tradition of separating the animal human body from the rational, spiritual human mind, person, or soul, and identifying humanity with the latter and disregarding the former' (Tallis, 2016: 69). Midgley, who cites Goodall, sought to refute the philosophy of René Descartes and his mechanistic account of animals. They are not incarnations of wickedness and have more than just basic needs. Tallis does, however, part company with Midgley in disputing the closeness between humans and even their primate cousins. It seems that philosophers have been reluctant to entirely surrender the claim to human exceptionalism.

Midgley continued to make important contributions to the thinking about human–animal relations for the next three decades. Her *Animals and Why They Matter* (Midgley, 1983) continued the debate. She contrasted the viewpoints of those Enlightenment thinkers who insisted on 'extending humane consideration to animals' to those who placed reason on a pedestal. For the latter, 'if animals were irrational, and value and dignity depend entirely on reason, animals cannot matter' (Midgley, 1983: 11). Midgley subjects Singer's claim that 'all animals are equal' to close examination. She sees concepts such as 'speciesism' as essential tools to break down prejudice, but these concepts are, however, 'notoriously obscure' (Midgley, 1983: 66).

One philosopher who created an initial difficulty for animal studies was Thomas Nagel, whose 1974 paper 'What is it like to be a bat?' (Nagel, 1974) seemed to limit the scope for a human to be able to understand another species. This is a paper that anyone approaching literary animal studies for the first time is likely to come across. His central thesis is that for each species there is something that it is like to be that particular species. He explains that he has selected the bat as a fellow mammal, but with sufficient difference, in terms of echolocation and being able to fly, to make it almost impossible for a human to imagine what it is like to be that species. The idea resembles Aristotle's concept of essence, which is the set of properties that make it what it is. For Aristotle this set of properties defined its difference in genera and species.

Nagel does not take us any further towards answering his question. He makes no reference to the bat workers who are engaged with addressing the question, either. Judging by those bat workers I have met, they have considerable empathy with their study object. It was the patient work of bat researchers that established that the morphologically similar pipistrelle species can be separated by the frequency of their echolocation call and slight variations in their ecology, for example. Nagel's essay is mainly concerned with the intractability of the mind–body problem. He rejects as overly reductionist all attempts to probe the consciousness of species, other than humans who can be asked to discuss it through introspection. Without being able to answer what it is like to be a bat, we cannot say that a bat has consciousness. There are two ways of looking at this question: one is to assume, until proved wrong, that the bat is an unthinking machine, rather as Descartes had described in the seventeenth century; conversely, under the precautionary principle, we should assume that bats and all other animals have consciousness until proved wrong. The latter position is consistent with Singer's challenge to speciesism.

The character Elizabeth Costello in Coetzee's *The Lives of Animals* takes issue with Nagel. For her, sympathy is a human faculty that allows us to share the being of another. She insists that 'there is no limit to the extent to which we can think ourselves into the lives of others, there are no bounds to the sympathetic imagination' (Coetzee, 2016 [1999]: 35). This imagination enables her to write about the life of an imaginary person by thinking her way into their existence.

Similarly, biologists have not accepted Nagel's idea that we cannot know what it is like to be another species. Estonian/German biologist Jacob von Uexküll (1864–1944) was particularly interested in how different species perceived their immediate environment. He suggested the term *umwelt* for the subjective experiential world of a species that was limited by its physiology and nervous system. One example was that of the tick, which although sightless, climbed to the top of vegetation by the overall sensitivity of its skin to light, from where it would fall, when it sensed the odour of butyric acid from the sebaceous follicles of all mammals, with the chance of landing somewhere on that animal from where it could attach to the cutaneous tissue of its prey. Each species has a different *umwelt* and in this sense, even for animals such as sea urchins, amoebae and jellyfish, it is possible for biologists to suggest what it is like to be that species. Uexküll's concepts are now taken as the starting point for the study of biosemiotics. The language of signs is not unique to humans, but is something that even the simplest of organisms can read and respond to. Species that are interacting with each other have *umwelten* that may overlap, part of the human *umwelt* will be to recognise the signs from the other species as to what might come next. This concept provides one way of looking at human–animal relations.

Yoon (2010) has used the concept of *umwelt* to explain how humans are able to recognise different species and organise them into some sort of classification. She suggests that taxonomists such as Linnaeus had a particularly well-developed *umwelt*, which allowed them to recognise morphological difference in the organisms they encountered. It is this same *umwelt* that is called on by Indigenous people when they are arriving at their own classification. Modern trends in taxonomy have moved away from detailed morphological measurements in favour of comparing the gene sequences of different organisms. From her own experience of sequencing the gene map of fruit flies, she found herself in a laboratory where all that there was of the animal was a drop of liquid in a test tube. While this method can help evolutionary taxonomists identify the path of evolution, it is at the expense of any sense of human–animal relationship.

In an essay written in 1977, art critic John Berger asked the question: 'Why look at animals?' He gives as an example that the domestication of cattle did not begin as a simple prospect of milk and meat, but they 'had magical functions, sometimes oracular, sometimes sacrificial. And the choice of a given species as magical, tameable *and* alimentary was originally determined by the habits, proximity and "invitation" of the animal in question' (Berger, 2009:

12, original emphasis). Urban dwellers have lost sight of this relationship where 'a peasant is fond of his pig, and is glad to salt away its pork'. For Berger the difficult part of that statement 'for an urban stranger to understand, is that the sentence is connected by an "and" and not a "but"' (Berger, 2009: 16). Berger compares the marginalisation of animals in zoos with that of humans in 'ghettos, shanty towns, prisons, madhouses [and] concentration camps'. The zoo is not somewhere where a stranger can encounter the look of an animal (Berger, 2009: 36–7). An animal studies approach requires us to look at animals and to allow them to look at us.

It was the look of the animal that interested Derrida in his long essay 'The animal that therefore I am (more to come)'. He takes the example of his cat gazing at him naked, to develop the idea of how we might cross the borders between human and animal: 'Crossing borders of the ends of man I come or surrender to the animal – to the animal in itself, to the animal in me and to the animal at unease with itself' (Derrida, 2002: 372). Derrida develops this point by offering two types of discourse, two types of knowledge, two grand forms of theoretical or philosophical treatise regarding the animal:

> In the first place are those texts signed by people who have no doubt seen, observed, analysed, reflected on the animal, but have never been *seen seen* [sic] by the animal. Their gaze has never intersected with that of an animal directed at them (forget about them being naked). If indeed they did happen to be seen furtively by the animal one day, they took no (thematic, theoretical or philosophical) account of it. They neither wanted nor had the capacity to draw any systematic consequence from the fact that an animal could, facing them, look at them clothed or naked, and in a word, without a word *address them*. (Derrida, 2002: 382, original emphasis)

Donna Haraway is grateful that Derrida has read and reread the canon so passionately that 'it could never be read the same way again' (Haraway, 2008: 20). She felt that he had correctly 'criticized two kinds of representations, one set from those who observe real animals but never meet their gaze, and others who engage animals only as literary and mythological figures' (Haraway, 2008: 21). However, she takes issue with Derrida by not considering those who have worked with animals and have accepted the interacting gaze. In particular she feels that he should have taken account of ethologists such as Jane Goodall, Gregory Bateson, Marc Bekoff or Barbara Smuts. She asks the question 'why did Derrida leave unexamined the practices of communication outside the writing technologies he did know how to talk about?' (Haraway, 2008: 21). Haraway highlights one of the difficulties for the student of animal studies. Ways of knowing about animals have advanced, particularly since the mid-twentieth century, across a very broad front involving a wide range of disciplines, each of which has a contribution to make. Some ideas need to be interrogated across the full range of these disciplines to strengthen the case for any conclusions that are drawn.

In her 2016 book *Staying with the Trouble*, Haraway suggests an approach to the seemingly impossible complexity of finding a way through the Anthropocene (although she prefers the term Chthulucene) by 'Promiscuously plucking out fibers in clotted and dense events and practices, I try to follow threads where they lead in order to track them and find their tangles and patterns crucial for staying with the trouble in real and particular places and times' (Haraway, 2016: 3). She uses the analogy of string theory to identify the pattern in the actual thing, and from this to pass on and receive, to make and unmake, and to pick up and drop threads. Through this practice and process she aims at 'becoming-with each other in surprising relays' (Haraway, 2016: 3). Since *Homo sapiens* became such a dominant species, some difficulties, such as having a constant fear of predators, have fallen away, but our relationship with and understanding of nonhuman animals, many of which are now facing extinction, has become more complicated. Although difficult, I share Haraway's view that it is incumbent on us to find a way through this trouble.

Another writer who was trying to bring animal welfare into public debate was ethologist Marian Dawkins, whose 1980 book *Animal Suffering: The Science of Animal Welfare* argued that animals have conscious experiences and the ability to feel pleasure and pain. Dawkins dates the birth of the study of animal consciousness as a legitimate field for scientific enquiry to 1976, with the publication by Donald Griffin of *The Question of Animal Awareness*. In a later book, *Why Animals Matter: Animal Consciousness, Animal Welfare and Human Well-Being* (2012), Dawkins approached the complex issue of difficulty of defining consciousness. In this book she asks whether it is necessary to understand consciousness before you can attend to animal welfare. By getting public acceptance that the health and well-being of the animals that we consume as meat is in their interest, there is no need to wait for the scientists to catch up with definitive proofs of exactly how consciousness works in nonhuman animals. Animal welfare legislation has advanced since early 1970, based on the five freedoms from hunger and thirst, from discomfort, from pain, injury or disease, to express normal behaviour, and freedom from fear and distress. This definition has been adopted by the RSPCA and is included with slightly different wording in the UK Animal Welfare Act 2006.

While this definition has served the purpose of guiding practical animal welfare management, science has been advancing. Dawkins returned to the subject in her 2021 book *The Science of Animal Welfare: Understanding What Animals Want*. This accessible book is aimed at the general reader and introduces some of the advances in science that should influence the way we think about animals, at least for those that are domesticated and under our direct management. The need to convince people that the consciousness of animals should be taken seriously has largely been achieved. She now advances towards the difficulty of not knowing what animals want. We cannot ask them in words, but by observing their behavior, ethologists can ask animals what they want. She stresses the importance of moving away from an approach to welfare based on human intuition to a more animal-centred mode of enquiry. There are further advances to be made in neuroscience by comparing the physical properties of human consciousness with those in animals.

Darwin and Mendel: the modern synthesis

Linnaeus had a clear idea about how to sort organisms into species. His sense of how they should be arranged at each level in the taxonomic system was based on the physical examination of morphology. Before Darwin, it was assumed that every species had been created by God and was immutable, but that assumption did not support the evidence that Darwin found from his collection of specimens, from both the living and fossil record, during the voyage of HMS Beagle. To ensure that his ideas would be accepted by taxonomists, he produced detailed descriptive work on barnacles from around the world. At the same time, he was corresponding with sheep and cattle breeders, and with pigeon fanciers. An important conclusion was that species change through a succession of small variations over time, so that eventually a new species may be formed. Gregor Mendel's experiments with pea plants between 1857 and 1864 established the basic principles of inheritance. However, it was not until 1900 that evolutionary biologists realised how these principles, where more beneficial traits would become more prevalent, could provide a mechanism of natural selection. This 'modern synthesis', also known as Neo-Darwinism, provided an explanation for how natural selection could work, but the actual business of taxonomy still had to rely on measuring and describing the anatomy of species and, if these measurements varied widely, on the subjective judgement of the taxonomist as to where to draw a boundary. Here it should be acknowledged that even great ideas can be put to bad use. For some, the association of these ideas with eugenics, and under Nazi rule with racial purity, is enough reason to stand well clear of all ideas that flow from this discovery. There are trigger words that enter discussion of what can be seen as a contentious field. They include 'reductionist' to discredit science based on molecular biology and 'determinist' to discredit the idea that all actions are determined by genetic inheritance and instinct.

Thomas Nagel made his position clear in the title of his 2012 treatise *Mind & Cosmos: Why the Materialist Neo-Darwinian Conception of Nature is Almost Certainly False*. Karl Popper proposed the falsification principle in the philosophy of science. All scientific knowledge is provisional and all science should attempt to disprove or falsify a theory. If Nagel had Popper in mind in his title, he does not include him in the references. What he proposes in place of the materialist theory is one based on metaphysics. As Aristotle understood, metaphysical ideas cannot be disproved by recourse to physics. While Popper might find Nagel's proposal to replace a scientific theory with one that is metaphysical to be non-science, even scientists now regard the Modern Evolutionary Synthesis, formulated in the 1940s, as a little tired.

The study of evolutionary biology in the third decade of the twenty-first century does not represent a single coherent approach but multiple approaches with different aims and methods. Epigenetics is the study of the modification of gene expression under environmental pressure. Not all scientists study animals at the molecular level, physiologists study the animal at process level and ecologists are interested in the way that each species is integrated into its environment. For example, Noble (2011) argues that a more integrative approach is required than the narrow view of genes taken in Richard Dawkins's *The Selfish Gene*, 'a multilevel approach in which genes and many other components of organisms that are inherited are viewed as cooperating in networks to express what we call phenotype' (Noble, 2011: n.p.). For Noble, 'Neo-Darwinism is capable of falsification. Indeed in its original form as a *complete* theory, it has already been falsified' (original emphasis). The field of evolutionary genetics is developing all the time, as it comes to be understood what genes can and cannot do, and how they work in cooperation with other physiological processes, some of which are influenced by environmental factors.

Neuroscience on sentience

On 7 July 2012, prominent neuroscientists of various persuasions gathered in Cambridge, England, 'to reassess the neurobiological substrates of conscious experience and related behaviour in humans and nonhuman animals'. At this conference, a document written by Philip Low and edited by other neuroscientists was tabled for signature by all present. This short document represented what was currently known about consciousness in nonhuman animals, summarised in the following declaration:

> The absence of a neurocortex does not appear to preclude an organism from experiencing affective states. Convergent evidence indicates that non-human animals have the neuroanatomical, neurochemical, and neurophysiological substrates of conscious states along with the capacity to exhibit intentional behaviours. Consequently, the weight of evidence indicates that humans are not unique in possessing the neurological substrates that generate consciousness. Nonhuman animals, including all mammals and birds, and many other creatures including octopuses, also possess these neurological substrates. (Low, 2012).

In this case it is the scientists who are leading the way. This declaration refutes the dualism of Descartes and adds scientific support for the animal welfare movement. It is very relevant in determining the scope of animal studies in the humanities.

David DeGrazia considers the philosophical and ethical issues raised by the new insights from science. For DeGrazia, 'sentient beings are capable of having pleasant or unpleasant experiences. This capacity entails having a quality of life or experiential welfare, from which it follows that sentient beings have interests' (DeGrazia, 2020: 17). He builds his case on a review of six features or phenomena that support an attribution of sentience. As with the Cambridge Declaration, he is clear that warm-blooded mammals and birds have sentience. There is a similar, albeit weaker, case to be made for cold-blooded reptiles. He is not convinced that amphibians are sentient, although they have some qualifying characters. Fish are more complicated and have to be considered under three higher taxa: the bony fishes, jawless fishes such as lampreys and hagfishes, and cartilaginous fishes such as sharks and rays. Of these, the case for sentience is strongest for the bony fishes, but a case can be made to include the more primitive fishes. A strong case can be made for cephalopods including octopuses, squid and cuttlefish. This again is in agreement with the Cambridge Declaration.

More difficult is the case for sentience in arthropods, including crabs, lobsters and insects. Research continues in these groups, with some scientists claiming that certain species, particularly bees which have been studied, might be conscious. DeGrazia (2020: 28) finds this claim to be 'more reasonable than the claim that they are not'. Some scientists claim that 'sentience and consciousness are interchangeable and therefore equally good bases for moral status' (DeGrazia, 2020: 30). For DeGrazia sentience involves both consciousness and the capacity for feelings – pleasant and unpleasant.

Politicians and scientists now take sentience and consciousness seriously, but that still requires judgement about what having moral status means. For Marian Dawkins an understanding of consciousness is necessary, but not sufficient to regulate our relationships with other animals. We need also to know what good welfare looks like from the animal viewpoint. It seems likely that future scientific studies will extend the list of species that should be considered to have moral status. One active question is whether the scope of study should be extended outside the animal kingdom. Recent discoveries in forest science have shown how trees can communicate with one another and adopt defensive measures when under threat. At least for this edition of this book I have assumed that trees are outside the scope of an animal studies reading in the humanities, apart from their importance in the environment of many animal species. This is, however, a field where new insights are coming along all the time.

This chapter has focused on the development of thinking about animals across a wide range of disciplines. Many of these ideas are central to the study of human–animal relationships in the social sciences. Some draw on literary texts and reports of performances involving animals. The next chapter focuses on the different approaches taken in animal studies and further exploration of the theoretical concepts that inform them.

Further reading

Bekoff, Marc and Pierce, Jessica (2017) *The Animals Agenda: freedom, compassion, and coexistence in the human age*. Boston, MA: Beacon Press.

Birch, Jonathan (2024) *The Edge of Sentience: Risk and Precaution in Humans, and Other Animals*. Oxford: Oxford University Press.

Dawkins, Richard (2016 [1976]) *The Selfish Gene*. Oxford: Oxford University Press.

Godfrey-Smith, Peter (2018) *Other Minds: The Octopus and the Evolution of Intelligent Life*. London: William Collins.

Gottschall, Jonathan and Sloan Wilson, David (2005) *The Literary Animal: Evolution and the Nature of Narrative*. Evanston, IL: North Western University Press.

Griffin, Donald (1982 [1976]) *The Question of Animal Awareness: Evolutionary Continuity of Mental Experience*. New York: Rockefeller University Press.

Higgins, Jackie (2021) *Sentient: What Animals Reveal about our Senses*. London: Picador.

Jackson, Christine E. (2014) *Menageries in Britain 1100–2000*. London: The Ray Society.

Kean, Hilda and Howell, Philip (eds) (2019) *The Routledge Companion to Animal–Human History*. Abingdon: Routledge.

Midgley, Mary (2002 [1978]) *Beast and Man: The Roots of Human Nature*. London: Routledge.

Paz, James (2017) *Non-Human Voices in Anglo-Saxon Literature and Material Culture*. Manchester: Manchester University Press.

Pliny the Elder (1991) *Natural History: A Selection*, translated by John Healy. London: Penguin Books.

Rudd, Gillian (2007) *Greenery: Ecocritical Readings of Late Medieval English Literature*. Manchester: Manchester University Press.

Tüür, Kadri and Tønnessen, Morten (eds) (2011) *The Semiotics of Animal Representations*. Amsterdam and New York: Rodopi.

Virgil (1983) *The Eclogues and the Georgics*, translated by C. Day Lewis. Oxford: Oxford University Press.

Zeder, Melinda A. (2015) 'Core questions in domestication research'. Special Series of articles by members of National Academy of Sciences elected in 2012.

References

Ahl, Frederick M. (1982) 'Amber, Avalon, and Apollo's singing swan', *The American Journal of Philology* 103:4, pp. 373–411.

Allen, Elizabeth et al. (1975) 'Against "Sociobiology"' *New York Review of Books*, 17 November.

Armstrong Oma, Kristin (2018) *The Sheep People: The Ontology of Making Lives, Building Homes and Forging Homes in early Bronze Age Norway*. Sheffield: Equinox.

Berger, John (2009) *Why Look at Animals?* London: Penguin.

Birkhead, Tim (2018) *The Wonderful Mr Willughby: The First True Ornithologist*. London: Bloomsbury.

Brumm, Adam et al. (2021) 'Oldest cave art found in Sulawesi', *Science Advances* 7:3, pp. 1–12.

Coetzee, J. M. (2016 [1999]) *The Lives of Animals*. Princeton: Princeton University Press.

Dawkins, Marian Stamp (2012) *Why Animals Matter: Animal Consciousness, Animal Welfare and Human Well-Being*. Oxford: Oxford University Press.

Dawkins, Marian Stamp (2021) *The Science of Animal Welfare: Understanding What Animals Want*. Oxford: Oxford University Press.

Descartes, René (1968) *Discourse on Method: The Meditations of Descartes*, translated by F. E. Sutcliffe. London: Penguin Books.

DeGrazia, David (2020) 'Sentience and consciousness as bases for attributing interests and moral status: considering the evidence and speculating slightly beyond' in L. S. M. Johnson et al. (eds) *Neuroethics and Nonhuman Animals*. Springer, pp. 17–33.

Derrida, Jacques (2002) 'The animal that therefore I am (more to follow)' translated by David Wills, *Critical Enquiry* 28:2, pp. 369–418.

Egerton, Frank N. (2013) 'History of ecological sciences, part 47: Ernst Haeckel's ecology', *Bulletin of the Ecological Society of America*, pp. 222–4.

Fudge, Erica (2004) *Renaissance Beasts: Of Animals, Humans, and Other Wonderful Creatures*. Urbana and Chicago: University of Illinois Press.

Haraway, Donna (2008) *When Species Meet*. Minneapolis: University of Minneapolis Press.

Haraway, Donna (2016) *Staying with the Trouble: Making Kin in the Chthulucene*. Durham, NC: Duke University Press.

Ingold, T. (2000) *Essays in Livelihood, Dwelling and Skill*. London: Routledge.

Leroi, Armand Marie (2015) *The Lagoon: How Aristotle Invented Science*. London: Bloomsbury.

Low, P. (2012) 'The Cambridge declaration on consciousness', *Proceedings of the Francis Crick Memorial Conference*, Cambridge University, 7 July, pp. 1–2.

Lucretius (2007) *The Nature of Things*, translated by A. E. Stallings. London: Penguin.

Midgley, Mary (1998 [1983]) *Animals and Why They Matter*. Athens, GA: University of Georgia Press.

Nagel, Thomas (1974) 'What is it like to be a bat?', *Philosophical Review*, October 1974.

Noble, Denis (2011) 'Neo-Darwinism, the Modern Synthesis and selfish genes: are they of use in physiology?' *The Journal of Physiology* 589:5, pp. 1007–15.

Robb, John (2020) 'Art (pre)history: ritual, narrative and visual culture in Neolithic and Bronze Age Europe', *Journal of Archaeological Method and Theory* 27, pp. 454–80.

Tallis, Raymond (2016) 'Beast and man: thirty-five years on' in Ian James Kidd and Liz McKinnell (eds) *Science and the Self: Essays in Honour of Mary Midgeley*. Abingdon-on-Thames: Routledge, pp. 65–84.

Villa, Paola and Roebroeks, Will (2014) 'Neanderthal Demise: an archaeological analysis of the modern human superiority complex', *PLoS ONE* 9:4: e96424.

Yoon, Carol Kaesuk (2010) *Naming Nature: The Clash Between Instinct and Science*. New York: W. W. Norton.

Zeder, Melinda A. (2012) 'The domestication of animals', *Journal of Anthropological Research* 68, pp. 161–90.

2
Theory for animal studies in the humanities

This chapter introduces some of the theoretical ideas that support the animal turn in the humanities. The turn towards animals was not a single event, there were in fact many turns in science and literature as knowledge accumulated, and new philosophical and ethical ideas developed. The body of ideas that underpins literary animal studies does not coalesce into a general theory. It is, however, an interdisciplinary way to approach the critical reading of literary texts. In this book I have cited authorities from across the full range of disciplines that inform literary animal studies, where possible selecting those that can be read by an informed, but not an expert, reader. There are many ways to follow the development of the body of ideas that advances the subjectivity of animals in critical readings.

Some readers will follow the long development in philosophy starting with Aristotle, through the setbacks of Aquinas and Descartes, to Deleuze and Guattari, Derrida, and then to Midgley, Plumwood and Bekoff. Others might take the natural history route from Aristotle again, Pliny the Elder, to Linnaeus, Ray and Willughby, the radical shift after Darwin, to the ethologists including Tinbergen, Marian Dawkins and Jane Goodall. A shorter route might come from cross-fertilisation of critical study in the humanities from the animal turn in the social sciences. The cross-over from human rights to animal rights was particularly important, with its commitment to action and ideas about what animal liberation might look like. Another might be a change of emphasis in environmental literary criticism, or ecocriticism, to foreground animals and allow them agency and subjectivity. In the following sections the ideas introduced in the last chapter are discussed in terms of their contribution to an animal studies reading of literary texts. Each theoretical viewpoint offers a basis for reading animals in literature, which complements alternative approaches.

Central to the development of literary animal studies is the recognition that animals have agency. McHugh identifies three interrelated imperatives for animal studies to:

> - conceptualize agency itself as more that simply a property of the human subject form
> - recover the spectrum of agency forms central to a variety of cultural traditions
> - [connect] the representational forms and material conditions of species life, the process whereby agency of literary animals comes to consist precisely in the way that cannot finally be enlisted in the tasks set for them. (McHugh, 2011: 10)

Approaching animal studies with these imperatives in mind demands that we pay close attention to agency in nonhuman animals. We need to see them as individuals that have choices, not as machines programmed by physiological and genetic codes. As was discussed in chapter 1, many species have sentience and the ability to feel pain. As science advances, more and more species are being seen as sentient. Authors from earlier times might not have had this insight, but still wanted to extend their humane sensibilities to at least domesticated animals.

The different ways of approaching literary animal studies is considered further in the following sections of this chapter. Concern for the welfare of domesticated animals has a long history. Recent advances in knowledge focus on what animals want, which may differ from what a human may project onto another species. Animal welfare considerations marked the first move away from a world where only human interests had moral standing. An animal welfare approach to literary animal studies is considered below.

Animal welfare

As discussed in chapter 1, animal welfare, as a humane imperative, started during the Enlightenment. When I was young there was an ancient notice to carters on the wall of a bridge in Hertfordshire instructing them to loosen the bearing reins on their horse before they went up the steep hill. This was to prevent severe injury to the horse's back if the tight reins that pulled the horses head in prevented the animals from taking a natural position as it pulled its load up the hill. Civic provision of drinking fountains for people and troughs for horses in Victorian England were based on similar concerns, this time shared by the desire for the poor to have access to clean drinking water and for horses to not suffer from dehydration. Later there was a concern that the troughs were a source of disease and responsible horse owners avoided them. Perhaps the key text for raising the awareness of animal welfare was Anna Sewell's children's novel *Black Beauty* (1877), considered further in chapter 7. This book from the nineteenth century was inspired by, and in turn informed, a growing sensitivity towards the welfare of domesticated animals. The domesticated species we have today have coevolved with the human societies that cared for them. In many cases they are dependent on this ongoing care. Only the most hardy breeds would thrive if left to survive on their own. Care for wild animals was seen as a separate issue covered by a separate branch of law.

There is an important limitation in the scope of animal welfare legislation and in the associated civic movement for the humane treatment of animals: that these provisions only apply to domesticated animals, including pets, farm animals and those used for vivisection and other scientific research. Wild animals come into the scope if there is cruelty exerted directly by humans on other species, as in badger baiting. Wild animals being cruel to each other is regarded as natural. Similarly wild animals suffering from starvation when they compete with humans for natural resources is outside the scope of welfare provision. In reading animal texts, the different value systems applied to domestic and wild animals will be important issues.

There has been progressive development in animal welfare, as new scientific insights about sentience and the ability to experience pain and distress have become better understood. These have had a particular impact on the use of live animals in performance, from cruelty as a spectacle in the Roman arena, through dog fighting and bear baiting, to the cruel training of big cats to perform in circuses. When animals are being prepared for performance, it is likely that concern for their welfare will take precedence over some of the more abstract positions taken by students of animal studies. While starting as a humane movement, animal welfare has advanced as science has found new insights into sentience and the way animals experience pain. Sentience and consciousness are therefore important aspects of theory in animal studies and are discussed in further detail below.

Sentience and consciousness

The 2012 'Cambridge Declaration on Consciousness', discussed in chapter 1, reiterated the scientific consensus that nonhuman animals are conscious beings and have feelings, both good and bad. From an animal welfare point of view it is their ability to suffer that creates an ethical duty for humans to take into account in their dealings with other animals. Scientists have established that all mammals and birds, and many other creatures, have neurological substrates complex enough to experience pain. Sometimes used as a synonym for consciousness, 'sentience' is the ability to experience sensations or feelings, in contrast to the ability to think. In this sense animals are being considered according to concepts in human psychology, particularly in behaviourist psychology, that differentiates between cognitive, affective and conative (thinking, feeling, doing) realms of behaviour. From a scientific viewpoint, these mental activities can be studied by describing the neurological components of the species' anatomy, from the electrical pulses that flow through these neurones when activated and by interpreting observed behaviour. The approach is still very much a humanist enterprise, which uses the test of how the neurological and physiological patterns of a particular species compare with our own to determine its moral standing and its qualification for humane compassion. Sentience's relevance in animal welfare is that the closer we look at the sensory capability of animals, the more species become candidates for humane treatment. The challenge comes when we try to discover if animals that are not like us are sentient.

The further away from mammals and birds, the more difficult it is to find convincing examples of sentience. Sometimes this is because we have not looked hard enough. Godfrey-Smith, in his book *Other Minds: The Octopus and the Evolution of Intelligent Life*, takes as his example the cephalopods (octopuses, squid and cuttlefish) as animals that are very different to us. 'If we want to understand *other* minds, the minds of cephalopods are the most other of all' (Godfrey-Smith, 2018: 10, original emphasis). A literature review commissioned by the London School of Economics (Birch et al., 2021: 79) considered evidence of sentience in published papers on cephalopod molluscs and decapod crustaceans (such as crabs, lobsters and shrimps), weighted according to reliability, for example, by giving greater credence to those papers that had been peer reviewed. The evidence was considered against eight criteria, all to do with the structure and functioning of the nervous systems. On this evidence they recommended that

> All cephalopod molluscs and decapod crustaceans be regarded as sentient animals for the purposes of UK welfare law. They should be counted as 'animals' for the purposes of the Animal Welfare Act 2006 and included within the scope of any future legislation relating to animal sentience. (Birch et al., 2021: 79)

They also noted that these taxa have been the subject of considerable research, while other animals that may be sentient had hardly been studied at all. It is likely that more and more classes of animals will be regarded as sentient as more research is done. How will this new emphasis on sentience change the narrative in creative works? One example is the 2020 Netflix film *My Octopus Teacher*, which explores the 'friendship' that developed between a film-maker and an individual octopus over many weeks of daily interaction. It is significant that these wonderful animals are much stranger than the bats Thomas Nagel felt were beyond human understanding. Despite being a mollusc, in adapting to live without a protective shell they have become remarkably intelligent.

In his essay 'What is it like to be a bat?' Nagel suggested that humans have no way of knowing what it felt like to be a bat. Some academics have side-stepped this problem. For example, Frans de Waal focuses on 'the world that animals live in, and how they navigate its complexity. Even though we can't feel what they feel, we can still step outside our own narrow *umwelt* and ally our imagination to theirs' (de Waal, 2016: 9). De Waal cites the work of ethologist Donald Griffin, whose analysis of echolocation calls showed how complex and effective this was as a navigation and hunting tool. Bat detectors that convert the ultrasound clicks into the human hearing range are now readily available.

I have listened to Daubenton's bats hunting moths over the river at Flatford Mill in Essex, made famous in Constable's landscape paintings, with the clicks getting faster as the bat closed in on its prey. Icelandic singer and performer Björk, in the film of her 2013 multimedia performance *Biophilia* at Alexandra Palace, London, included 'Bat sounds' as the last number in her set. As well as the hunting sequences where the bats close in on their prey, she included the chatter that bats make in their communal roosts before they leave to go hunting. These sounds were transmitted without interpretation, for the human audience to make of them what they would, although by choosing *Biophilia* for the title of the overall performance, she is assuming that hearing these sounds will generate positive feelings towards other species among her human listeners.

Scientists have not been deterred by Nagel. Tim Birkhead, in the subtitle for his 2012 book *Bird Sense: What It's Like to Be a Bird*, accepts that, 'In a a sense Nagel is right: we can never know *exactly* what it is like to be a bat or indeed a bird' (Birkhead, 2012: x, original emphasis). Birkhead observes that the point is 'subtle and pedantic perhaps, but that's philosophers for you' (Birkhead, 2012: x). For Birkhead, birds have characters that we can identify with, for example, that they are bipedal, rely mostly on vision and hearing, and are diurnal. But Birkhead cautions that this similarity can be misleading. It is the abilities that are hard for us to understand that are of interest to him: the swift screaming round a building, the emperor penguin diving to depths of 400m, and the urge that some species have to put on fat in preparation for a long migration. The development of miniaturised recording devices and cameras that can be attached to individual birds enables us to see the world as they do, at least visually, and helps us to get a better sense of what it is like to be another species. Our knowledge of them may be incomplete, but it is sufficient to inform our ethical choices relating to animal welfare.

Animal welfare is concerned with making sure that animals under our care do not suffer, but for Bekoff and Pierce, such concerns do not question 'the underlying conditions of captivity or constraint that shape the very nature of their lives' (Bekoff and Pierce, 2017: 6). Such constraints are obvious for farm animals and companion animals, but increasingly so in the Anthropocene, a term originally proposed as a new geological epoch which has been widely adopted in the humanities and social sciences to signify the point where human activities started to have such a profound impact on the environment. During the writing of this book the term was not held to meet the very exacting conditions for a geological epoch, but as it is now entrenched in the humanities I have continued to use it (Witze, 2024). In the Anthropocene, animals that should be wild are often constrained by human activities. For example, what is it like to be a lesser horseshoe bat at risk of greater mortality when a road is widened between its traditional roost and feeding grounds? Bekoff and Pierce propose instead to look at ways that animals can enjoy freedom in what they call the science of animal well-being (Bekoff and Pierce, 2017: 7). Marian Dawkins also looks to simplify animal welfare without the need to refer to technical neurological terms. For Dawkins, the first principle of animal welfare is that they should have adequate food and water, and be kept in a safe comfortable environment. In addition to these prerequisites for animal health, the second is to ask 'what animals want' (Dawkins, 2021: 8). Such preferences can be inferred from observable behaviour and from the choices that animals make when they are presented with options.

Consciousness and sentience can have precise meanings, established by reference to material criteria set by (human) scientists. More often the terms are used interchangeably and with much looser lay meanings. The concept of 'what animals want' is well-aligned with the underlying principles of animal studies in the humanities. Although it is humans who decide what the animals in their care want, it is placing the onus on those responsible to try to see wants from the animal viewpoint. This issue will be explored further in the discussion of posthumanism. The science of sentience and consciousness is advancing quite rapidly and it is likely that more and more classes of animals will come to be considered as sentient. For the purpose of this book I have assumed that all multi-cell animals (metazoa) are within the scope of animal studies. To exclude any animals because their sentience was unproven would miss out on interesting works, particularly in poetry and documentary film.

While this is a convenient boundary for animal studies, it should perhaps be questioned whether excluding single-celled animals (protists) and all plants is just extending the boundary to a point where speciesism becomes acceptable. The meanings that human observers attach to animals can determine the values we deploy. In human–animal studies it is sometimes necessary to study the human. This aspect is discussed in the next section.

The social construction of animals

The development of human–animal studies in the social sciences has drawn on the social construction model. Under this model the mind is a more or less blank slate on which what we know about animals is constructed through discourse. Further, we construct our own identity in relation to animals. There is a potential clash here, because much of what we know about animals has been produced by scientists, working to a quite different model in which evolution has played a major part. Bruno Latour's actor–network theory is an attempt to bridge the gap between the social sciences and natural sciences, in particular by confronting those 'who continued to imagine a social world without objects set off against a natural world without humans' (Latour, 2017: 3).

Edward Wilson advanced his hypothesis that humans have an innate (that is inherited) love or hate of other living things that he called 'biophilia'. This hypothesis, which has not yet been sufficiently tested to be raised to the status of a theory, is in direct opposition to the social construction model. Although the biophilia hypothesis continues to be controversial, it lives on in evolutionary psychology in the idea that at least some of what we know and feel about animals is genetically determined. Our fear of predators or poisonous snakes would, for example, have an evolutionary advantage. The relative merits of a materially determined versus a culturally determined view of nature are hotly contested.

Human–animal study in the social sciences 'explores the spaces that animals occupy in human social and cultural worlds and the interactions humans have with them' (DeMello, 2012: 4). This aspect of the animal turn sits within the ways of seeing the social world through the social forces that shape our lives. For DeMello this approach dates back to 1959, when C. Wright Mills's book *The Social Imagination* established a means by which the relation between self and society can be understood. This approach, and the claim that our identity and view of the world, is socially constructed through discourse and performance, is well established in the social sciences and the humanities. From this practice, the animal turn shifts the focus from solely human actors to highlight the part that animals play in the social process. Classing animals as wild, domestic, pet, rare, pest or alien is clearly more meaningful to humans than to the animals. These classifications determine how a particular species is treated by human society. Other classifications, such as endemic, migratory, resident and commensal, although constructed through human discourse, would lose their meaning if there is no material evidence to validate the use of that appellation. Perhaps the most problematic term for a social constructionist standpoint is species.

A social constructionist reading of the Linnaean system of classification would have the taxonomists looking back to earlier models, such as the great chain of being, that placed humans as separate from and superior to the rest of the animal kingdom. Some aspects of taxonomy are based on human judgement, for example, the divergent views of the lumpers and splitters when drawing the line between very similar species. Under the biological species concept, an organism is a separate species if it can only breed with another of the same species. This concept relies on observing the choices made by the animals themselves, rather than judgements based on morphology alone. While this concept can be problematic, it does indicate that scientists are trying to eliminate social construction from their judgement about how to classify an organism.

Any idea that such classification could rely on our innate world view, conditioned by the *umwelt* of *Homo sapiens* is rejected in the social construction model as essentialising. For DeMello, othering and essentialising are practices that are closely associated with racism, sexism and speciesism (DeMello, 2012: 258–9). The practices of early taxonomists in splitting different races of humans to the sub-species level makes them suspect in harbouring these types of attitude. Even though taxonomy has not been able to show any essential basis for racial differences, and all humans are classified firmly within one species, these accusations are still part of the argument between social construction and essentialist ways of seeing. Now that species relationships are being revised from genetic analysis, some of the taxonomy based on the subjective assessment of morphology has been overturned. It is harder to make the case that a taxonomy is socially constructed when it is determined by evidence of the branching of the genetic tree, sometimes millennia before humans were around to socially construct meaning.

For DeMello, human–animal studies is a way of seeing animals wherever they exist in the human world. She takes the example of her pet rabbit, which has a different meaning and set of rules to those that are wild or kept for meat. I suggest that the rhinoceros is another example; there are several species, all rare. In Africa, the white and black rhinoceroses are included in the 'big five', along with the lion, leopard, cape buffalo and elephant. These were the prize prey for big game hunters because they were the most dangerous to hunt on foot. Trophy hunting is about constructing an identity in the hunter as brave and skilful, although very often most of the work was done by African trackers. Theodore Roosevelt was pictured in 1909 with his gun resting on the back of a rhinoceros that he had killed. The term 'big five' is also used to market safaris that promise close views for tourists armed only with cameras. Close views are almost certain because these dangerous animals have been habituated to ignore humans, provided they stay seated within their vehicle. As far as the animals are concerned, the humans are not there. In this scenario, humans see the animals, but the animals do not meet their gaze. The narratives that are brought home from these trips also help to shape the way people see animals in the wild. However, habituation is dangerous for the rhinoceros.

Because their horn is prized in Chinese traditional medicine, habitation makes them more vulnerable to poaching. For the impoverished people living near the game concessions, the rhinoceros is a symbol of financial security for their family. In Chinese medicine, the ground-up horn, which is mostly keratin, as in hair or fingernails, is believed to be an aphrodisiac. Because of its cost, a wealthy person might display a whole horn as a signifier of their wealth. This is one class of animals with many meanings in the construction of human identities, for example, intrepid big game hunter or ecotourist. Big game animals are big business; hunting and ecotourist safaris are very expensive. The poacher, the smuggler, the wealthy customer for rhino horn are also attracted to the species by their monetary value. In this way wild animals become enmeshed with economics in a world where wealth is not shared equally. The study of how animals are used to construct human identities is an important aspect of animal studies in the humanities. Creative works can be informed by the ideas about animals that are socially constructed. Also creative works as discourse play a part in the construction of the relationship between humans and animals.

For Armstrong, 'once you start noticing them, animals and human-animal relations appear everywhere in the literary canon' (Armstrong, 2012: 342). He considers three ways to look at animals in literary texts. The default way is to consider their symbolic value. His second way is 'reading from animals to animal practices [that] provides new ways into the texts and their economic, social and historical contexts'. His third way is in 'exploring how human-animal narratives fulfil one of the longest standing and most important roles of fiction: the exploration and expression of structures of feeling and sensibility' (Armstrong, 2012: 342–3). The social construction view of how meanings are constructed from texts and performance is well established in literary studies. Despite the fact that much of what we know about animals has come to us from advances in science, the concept of social construction has relevance in animal studies. While it foregrounds the role of the human in socially constructing the meaning of animals and their relationship with humans, it can also give us an insight into human identity in a multispecies world.

Stop and think

Animal studies covers the animal nature of *Homo sapiens* and has regard for the agency and sentience of other animal species. Apart from that, it is not a single method. The relationships between all the myriad species on Earth is too impossibly complex to understand with a single method. Even the sciences have to simplify their fields of enquiry to assume that much of what happens goes on in the background to their study of a single species, physiological or neurological process, or activity. The discussion of theoretical ways of approaching this complexity that follow must always allow for the complex, messy, unpredictable and wonderful world we encounter when we start to take other animal species seriously. Where do you stand in relation to other species of animal: have you always had close relations, for example, with family pets, or from an interest in nature from childhood? Have you, like some of the writers we will encounter in future chapters, ever experienced an epiphany after which you had heightened sensitivity to one or more animal species?

The animal rights turn

The animal rights turn is founded on similar concerns to those of the animal welfare movement, and sought to harness the same sense of urgency and need to confront underlying prejudice as the Black and women's liberation movements. As discussed in chapter 1, Singer and Regan made the case for extending this principle of these liberation movements to other animal species. Speciesism was just as objectionable as racism or sexism. With its birth in the rights movements of the 1970s, there is an emphasis on action. For some this will be militant, as with the acts of sabotage at vivisection laboratories by the Animal Liberation Front. Others prefer a gradualist approach that uses discourse and performance to change attitudes. For criticism in the humanities, particularly of works whose creators have studiously avoided didactic positions, a prior commitment to activism on the part of the critic can be problematic. On the other hand, any move towards giving animals a voice in creative works and in criticism is already entering the political arena. Advocacy and activism in reading animal narratives are explored in greater depth below.

By drawing the comparison between speciesism and the othering of women and non-white races, Singer and Regan made the case for animal rights to be to be promoted alongside the rights movements for marginalised peoples. A rights-based approach tends towards activism, rather than slow lobbying for improved animal welfare based on the gradual changing of public attitudes. The extremist wing of the animal rights movement worked through (illegal) acts of sabotage, for example, when the Animal Liberation Front 'rescued' laboratory animals and battery hens. Others look to acts of theatre, such as the photographs of naked celebrities in the People for the Ethical Treatment of Animals campaign against wearing fur. The focus of all of these protests was on what was in the best interest of the individual animal. In contrast, the environmental activist movement campaigned on behalf of more generalised entities, such as the planet, ecosystems at the biome or catchment level, and biodiversity. Although they have some concerns in common, these two activisms were often in opposition.

To address this mismatch Amy J. Fitzgerald, in *Animal Advocacy and Environmentalism: Bridging the Divide*, shows how animal rights can intersect with the environmental movement. She takes as her examples the wearing of fur, the practices in zoos and menageries, and what she calls industrial animal agriculture. One area of disagreement is in attitudes to science. Environmentalism is informed by science, but in animal advocacy, with its origins in opposition to vivisection, science was often mistrusted. Fitzgerald shows how advances in science, for example, in ethology, which describes the rich mental and emotional lives of animals, have shown how science can support a more humane approach to the treatment of individual animals (Fitzgerald, 2019: 162). Similarly the outright opposition to the wearing of fur takes on a new perspective if it is seen against the dependence of Indigenous people on the fur trade. Fitzgerald also makes the case for joining forces with ecofeminists, where the environment, animals and denigrated social groups, are all suffering at the hands of patriarchy, colonialism, anthropocentrism and speciesism (Fitzgerald, 2019: 186). This interventional approach, often intersectional across more than one aspect of oppression, has been taken up in the movement known as 'critical animal studies'.

Critical animal studies

The 'critical' that prefixes critical animal studies signifies that this is to be more than disinterested academic study of human–animal relationships. Those who take up this branch of animal studies are already committed to action, at least in their personal lives, for example, by adopting a vegan diet and refusing to be present at any biological experiment using live animals. The dedication of Anthony J. Nocella II and Amber E. George's edited volume *Intersectionality of Critical Animal Studies: A Historical Collection* (2019) reads: 'This book is dedicated to everyone that has suffered and was murdered at the hands of sexism, racism, classism, ableism, ageism, fascism, speciesism and anti-LGBTTQQIA. // Until all are free …'

Many academics operate within organisations where strident political standpoints are discouraged. Nik Taylor and Richard Twine's edited volume *The Rise of Critical Animal Studies: From the Margins to the Centre* (2014) addresses how this activist line of enquiry can be brought into the mainstream. In his contribution to that book, Nathan Griffin suggests one way in which critical animal studies can be pursued within the current academic culture of audit and goals. For Griffin, critical animal studies is 'a compassionate, interdisciplinary approach to working against oppression, and reflexive research practice allows a level of self-awareness and critical reflection that can be valuable in this pursuit' (Griffin, 2014: 115). It values passion and subjectivity over a neutral appraisal of hard data. For this approach to be effective, it has to acknowledge the research context and the pressures on the researcher. Possible methodologies for critical animal studies can include the collection and interpretation of biographical documents to better understand the subjectivity of the researcher's lived experiences. Other methods are performative social science and visual methods. It is therefore possible to see how practices in the humanities could be harnessed to advance a cause under the banner of critical animal studies.

Most creative work is not produced to be didactic or political, although there is room for a feminist or postcolonial reading of many works. One poet who sets out to promote a cause is vegan pacifist John Kinsella, for example, in his *Activist Poetics: Anarchy in the Avon Valley*. For Kinsella 'poetry has no point unless it's a prompt or aid to political or ethical change' (Kinsella, 2010: 16). Activist poems can include those that are radical linguistically, and those that are a straight declaration. Poems can stop bulldozers, not by direct prohibition, but 'because the intricacies of language challenge, distract and entangle the bulldozer' (Kinsella, 2010: 17). Kinsella explains his own process and how it differs from his collaborator

Coral Hull in the collaborative poetry collection *Zoo,* based on their visits to Taronga Park Zoo:

> In *Zoo* the majority of Hull's pieces are direct action in nature, mine work by allusion and circumlocution. … Where Hull will say something outright and then build layers of metaphorical allusion, I'll start with metaphorical allusion and leave the reader to distill the politics (Kinsella and Hull, 2000: 130–1)

Both writers were against the idea of zoos before they made their visit. For Kinsella, zoos are concentration camps. In *Zoo*, the resulting collection of poems, Kinsella's poems are lyrical, while Hull's tend to be prose poems. This collection is about zoos in general and is not specific to the visit that began their collaboration. Even when works have not been created with activism in mind, they can be read and subjected to critical analysis to elicit political themes.

The animal turn, in both the social sciences and the humanities, has been energised by the animal rights movement espoused by Singer and Regan. In a sense, all works in the humanities have a moral purpose, and any that allow for the subjectivity and agency of individual animals are already confronting established social norms. It is likely that anyone attracted to animal studies in the humanities will have some animating purpose to spur their interest. As with Kinsella, work can be created with activism in mind, but even work that has no explicit message can be read with and against texts that transform the reading into one that has an overt political meaning. Exploring animal studies in the humanities can be transformative, not least for the scholar. This transformation is more likely if the research process is reflexive and draws on the researcher's lived experiences. As we draw closer to animals, our knowledge gives way to feeling. This aspect is explored in the next section.

Affect, empathy and altruism in kinship between species

The idea that humans can achieve kinship with other species is based on the study of commensalism between species, on ideas from philosophy that reject human claims to exceptionalism, on the rejection of the dominant humanist world view, and on practical experience of living with companion animals. Other species of animal are seen to have abilities that were thought to be unique to our own species. Human exceptionalism is no longer a valid basis for discourse about humans and other species. There is debate about whether or not nonhuman animals can show altruism to conspecific individuals, or to those of other species. Evolutionary psychologists struggle to fit behaviour that may not be in the best interests of the individual into how it may be selectively preferred in future generations.

A case can be constructed that altruism between closely related individuals of a species can confer an evolutionary advantage. An example is among white-browed sparrow weavers in the Kalahari desert, where close relatives of the biological parents, including older siblings, share the care of young. Does this 'kin selection' offer a way forward in the animal turn, where the emphasis is on the quality of relationships between species? Donna Haraway has argued that humans must establish such kinship relations across the species boundary if we are to confront the challenges of a heating world, mass extinction and breakdown in the social order. To understand how such a mutually supportive relationship between species might work, we need to look at affect, empathy and altruism in the construction of kinship relationships.

For some philosophers, particularly Midgley, feeling empathy is part of what it is to be human. Affect and empathy flow from our essence, but cannot be explained by physics and must be accepted as metaphysical. As the nature of this essence is unique to *Homo sapiens* it must be inherited or depend on inherited characters, but as it is metaphysical, we admit that we do not know how. From an animal studies viewpoint, the degree to which we have feelings for and empathy with other species will determine how cross-species kinship can work. Mary Midgley was one philosopher who advanced the idea that empathy across the species barrier was integral to the essence that makes us human. She was influenced by reading Konrad Lorenz's *King Solomon's Ring: New Light on Animal Ways* (1952), a joyful account of his encounters with animals. This popular book was influenced by ethology but allowed for Lorenz's feelings about these animals to shine through. Reading widely in ethology, biology, psychology and environmentalism, Midgley was inspired to write *Beast and Man: the roots of human nature* (1978). She took the view that if you want to understand human attitudes to animals you should pay attention to people whose day-to-day work is understanding them (Kidd and McKinnell, 2016: 2–3). She was adamant that the species barrier is very real: while the differences across *Homo sapiens* are slight, those between the different species of animals are fundamental to their essence and *umwelt*. Thinking back to her childhood home, with its dog and cats, she now saw it as 'a "mixed community", a completely familiar inter-species collective, structured by social bonds of trust, friendship and care' (Mac Cumhaill and Wiseman, 2022: 278). Taking a broad view that allowed for cross-species interaction, the distinctive essence and *umwelt* of each species, and complexity of individual differences and development, Midgley made a major contribution to the philosophy of the empathy that humans have for other species.

Literary scholars, particularly those working on the Romantic period, have shown a particular interest in affect. Ottum and Reno survey the scope for the affective turn in the humanities to inform the critical readings of Romantic texts. Affect is seen as an integral part of the human response to the natural world. It is not possible to separate affect from cognitive or conative action. That affect is a physical sensation that can be measured, if not understood, by physiological and neurological responses, adds to its importance. For Ottum and Reno, the utility of affect is that it is open-ended. It leads to feeling conscious emotions. While affect remains contested, it deserves much more intensive study (Ottum and Reno, 2016: 6). Studies of Romantic literature are firmly within the field of ecocriticism, but many writers in the English and American romantic tradition were just as concerned with animals. I will suggest in the chapters that follow that animal studies can bring a new way of looking at texts to complement an ecocritical reading.

Zoologists have actively discouraged their students from letting empathy inform the way they conduct their research and report their findings. Primatologist Jane Goodall was criticised for the close relationships she formed with her research subjects and for giving them names rather than numbers. If she had maintained the recommended distance, she would never have seen anything. Without her observations on the social life and relationships of the chimpanzees of Gombe, we would still be in the dark about the social relations of our close kin. Goodall carried on using close interaction with the study population until the chimpanzees suffered a polio epidemic, and the risk that diseases could cross the species barrier with catastrophic consequences became evident. Now all research is done from a distance.

One zoologist has suggested that *Homo sapiens* has evolved to show affect, positive and negative, towards other species. Edward Wilson's *Biophilia* published in 1984 made this bold claim, but so far has had limited success in showing how that might work. A subsequent book, edited by Kellert and Wilson, was given the title *The Biophilia Hypothesis* to make it plain that, at least for now, the claim that humans have evolved to love or hate other species is a hypothesis for which a falsifiable proposition has not been proved, and therefore it cannot yet be raised to a theory (Kellert and Wilson, 1993: 21). Limited success in demonstrating that altruism could confer fitness on individuals of a species has relied on building mathematical models for kin and group selection. Midgley was dismissive of Wilson's attempt to extrapolate from the social life of ants to that of more complex animals. Not everything can be explained by a reductive and essentialising model that placed too much emphasis on genetics. For Midgley there was scope to apply more metaphysical concepts to human empathy. While the scientists are still looking at the physical processes of feeling, it is to the philosophers that we need to look for the concept of empathy. However, the meaning of the concept may vary between disciplines.

Neuroscientists and physiologists are still exploring the physical indications that are experienced as affect in humans and nonhuman animals (Paul et al., 2020). For the present, we should assume that the unique essence of nonhuman animals includes the capability to feel. It should not, however, be assumed that all humans feel the same way. Autism and other divergence from typical neurological reactions can have a marked influence on the affective response to other species. In so far as animal studies makes common cause with marginalised others, it is incumbent on us to allow for diversity in the way that affect is experienced. These alternative readings (as, for example, discussed in Carlson, 2018) will be explored in the following chapters. Whether kinship across species lines can be reciprocated is an open question, although for the companion animals in Haraway's example and in Midgley's mixed community, it seems possible. Dogs have coevolved with humans for millennia and it may be that reciprocated feelings of affect between the two species, similar to those humans experience between their own kin, have contributed to the evolutionary fitness of *Canis lupus familiairis*.

With companion and domesticated species, we are able to have feelings for individual animals. Other animals might be loved for their iconic status, even when we have only a remote chance of seeing them in the wild – polar bears and tigers come to mind. In Britain, the robin engenders an affective following. Because robins are highly territorial, it is easy to think that the robin we see picking invertebrates out of the freshly turned soil in our garden is the same individual, but we cannot be sure. When Peter Scott and his family established a reserve for migrating geese and swans on the Severn estuary, they found that each individual Bewick's swan (the European subspecies of the taiga swan *Cygnus columbianus bewickii*) had a unique pattern in the yellow of its bill. By charting these differences they were able to follow the fortunes of individual pairs of birds as they returned each year with or without that year's young. Although the purpose of this exercise was to collect scientific data, the affect they felt for the individual birds was an added bonus. It is also possible for humans to have affect for a species, or for some entity such as a murmuration of starlings where individuals seem to lose their identity in the patterns that whirl across the sky before flying in to roost. Once in the roost it is individuals that squabble all night as they jostle for space. From an animal studies viewpoint, affective feelings towards an individual of a different species provides at least the opportunity to meet the gaze of that individual, which Derrida suggests is necessary if we are to take nonhuman animals seriously.

Affect at the individual level brings with it a commitment to the well-being of that individual as expressed in animal welfare attitudes and provisions. Affect at the species level can bring into play a commitment to the continued presence of a thriving population of that species. Kinship between humans and a diverse cast of other species, not all of which are likely to be within the field of perception of an individual human, is more challenging than affect for a companion animal that shares our home. At a time of mass extinction, many conservationists try to stress that these threatened species deserve our affect. In this way they hope that we can extend our feelings of kinship to animals we have not met, or if we have we did not see, so that we bring them into the class of organisms that deserve our moral concern. The new field of extinction studies probes how such feelings work, both in those that are already committed to taking positive action and where these species have a presence in creative works.

Taking a cultural studies approach, Ursula Heise uses the special case of narratives about extinct and endangered nonhuman species to ask, 'why we care, not just as individuals but as communities or cultures' (Heise, 2016: 5). This way of seeing these narratives departs from the science and practice of conservation to focus on the attitudes of both the reader and writer of these narratives. She argues that 'biodiversity, endangered species, and extinction are primarily cultural issues, questions about what we value and the stories that we tell, and only secondarily issues of science'. This view is shared by Rose et al. Extinction studies have to be 'attentive to the simultaneously biological and cultural complexity of our world, insisting that extinction is an inherently and inextricably *biocultural* problem' (Rose et al., 2017: 5, original emphasis). For Rose et al., 'the biocultural complexity of the time of extinction … demands considered, lively, and creative responses from the humanities' (Rose et al., 2017: 2).

This focus on loss of biodiversity places the critical study of extinction narratives on the boundary between ecocriticism and animal studies. Most of these narratives could be read from either perspective. The focus on species as the embodiment of the animal other is a further complication. Looking at animals through the collectivity of species rather than as individuals requires us to understand how affect works when it is not on a one-to-one basis across the species boundary. I have taken the special field of extinction studies to be within the scope of animal studies. While Heise has been concerned about how we construct our own identity in relation to endangered species, extinction studies also raise issues relating to cross species affect and empathy, when abstract actors such as species and communities are involved.

Stop and think

If affect, emotion and empathy are only really experienced as internal to the individual, how confident are you that you would be able to describe your own emotional state? How would you detect the emotional state of another person? How confident would you be in reading the feelings of a nonhuman species? If it is so difficult would it be best to keep emotion out of it altogether and stick to the observable facts in interaction between species? Is it possible to approach works in the humanities on a solely factual basis devoid of feeling? These are difficult questions. Science is approaching them by searching for neurological markers and physiological responses to emotional states. Philosophers such as Mary Midgley have accepted that we are metaphysical animals and that empathy and feeling are components of the essence that makes us human.

From ecocriticism to animal studies

Ecocriticism covers a wide range of environmental concerns that are read with and against creative works in the humanities. The journal *Interdisciplinary Studies in Literature and the Environment* sets out its scope as: 'celebrating the rich confluence of environmental humanities, ecocriticism and environmental justice' (Oxford University Press, n.d.). Ecocriticism came into its own after the 1992 United Nations Conference on Environment and Development in Rio de Janeiro, otherwise known as the Earth Summit. The three conventions flowing from this summit define the linked environmental issues of climate change, loss of biodiversity and sustainable development. Ecocriticism embraces all of these pressing issues. It may be concerned with anthropogenic climate change or global extinction processes, on the other hand it can involve quite local experience of the natural world that gives meaning to a sense of place and the feelings of identity that are constructed from this experience. Animals, including humans, may be affected by climate change insofar as it forces changes in the ecosystems that they rely on for food, water and shelter.

Ecosystems can be at the scale of a catchment or forest system, or very local as in a pond or puddle. Ecology can be subdivided into systems ecology, which considers how the living plants and animals interact to form a functional system; population ecology where the size, breeding success and mortality of a single species is studied, and behavioural ecology where inter and intra-species behaviour influences the life outcomes of individuals and species. Systems ecology depends on systems thinking in terms of inputs, outputs and controls, and is very often descriptive. Population ecology is concerned with building quantified models. Relationships with other species tend to be simplified, as in predator–prey pressures. Behavioural ecology is concerned with areas such as display and courtship, parenting strategies and family bonds, and altruism between species. All of these versions of ecology can involve animals, but often address them at the level of species or population. Human–animal studies recognises that humans are animals that are subject to the same ecological pressures as other animals. There is therefore an overlap between ecocriticism and literary animal studies.

Animals occur widely in literature and it is the task of literary animal studies to explore the meanings flowing from their presence in a text, and their relationship to the human subjects. As a discipline, literary animal studies draws on the philosophical understanding of animals, the construction of meanings that relate to them, the rights of all sentient species and the semiotics of animal behaviour. Recognising the subject status of individual animals, rather than the objects of population or species studied by some ecologists, is an important aspect of literary animal studies. However, as we come to understand how the individual fits into the social world of its own species, we reach the boundary where other species and the environment as a whole come to play a part. Many investigations in animal studies will therefore draw on insights from ecology that are equally relevant in ecocriticism. Many of the literary texts studied under animal studies, may also be considered from an ecocritical standpoint.

Animal studies allow animals to have agency, and foregrounds them as subjects in the narrative rather than objects to be observed from afar. For example, a shepherd that knows their sheep as individuals will see them differently to those who see them collectively within a landscape. An environmentalist will see them as sources of greenhouse gas and modifiers of the habitat. Recognising the interconnection between the cultures of sheep and shepherds in a cultural landscape will offend those who see all domesticated sheep as bad. In this single example, an ecological reading of texts that feature sheep might focus on climate change, the ethics of domestication, the modification of the natural landscape and its effect on biodiversity, all intermingled. An animal studies reading will be concerned with the welfare of the animals, their agency and their recognition as subjects rather than objects. Both viewpoints will explore the coevolution of humans and sheep over ten millennia, the cultural meanings associated with sheep and shepherding and the ethical issues involved in their slaughter and consumption. The ethical considerations and cultural meanings associated with the consumption of meat are particularly challenging.

For some, the issue of meat for consumption is straightforward. If we are serious about overcoming speciesism, we should allow nonhuman animals the same rights that we extend to all humans, including not eating their flesh. That we may prefer not to address this issue head on is a problem in literary animal studies. Carol Adams suggested that the word 'meat' is problematic: 'Through butchering, animals become absent referents. Animals in name and body are made absent for animals as meat to exist' (Adams 2024 [1990]: 23). Adams' book, which celebrated 35 years in print in 2025, is a key reader for vegan studies. In her book she makes the explicit link between the othering of women in a patriarchal world, and the othering of animals reared for meat. 'My becoming a vegetarian had seemingly little relationship to my feminism – or so I thought. Now I understand how and why they are intimately connected, how being a vegetarian reverberates with feminist meaning' (Adams 2024 [1990]: liii). Feminism and animal studies are discussed further in chapter 4. Melanie Joy introduces the term 'carnism' as 'a sub-ideology of speciesism that dichotomises non-human animals into "edible" and "non-edible" categorisations and legitimates the exploitation and consumption of animal others – and thus presents an apt case study of speciesism'. She suggests that defences that support carnism form 'an invisible but potent feedback loop [that] construct fictitious cultural narratives that both validate carnism and invalidate veganism' (Weitzenfeld and Joy, 2014: 21–2).

Such narratives should be identified and be subjected to critical analysis. Can we do that without risking racism if we praise some Indigenous cultures for their vegan practice and condemn others for carnism? The Jain in India go as far as avoiding root vegetables to mitigate the risk that soil invertebrates might be harmed in their harvesting. The Inuit inhabit territories where hunting is possible, but agriculture is either very difficult or impossible. It may be necessary to look closely at what seems to be a human right, to validate transferring it seamlessly to a nonhuman animal. If problems arise considering a text using a literary animal studies framework, it may be given new depth by a further reading using ecocriticism.

Animal studies, with its focus on the individual animal, particularly if it is a human that is deciding what is good for it, may give us a one-sided view. For the consumption of meat, ecocriticism will add issues such as the impact on climate change from the emissions of methane, eructed (burped) from the rumen of cows and sheep reared for meat and dairy. It would further question the risks to biodiversity from intensive grazing and the use of pesticides. From those perspectives it might support arguments in favour of eating very little or no meat. However, an ecocritical reading would make a distinction between intensive rearing and the part played by extensive grazing in promoting high nature value landscapes. Katz-Rosene and Martin address these issues in *Green Meat?* (2020).

Katz-Rosene and Martin acknowledge that meat consumption on the scale of the affluent west is not sustainable, but stress that their book is not for 'hardline carnivores or vegans'.

> If anything, our foremost intention as editors – and that of our contributors – is to reiterate the importance of thinking carefully about *what* you eat, *where* it comes from, and *how* it is produced. What are the impacts of your diet on you, your community/communities, and your planet? This critical thinking about food and diet is a responsibility that we believe we have as editors, who are part of a consumption-driven class of settlers in what is presently known as Canada, all while living in a particularly challenging epoch of global environmental change – and the social, political, and economic changes that come along with it. (Katz-Rosene and Martin, 2020: xi, original emphasis)

The editors question the assertion by George Monbiot and others that cutting out all meat and dairy is the way to save the planet: 'the suggestion strikes the "critical thinker" in some of us as perhaps too simplistic a claim, an ostensibly singular truth that masks a vast, complex array of competing truths' (Martin and Katz-Rosene, 2020: 1). Indigenous communities' dependence on hunting for wild meat and fish raises such competing issues.

Thompson, Pritty and Thapa conducted a small-scale study of eco-carnivorism in the Gardenhill Foodshed in northern Manitoba. They aimed to demonstrate how such a diet can 'operate in harmony with Indigenous values, culture, health, and the environment' (Thompson, Pritty and Thapa, 2020: 107). These authors draw on the cultural importance of consuming meat, including social sustainability, or *mino bimaadiziwin* in the Oji-Cree language. 'Food for Indigenous communities is not merely a commodity but a celebration of culture and relationship with the environment, spirit, land, and animals' (Thompson, Pritty and Thapa, 2020: 110). How does this statement relate to Joy's 'fictional cultural narratives'? Indigenous story-telling narratives are discussed further in chapter 8. There are many other examples where an animal studies reading of literary works exposes similar layers of complexity. Meat eating, for which indifference is as potent a critical issue as commitment to either veganism or carnism, is one of the most problematic aspects of animal studies. There is a saying among farmers that if you cannot handle 'deadstock' you shouldn't handle 'livestock'. The same might be true for animal studies: in considering how nonhuman animals live we must confront how they die: through slaughter for meat, euthanasia as a welfare intervention, predation by nonhuman carnivores or starvation by humans reserving crops for themselves. The relationship with animals by those who adopt a vegan diet is itself a field of study that can complement an animal studies or ecocritical reading.

A specifically vegan reading might add new insights for some literary texts. The emerging discipline of Vegan Studies addresses

> what it means to read as a vegan, to recognise vegan characters as something other than as curiosities and sources of ridicule but, rather, as evidence of profound social, cultural and political resistance against a variety of injustices and an attempt to recognise non-human animals as deserving rights *and* having suffered the matrix of oppressions – racial, patriarchal, and gender-based – that also impact specific human animals. (Wright, 2022: 107, original emphasis)

For a fuller discussion of vegan studies see Wright and Quinn (2022).

Animal studies is, of necessity, interdisciplinary, and practitioners will call on many different ways of studying animals and the texts in which they appear. Ecocriticism is one of the disciplines that may be called in aid.

Posthumanism in animal studies

It could be claimed that any departure from the dualism of Descartes, with its claims for human exceptionalism, is posthumanist. A fully posthumanist approach means turning away from humanism completely. This rather drastic view argues that any attempt to adapt humanism through humane animal welfare, social construction (by humans) of animals, or (human led) campaigns for animal rights, is fatally flawed by its reliance on humans taking the lead. Not all those who write under the posthumanist banner are committed to this purist view. A posthumanist position can also be approached by allowing other species to have agency and desires that should be met. Human interests should not trump those of other species. Claims for human exceptionalism by virtue of literacy, reasoning and moral judgement should be set aside, so that we can attempt to see what it is that animals want.

If animals are to be considered on their own terms, the humans who create works, the critics who interpret them, and the people who read texts or watch film or performances, must hold back on privileging the human experience. This is very difficult to do. Creative works are the product of the human imagination, perceived through a human *umwelt*, expressed in the language and semiotic code of *Homo sapiens* and judged according to the moral code and sense of what is good that comes from the metaphysical human essence. Despite these difficulties, posthumanism is now well established in the academy and is seen to be a valuable standpoint for reading creative works.

The idea that kinship across species lines is both necessary and possible is central to Haraway's version of posthumanism (Haraway, 2008). While she is not entirely comfortable with the posthumanist label, most of her books are read as though they are posthumanist in intent. She does not submerge the human in her discourse, rather she admits nonhuman animals to affective relationships that have in the past been considered as unique to *Homo sapiens*. Affect is a slippery concept, we all have feelings that are evident to us, but others cannot observe them directly and have to rely on how we say we feel. This is difficult enough for ascertaining feelings in humans, but we cannot ask individuals of other species how they feel. Philosophers, scientists, psychologists and literary scholars have all grappled with affect.

Posthumanism is not a single coherent method. Cary Wolfe in *What is Posthumanism?* does not give a straight answer. He is clear, however, that it is not 'liberal humanism' which has been the dominant position in the humanities until the start of the twenty-first century. He is particularly clear that:

> we should *not* try to imagine some super-discipline called 'animal studies' … but rather recognise that it is only in and through our disciplinary specificity that we have something specific and irreplaceable to contribute to this question of the 'animal' that has recently captured the attention of so many different disciplines: not something *accurate* to contribute but something *specific*. (Wolfe, 2010: 115, original emphasis)

He argues instead for the practice of 'transdisciplinarity', in which a distributed network of observers are using their own disciplines, which can call into question the conclusions of each other. Citing Cora Diamond, he gives as an example how literature can confront philosophy, when thinking about our moral responsibilities. There is, however, always a risk that in our reliance on critical consciousness and by using characters that are specific to human thinking, we therefore reinstate the human/animal divide (Wolfe, 2010: 118). He makes the case for a posthumanism in which the discourse or critical procedure takes account of its own distinctions, forms and procedures (Wolfe, 2010: 122). Braidotti and Bignall also see posthumanism as transdisciplinary. Citing Deleuze and Guattari, they suggest that there should be a parallelism between philosophy, science and the arts. The result should be 'a clamorous and multiperspectival set of discussions taking place within the hybrid and marginal disciplinary terrains of the "new Humanities"' (Braidotti and Bignall, 2019: 5).

Escaping from 'speciesism' is very difficult. For Wolfe this is particularly true when cultural studies are addressing 'racism, sexism, classism and other -isms'. Each of these radical approaches can still remain committed to systematic discrimination against any other on the basis of species (Wolfe, 2003: 1). He maps the interplay between humanism and posthumanism on two axes – external relations and internal disciplinarity – placing Derrida close to posthumanism on both axes, and Haraway close on the external relations axis, but a little less close on internal disciplinarity. In contrast he cites Richard Rorty as close to posthumanism for external relations and close to humanism for internal disciplinarity (Wolfe, 2003: 125). To support this positioning, he cites Rorty's rejection of philosophies based on both idealism and realism. He also rejects philosophy as the 'mirror of nature'. Despite Rorty's attack on philosophy, he makes no effort to rethink the hierarchy of human/animal or indeed to include animals in liberal 'conversation'. Singer and Regan are placed close to posthumanism for external relations, but close to humanism for internal disciplinarity. To take a posthumanist view on both axes will require a fundamental change in the way we think. Even Derrida, who Wolfe places closest to this ideal, is still present to meet the cat's gaze. Does he allow for the power relations between the human and the cat? Has it been neutered, does it find its own food, are there parts of the home where it is not allowed? Are the stray cats of the district rounded up for neutering or euthanasia?

Bruno Latour holds that the distinction between the natural (material) world and the social world of *Homo sapiens* is artificial. At a time when all nonhuman animals are affected by what humans feel and do, this separation is plainly wrong. At the same time, our social world is directly influenced by nonhuman animals in our social culture, and in the material reality of living together in a biosphere with finite resources. Latour (2005) proposes the concept of actor-network theory (ANT) to reconcile these seemingly separate field of enquiry. Although developed within the social sciences, this theory readily translates to a posthumanist reading in the humanities. Latour does not exclude the human from such a reading, but he brings forward the part played by nonhuman 'actants' that can have an effect on human societies. His actants can include plants and inanimate material. Networks are in a constant state of flux. The network only comes into existence when effects are produced. It should be stressed that a posthumanist reading is not an attempt to follow the sciences in excluding human affect from 'objective' study, rather it embraces the subjectivity of nonhuman animals and the relationship that we have with them through creative practice in the humanities.

In practical terms, posthumanist practice in animal studies (Wolfe finds that term problematic as well) is best served by making repeated readings, each with a different way of looking at the problem.

Stop and think

As a thought experiment, think of an animal with no natural predators that is monopolising primary production of photosynthesising plants. Red deer in the Scottish Highlands would be an example. Consider the proposed solutions suggested by humans for restoring ecological balance: culling by shooting or the reintroduction of an apex predator such as the grey wolf. Now imagine that the species that is taking more than its share of natural resources is *Homo sapiens*. Obviously the drastic measures we impose on other species are out of the question for our own species. There is some way to go before we are truly democratic at the inter-species level. Can we be posthumanist if we make excuses and exemptions for our own behaviour? Do these excuses include the idea that humans are exceptional in both intellect and moral worth? The best we can do is to acknowledge how and when we are still privileging the interests of our own species, while making our best efforts to take account of the needs of the nonhuman kin we share the world and its resources with. For the avoidance of doubt, I am not suggesting some final solution for human overpopulation, but I am suggesting that a posthumanist account needs to acknowledge the way that we privilege our own species.

Post-*Homo sapiens*

Exploring a world where humans have become extinct is a logical extension from posthumanism. No species lasts forever, and at some stage, hopefully in deep time, *Homo sapiens* will become extinct. In the worst case scenario, our own species will become a casualty in the mass extinction event that seems to be in progress. Climate change of a magnitude to make life impossible for many species may also threaten humans with extinction. These ideas have preoccupied people at least since the *New Testament*'s 'Book of Revelations'. Biblical references in literature have introduced the idea that we are facing an apocalypse. In addition, Mussgnug draws attention to a loose genre of 'last man' stories that focus on 'experiences of solitude, the disruption of the closed order, crises of identity, and the encounter with a reality that eludes human understanding'. He traces this genre from Mary Shelley's *The Last Man* (1826) (Mussgnug, 2012: 334). The idea persisted from the interplay between early science fiction and Gothic literature, to twentieth-century eco-thrillers (Mussgnug, 2012: 336). From the 1970s, he suggests that authors turned to encounters between species and imagining a posthuman future (Mussgnug, 2012: 338). Not everyone views the extinction of our species as an apocalypse to be feared.

For MacCormack, the extinction of *Homo sapiens*, or at least the species continuance in very small relict populations, is to be welcomed. 'The conclusion of human extinction, seems unthinkable because the idea of a world without humans is understood as an apocalyptic end rather than an opening of the world' (MacCormack, 2020: 48) In Her *The Ahuman Manifesto* she puts forward an activism that will move away from animal rights to absolute abolition (MacCormack, 2020: 14). 'Abolitionists advocate the end of all use of animals for all purposes' (MacCormack, 2020: 15). They would abolish all interaction with animals that assume that humans are superior (MacCormack, 2020: 145). In practical terms, supporters of this manifesto would practise veganism and, as 'anti-breeders', avoid reproduction (MacCormack, 2020: 147). Removing all human dominance over animals is based on an understanding that 'the world is formed of chaotic flows' (MacCormack, 2020: 26). Writing against the idea of human compassion that drove both the animal welfare turn and that towards animal rights, she claims that the death of our species would be a far greater affirmation of ethics.

Mass extinction can also be a time for new species to emerge, just as mammals radiated to take the place of dinosaurs after the last mass extinction, small isolated groups of human survivors might adapt to a degree that they become one or more new species in the genus *Homo*. There have been a number of such adaptations in the hominid line over many thousands of years and this could happen again. It should not be assumed that we would regard any such change as progressive. Evolution does not work that way. Our own attitudes of exceptionalism might think these new people are brutes, just as we tend to look down on Neanderthals. Another possibility is that *Homo sapiens* becomes so dependent on computers for every aspect of life, that they become a hybrid between an animal and a cyborg. If our own species survives this mass extinction, what will it be like living without a host of animals that we take for granted? All of these possibilities are at present speculative and while they might feature in some science fiction texts, there is no firm basis for prediction of how it will all work out. Any reading of creative works that speculate about the future of our own species in deep time is likely to tell us more about how we currently contemplate the future than what that future will actually be like.

Potential obstacles

The first obstacle to overcome is to decide which animals are within the scope of an animal studies reading. Approaching from the viewpoint of sentience, there is a temptation to limit the scope to the 'higher animals', but with the caveat that the range of species of animal that have sentience and the ability to feel pain is expanding all the time with advances in neuroscience. Limiting the scope of animal studies to those texts which consider only animals with proven sentience would exclude many interesting texts and performances that consider insects, invertebrates and other multi-cellular animals. For this book I have assumed that the scope of animal studies extends to all species in the animal kingdom of complex multi-celled organisms that do not produce their own food. The kingdom includes living and extinct species, which brings the field of extinction studies within the scope of an animal studies reading.

Dwelling on sentience will also guide us to give preference to those species for whose welfare we have a moral responsibility, that is, domesticated animals and the humane treatment of harvested wild animals. We should at this stage challenge the wild/domestic binary. This will not be easy, particularly reading texts in nature writing that cover wild animals to the exclusion of those that are not wild. The boundary between 'wild' and 'not wild' is itself problematic. Wild animals can be habituated so that they ignore the presence of humans, for example, in a safari vehicle, or tamed so that they interact with humans to be fed. The distinction is based on the assumption that the social world inhabited by humans is entirely separate from the natural world inhabited by wild animals. Following Latour, the best course is to assume that there is an interaction between all species, including *Homo sapiens*, that share the same space.

A further question is whether we consider animals as individuals, populations or the whole species. For readings concentrating on agency and the subjectivity of the animals, it is the individual that possesses such attributes, with the possible exception that some biologists would argue that a nest of social insects could be considered as a super-organism. With the loss of biodiversity in response to climate change and other factors now a major concern, it is tempting to bring a species perspective within the scope of an animal studies reading. Expanding the scope in this way begs the question, how does an animal studies approach differ from an ecocritical reading? As discussed above, the answer is that they may well overlap, but ecocriticism includes wider environmental concerns. Some ecocritical readings may place animals in the background or ignore them altogether, for example, those pastoral studies that have a lot to say about the culture of shepherds. They may, however, say very little about the social relations that the sheep have with each other, with the shepherds that tend them, with the dogs that herd or guard them, and with the predators that threaten them. In such texts an animal studies reading may need to look between the lines to discover the agency and subjectivity of the animals in a pastoral system.

Can an animal studies reading be politically neutral? For some people, particularly those who embrace the term 'critical animal studies', the answer is that all animal studies readings should be committed to activism, by personal witness or by political engagement. Most of those drawn to animal studies in the humanities will be guided by moral principles and a belief that action should be taken. Most of the texts, films and performances they study will have a subtext that supports at least organic change through advancing understanding about animals, the threats they face, and the danger that we will only realise what we have lost when they have gone. It is important to take an open-minded approach that takes account of other standpoints, for example, of Indigenous peoples who have different ways of looking at animals, who will resent being dispossessed from their ancestral lands by colonial powers and their neo-colonial equivalents. Above all it is important to listen to the animals, to allow them agency and subjectivity. At the same time, to listen to the voices of Indigenous people for whom animals have spiritual as well as a material presence, and who may well have a better understanding of what the animals want.

Getting started in animal studies: key tenets

This section is an aide-mémoire of the principles discussed above. These are the important points to bear in mind in an animal studies oriented reading of literary works:

- *Homo sapiens* is not exceptional and has much in common with other animal species.
- The scope of an animal studies reading is not restricted to the 'higher animals', but should include all animals that have attracted the attention of creative practitioners in the humanities.
- The term 'species' is a human construct with room for disagreement about the boundaries between species, but the material and behavioural differences on which judgements are made are real.
- The Linnaean method of naming species is not superior to those used by Indigenous peoples and can obscure the way that other cultures have related to and named the animals that they knew intimately.
- Our understanding of sentience is advancing rapidly and it is not safe to assume that unfamiliar animals lack sentience.
- The ability to feel pain is similarly problematic and we should keep an open mind.
- Our relationship with other species should be based on what animals want and should allow for each individual to have agency.

- The 'human subject/nonhuman animal object' divide is artificial and all animals should be allowed to be subjects.
- The nature/culture divide is also artificial, the social world is influenced by material effects and social effects transform the natural environment.
- The wild/domesticated distinction is also problematic; limiting an animal studies reading to one category will miss the nuances of their inter-relationship in a multispecies world.
- The effect an animal has on the human imagination is a valid topic for an animal studies reading, we are not separate from the animal world.
- All animal studies readings have the potential to confront entrenched political positions, but those in the service of a single ideological standpoint are at odds with an open-minded approach that embraces the complexity of entanglements in a multispecies world.

Further reading

DeMello, Margo (ed.) (2012) *Animals and Society: An Introduction to Human-Animal studies*. New York: Columbia University Press.

Edwards, Karen L., Ryan, Derek and Spencer, Jane (eds) (2020) *Reading Literary Animals: Medieval to Modern*. New York and Abingdon: Routledge.

Gross, Aaron and Vallely, Anne (eds) (2012) *Animals and the Human Imagination: A Companion to Animal Studies*. New York: Columbia University Press.

Marvin, Garry and McHugh, Susan (2019) *Routledge Handbook of Human-Animal Studies*. New York and Abingdon: Routledge.

Midgley, Mary (1998) *Animals and Why they Matter*. Athens, GA: University of Georgia Press.

Turner, Lynn, Sellbach, Undine and Broglio, Ron (eds) (2018) *The Edinburgh Companion to Animal Studies*. Edinburgh: Edinburgh University Press.

References

Adams, Carol J. (2024 [1990]) *The Sexual Politics of Meat: A Feminist-Vegan Critical Theory*. London: Bloomsbury Academic.

Armstrong, Philip (2012) 'Literary animal encounters' in Margo DeMello (ed.) *Animals and Society: An Introduction to Human-Animal Studies*. New York: Columbia University Press, pp. 342–5.

Birch, Johnathan, Burn, Charlotte, Schneil, Alexandra, Browning, Heather and Crump, Andrew (2021) *Review of the Evidence of Sentience in Cephalopod Molluscs and Decapod Crustaceans*. London School of Economics.

Bekoff, Marc and Pierce, Jessica (2017) *The Animals' Agenda: Freedom, Compassion, and Coexistence in the Human Age*. Boston: Beacon Press.

Birkhead, Tim (2012) *Bird Sense: What It's Like to Be a Bird*. London: Bloomsbury.

Braidotti, Rosi and Bignall, Simone (2019). *Posthuman Ecologies: Complexity and Process After Deleuze*. New York: Rowman & Littlefield.

Carlson, Marla (2018) *Affect, Animals and Artists: Feeling Around the Edges*. Ann Arbor: University of Michigan Press.

Dawkins, Marian Stamp (2021) *The Science of Animal Welfare: Understanding What Animals Want*. Oxford: Oxford University Press.

de Waal, Frans (2016) *Are We Smart Enough to Know How Smart Animals Are?* London: Granta.

Fitzgerald, Amy J. (2019) *Animal Advocacy and Environmentalism*. Cambridge: Polity.

Godfrey-Smith, Peter (2018) *Other Minds: The Octopus and the Evolution of Intelligent Life*. London: William Collins.

Griffin, Nathan Stevens (2014) 'Doing critical animal studies differently' in Nik Taylor and Richard Twine (eds) *The Rise of Critical Animal Studies: From Margins to the Centre*. Abingdon: Routledge, pp. 111–36.

Haraway, Donna (2008) *When Species Meet*. Minneapolis: University of Minneapolis Press.

Heise, Ursula (2016) *Imagining Extinction: The Cultural Meanings of Endangered Species*. Chicago: University of Chicago Press.

Katz-Rosene, Ryan M. and Martin, Sarah J. (eds) (2020) *Green Meat? Sustaining Eaters, Animals, and the Planet*. Montreal: McGill-Queen's University Press.

Kellert, Stephen R. and Wilson, Edward O. (eds) (1993) *The Biophilia Hypothesis*. Washington DC: Shearwater.

Kidd, Ian James and McKinnell, Liz (eds) (2016) *Science and the Self: Animals, Evolution and Ethics: Essays in Honour of Mary Midgley*. Abingdon: Routledge.

Kinsella, John (2010) *Activist Poetics: Anarchy in the Avon Valley*. Liverpool: Liverpool University Press.

Kinsella, John and Hull, Coral (2000) *Zoo*. Bowraville, NSW: PaperBark Press.

Latour, Bruno (2005) *Reassembling the Social: An Introduction to Actor–Network Theory*. Oxford.

Latour, Bruno (2017) *Facing Gaia: Eight Lectures on the New Climate Regime*. Cambridge: Polity Press.

MacCormack, Patricia (2020) *The Ahuman Manifesto: Activism for the End of the Anthropocene*. London: Bloomsbury Academic.

Mac Cumhaill, Clare and Wiseman, Rachael (2022) *Metaphysical Animals: How Four Women Brought Philosophy Back to Life*. London: Chatto & Windus.

McHugh, Susan (2011) *Animal Stories: Narrating Across Species Lines*. Minneapolis: University of Minnesota Press.

Martin, Sarah J. and Katz-Rosene, Ryan M. (2020) 'Introduction' to Katz-Rosene, Ryan M. and Martin, Sarah J. (eds) *Green Meat? Sustaining Eaters, Animals, and the Planet*. Montreal: McGill-Queen's University Press, pp. 3–28.

Mussgnug, Florian (2012) 'Naturalising apocalypse: last men and other animals', *Comparative Critical Studies* 9:3, pp. 333–47.

Nocella II, Anthony J. and George, Amber E. (eds) (2019) *Intersectionality of Critical Animal Studies: A Historical Collection*. New York: Peter Lang.

Ottum, Lisa and Seth T. Reno (2016) *Wordsworth and the Green Romantics: Affect and Ecology in the Nineteenth Century*. Durham, NH: University of New Hampshire Press.

Oxford University Press (n.d.) *ISLE: Interdisciplinary Studies in Literature and Environment: About the Journal*. Available at: https://academic.oup.com/isle/pages/About (accessed 10 August 2025).

Paul, Elizabeth S., Sher, Shlomi, Tamietto, Marco, Winkielman, Piotr and Mendl, Michael T. (2020) 'Towards a comparative science of emotion: affect and consciousness in humans and animals', *Neuroscience and Behavioural Reviews* 108, pp. 749–70.

Rose, Deborah Bird, van Dooren, Thom and Chrulew, Matthew (2017) *Extinction Studies: Stories of Time, Death and Generations*. New York: Columbia University Press.

Taylor, Nik and Richard Twine (eds) (2014) *The Rise of Critical Animal Studies: From the Margins to the Centre*. Abingdon: Routledge.

Thompson, Shirley, Pritty, Pepper and Thapa, Keshab (2020) 'Eco-carnivorism in Garden Hill First Nation' in Ryan M. Katz-Rosene and Sarah J. Martin (eds) *Green Meat? Sustaining Eaters, Animals, and the Planet*. Montreal: McGill-Queen's University Press, pp. 107–32.

Weitzenfeld, Adam and Joy, Melanie (2014) 'An overview of anthropocentrism, humanism, and speciesism in critical animal theory' in Anthony Nocella J., II (ed.) *Defining Critical Animal Studies: An Intersectional Social Justice Approach for Liberation*, vol. 448, Counterpoints, New York: Peter Lang, pp. 3–27.

Witze, Alexandra (2024) 'Geologists reject the Anthropocene as Earth's new epoch – after 15 years of debate', *Nature News*, 6 March.

Wolfe, Cary (2003) *Animal Rights: American Culture, the Discourse of Species, and Posthumanist Theory*. Chicago: University of Chicago Press.
Wolfe, Cary (2010) *What is Posthumanism?* Minneapolis, MN: University of Minnesota Press.
Wright, Laura (2022) 'Book review: Emilia Quinn. *The Monstrous Vegan: Reading Veganism in Literature*', *Literature and History* 31:1, pp. 105–7.
Wright, Laura and Quinn, Emilia (eds) (2022) *The Edinburgh Companion to Vegan Literary Studies*. Edinburgh: Edinburgh University Press.

3

Posthumanism after Cary Wolfe: humans and animals in literary non-fiction

This chapter covers works of non-fiction that are open to an animal studies reading. It introduces the type of works that have been influential in how we view animals and shows how some of the theoretical ideas in the last chapter could guide our reading of animals in non-fiction prose. In particular it considers how posthumanism, as described by Cary Wolfe in his 2010 book *What is Posthumanism?*, can help give a voice to animals by giving their interests at least an equal weight to that of the humans who interact with them.

Posthuman readings after Wolfe

As we have seen in the previous chapters, influences on animal studies from ethology have provided evidence that nonhuman animals can have agency and subjectivity; from philosophy, that asks us to consider what it is that animals want; and from sociology, that shows how the social worlds of humans and nonhumans are intertwined. These developments invite us to question the tenets of liberal humanism. Animals are not the machines that Descartes had suggested and humans are not exceptional, in that many of the attributes that are claimed as markers of humanity are shared with nonhuman others. As soon as we acknowledge these difficulties with the traditional models associated with liberal humanism, we are leaning towards a posthumanist outlook.

Liberal humanism tends to put the interests of the human species above all others. The emphasis is on literature that speaks to what is constant in human nature (Barry, 2017: 19–23). We cannot know what it is to be a nonhuman animal, but in invoking human nature we should at least acknowledge that our nature has evolved over time, and that some aspects will be shared with other species. We have to set aside any claims for human exceptionalism. Liberal humanism's claim that the purpose of literature is the enhancement of life and the propagation of humane values would seem to pave the way to extending humane care to other species. But Cary Wolfe is particularly distrustful of liberal humanism's tendency for such pluralism, which expands consideration to previously marginalised groups, but without questioning 'the schema of the human who undertakes such pluralisation' (Wolfe, 2010: 99). In his discussion of American literature, Wolfe warns of an American exceptionalism based on assumptions that are embedded in theory and methodology (Wolfe, 2010: 242–3). He argues that these assumptions and commitments lead to an ideologically specific form of liberal humanism. This would be at odds with liberal humanism's claim to be free from socio-political influences (Barry, 2017: 19–20).

As discussed in chapter 2, there is not yet a consensus on what posthumanism means and still less an established methodology on how to deploy the concept in an animal studies reading. Cary Wolfe has extended thinking about posthumanism into the critical reading of works in the humanities, including poetry, fiction and film. He suggests

> that we should *not* try to imagine some super-discipline called 'animal studies' (an understandable desire, of course, for all who work on cultural studies of non-human animals) but rather recognize that it is only in and through our disciplinary specificity that we have something specific and irreplaceable to contribute to the 'question of the animal' that has recently captured the attention of so many different disciplines. (Wolfe, 2010: 115, original emphasis)

It is particularly important to recognise that the 'critical consciousness' of liberal humanism places the human above the nonhuman and 'reinstates the human/animal divide' (Wolfe, 2010: 119). For Wolfe posthumanism has to take account of its own internal logic and procedures, and be able to show how these differ from those of liberal humanism (Wolfe, 2010: 122). Noting that there are many contradictory definitions of posthumanism, Wolfe chooses to see this uncertainty as an opportunity rather than a barrier (Wolfe, 2010: xi).

In applying posthumanist thinking to animal studies, Wolfe suggests that it should be addressed at two levels: 'the level of content, thematics, and the object of knowledge (the "animal" studied by animal studies) but also the level of theoretical and methodological approach (*how* animal studies studies 'the animal")' (Wolfe, 2010: 99, original emphasis). The examples that follow show how writers of creative prose bring animals, with agency and individuality, to life in a form that can be subjected to critical analysis by animal studies.

Literary non-fiction should be both literary and factual

Potentially, the category of literary non-fiction is very broad. While most focus is likely to be on non-fiction works that have been classified as nature writing or animal writing, animals can also play a central role in biography, hunting memoirs, travel writing, wildlife interpretation, farm and equestrian memoirs, and popular science writing. All share the commitment to truthfulness in the description of actual animals and events, although these can sometimes be an amalgam of different real encounters for dramatic effect. All should be written in a literary style rather than the professional modes of expression of biologists, farmers or land managers. The departure from writing in literate English to the style of the professional scientist happened gradually through the twentieth century.

Erasmus Darwin (1731–1802) saw himself as both a scientist and a poet. He translated Carl Linnaeus's botanical taxonomic classification *Systema Naturae* (1735) as a long poem in *The Loves of Plants* (1789), which brought Linnaeus to a literate audience. In another long poem, *The Temple of Nature*, published posthumously in 1803, he set out his own ideas about evolution. Samuel Taylor Coleridge, at first an admirer of Darwin, came to dislike his verse style. I mention Erasmus Darwin here, even though he was writing on plants not animals, and in verse not prose, to illustrate the point that literary styles are often contested. Today Darwin is seen as a scientist and Coleridge, even though he was an accurate observer of the natural world, as a poet.

Erasmus's grandson Charles Darwin (1809–82) also wrote in a literary style. With only a small degree of rearrangement, Ruth Padel was able to transpose his writing as poetry in *Darwin: A Life in poems* (2010). George Levine makes the case that

> Darwin's enormous cultural success – in the short run at least – depended as much on the form of his argument and the nature of his language, as it did on the power of his ideas and his evidence. [Levine didn't] want to minimise these latter; the quality of the writing itself depends on the nature of the evidence and the way that it is deployed. The qualities required for good science – not least precision – are not much different from the qualities required for good literature. (Levine, 2011: 5)

This precision, even when it is speculating about the natural world, is then an important quality to look for in reading animals in non-fiction.

Careful observation of animals

A commitment to a 'true to nature' description of animals has given us the classic natural history of a single locale in Gilbert White's *Natural History and Antiquities of Selborne* (1789). This work was carefully edited from his scientific correspondence with Thomas Pennant and Daines Barrington. The developing field of natural theology meant that the study of nature was seen as a proper occupation for a clergyman. White's book brought together 30 years of detailed observations from journals and from his scientific correspondence. The long-term study, across the seasons and from year to year, enabled him to build an understanding of each species. There is uncertainty in much of his discourse, for example, over where swallows and house martins go in the winter, leaving it to future scientists to fill in the gaps in our understanding of these and other species. What is significant is that where he is uncertain he tells us. The correspondence from which his account was drawn allows for debate where facts are missing, but not to fall back on the fables of antiquity.

There have been many editions of this book, mostly missing the section on antiquities, and it is still in print. The editors of these editions, who include Richard Jeffries, Richard Kearton, E. M. Nicholson, James Fisher, R. M. Lockley and, for the version I have, Richard Mabey, is a roll call of important writers on animals and the natural world. For Abberley et al. modern nature writing owes a great deal to Gilbert White who, in *The Natural History of Selborne,* 'presented nonhuman creatures as forming a dynamic ecological community. Its sympathetic and precise attention to animal behaviour, as well as its close focus on a particular locale, have had a powerful influence on nature writers over the past two centuries' (Abberley et al., 2022: 38). These works will inform 'the content, thematics, and the object of knowledge' that is the animal that is studied by animal studies (Wolfe, 2010: 99). *The Natural History of Selborne* is a classic book in the nature writing genre. While it can be given an ecocritical reading for its construction of the English countryside and for its parochial focus at a time of political and agricultural revolutions, it is White's way of looking at and thinking with animals that concerns us here.

The value of study close to home was rediscovered during the COVID-19 pandemic, when many naturalists were unable to make the excursions to favourite places, some of which were in other continents. White learned to really look at and listen to the animals he studied. This is the gaze of the naturalist in the field, taking in the details of behaviour, which sets it apart from what White called the 'faunists', who worked from dead specimens in museums and laboratories. He watched house martins building their mud nests under the eaves, and recorded how they allowed time for each layer to dry before adding another. His separation of the three species of leaf warbler, which was based on close observation of their field behaviour, song and the small differences in their plumage, was later confirmed by genetic analysis.

Some naturalists will go to great lengths to avoid being seen by the animals that they are studying. Photographer Richard Kearton hid inside a hollowed out cow skin to get closer to his subjects. White just made himself unthreatening. All the birds and animals he observed were living alongside humans in the English village that had been shaped by generations of farmers. The house martins and swifts under the eaves and the barn swallows in the barns had adapted themselves to human buildings and could be said to be commensal with *Homo sapiens.* The following passage is an example of how

White watched birds and his understanding that he too was being watched.

> A farther instance I once saw of sagacity in a willow-wren [willow warbler], which had built in a bank in my fields. This bird a friend and myself had observed as she sat in her nest; but were particularly careful not to disturb her, though we saw she eyed us with some degree of jealousy. Some days after we passed that way and were desirous of remarking how this brood went on; but no nest could be found, till I happened to take up a large bundle of green moss, as it were carelessly thrown over the nest, in order to dodge the eye of any impertinent intruder. (White, 1987 [1789]: 142)

Leaving aside for the moment the anthropomorphism implicit in words such as: 'sagacity', 'jealousy' and 'impertinent', the key point in this passage is that White met the gaze of the willow warbler and adapted his own behaviour to avoid flushing it from the nest. Is this the *'seen seen'* that Derrida had in mind?

This bird was not habituated to behave as if White was not there, but was continuously making an assessment of the trade-off between her own safety and that of her clutch. Covering the nest when it was vacated would help conceal it from the 'impertinent' eye of egg-stealing children and magpies. Both of these behaviours would increase the probability that the young would be safely fledged, and therefore contribute to fitness under pressure from human and other predators. White was writing long after Descartes claimed that all nonhuman animals are automata and before Darwin and Wallace came up with the concept of natural selection.

Stop and think

How does the naturalist's field craft deployed by White contrast with Derrida being *'seen seen'* by his cat? Derrida chose his domesticated cat for his example, but can the principle be extended to wild animals? Is White's attribution to this bird of the human qualities of jealousy and sagacity anthropomorphic, or does it suggest that White is allowing for a nonhuman animal to have powers of reasoning and affect? How can such careful observation with an open mind about what it all means be compared with allowing the animals themselves to speak? Is this receptiveness to the meanings of the other threatened when scientists have decided they have enough data to say what it means?

Field work and narrative

Although White is seen as the model for patient observation in the field, the reality in the nineteenth century was that taxonomy was where reputations were made, thereby creating a demand for a ready supply of dead specimens. Ornithologist Edmund Selous (1857–1934) was at first very much at home with this tradition. However, Birkhead claims that in 1898 Selous had an 'epiphany' (Birkhead, 2022: 214). He had been watching a European nightjar as it sat on its nest. This species is famous for its camouflage and Selous spent some time gazing at the stationary shape before he was convinced that he was looking at a bird and not a piece of bark. After this experience he gave up shooting birds to savour the affect that he experienced in observational field work. For Birkhead this was an important shift to empathy in our relationship with wild animals.

Field naturalists were 'hated and derided by museum experts – who considered themselves the *real* scientific experts – Selous made empathy for birds respectable and, in doing so, changed the world' (Birkhead, 2022: 215, original emphasis). His approach was to watch and think about why birds were behaving in particular ways by '*inference*' (Birkhead, 2022: 215, original emphasis). Here he is wondering about the behaviour of a duck feigning injury to lead a human away from its young:

> Darwin, if I remember rightly, found it difficult to believe that birds, when they thus distract attention from their young to themselves, do so with full consciousness of what they are doing and why they are doing it. When the female wild-duck, however, acts in this manner, it is difficult, I think to escape this conclusion. She flaps for a long way over the surface of the water, pausing every now and again and waiting as though to see the effects of her ruse, and continues her tactics as soon as you get up to her. Having thus led you a long

> distance away, she rises, and leaving the river flies an extended circle, which will ultimately bring her back to it by the other bank when you are well out of the way. (Selous, 1901: 58–9)

Selous could have offered a simple description of this behaviour, but by empathising with the bird, he came to the conclusion that this behaviour is considered. Margaret Nice cites Selous's description of his guiding principles: 'joy in all wild life and its surroundings, with another joy in Darwin and a social shunning disposition – and an intellectual love of truth too' (Nice, 1935: 90). She summarises his method as 'observation – tireless and heroic; studied independence of contemporary naturalists; interpretation of his findings in the light of Darwin; and an intense hatred of killing' (Nice, 1935: 90).

Kuklick shows the similarity between naturalists such as Selous, for whom fieldwork should be heroic, with those of anthropologists, who immerse themselves within the culture of the society they are studying. For Selous to study the mating habits of ruff in Holland he was subjected to 'wretchedness, cold, and discomfort' (Selous cited by Kuklick, 2011: 14). This way of working allowed its practitioners some licence in departing from strictly scientific observation.

> Because fieldwork was understood to test and build character, it is not surprising that its practitioners were inclined (and permitted by their audiences) to develop deliberately personal investigative styles, as opposed to the ostensively affectively neutral style normative in laboratory research. (Kuklick, 2011: 14)

It is this admission of empathy that makes the nature writing of naturalists such as Selous readable as literature. Empathy can allow for the nonhuman species to have subjectivity and agency. This turn in field natural history can therefore align such nature writing with the principles of animal studies discussed in the previous chapter, and in particular with how animal studies approaches the animal (Wolfe, 2010: 99).

Field ornithology and the Second World War

Although birds are problematic from an animal studies point of view, as being closer to the dinosaurs than to the mammals that we might have some chance to understand, they have been very popular for study by both amateur bird watchers and professional ornithologists. Interest in such studies was gathering pace in the 1920s and 1930s, but it was during the Second World War that ideas were consolidated. Max Nicholson, in *The Art of Bird Watching* (1931), put forward the idea that bird watchers could collaborate to gather data to inform the conservation debate. The British Trust for Ornithology (BTO) was founded in 1932 to implement his ideas. David Lack had begun an in-depth behavioural study of breeding robins around Dartington in Devon, which was published as a monograph *The Life of the Robin*, in 1943. James Fisher published his *Bird Watching* in 1941. He begins the first chapter:

> Though they are by no means the most ubiquitous, numerous, curious, or diversified forms of life, it is nevertheless a fact that birds have more attention paid to them than any other corresponding group of animals. Many attempts have been made to discover why so many people like birds. Nobody has so far given a really satisfactory answer, though when it comes, it will probably be found partly from a sort of mass observation and partly from the long and detailed history which bird watching has enjoyed particularly in Britain. (Fisher, 1945 [1941]: 13)

Having got off to a promising start, this movement, guided by Nicholson, Fisher and others, was put on hold. Nicholson worked in central government organising shipping across the Atlantic and for the invasion of Europe. Lack moved to research on radar and was able to show that the 'angels' which mariners reported on their screen were migrating flocks of birds. Fisher studied rooks for the Ministry of Agriculture. Four bird watchers, Peter Conder, George Waterston, John Barrett and John Buxton, found themselves prisoners of war at Oflag VI B in Warburg, Germany, from where they were able to conduct in-depth studies of the birds that nested within the confines of the camp and to count those that migrated above it. Buxton, who was to return to civilian life as an English literature academic was to write a Collins' New Naturalist monograph on the redstart by drawing on the dawn to dusk observations of the birds he and others made when confined as prisoners of war (Niemann, 2012).

After the war, James Fisher, who became editor of Collins' New Naturalist, was very influential in publishing writing by naturalists.

Not all of these were in a literary style, although the writing in Buxton's *The Redstart* has been highly praised. Waterston spent part of his time as a prisoner plotting how to set up a chain of bird observatories to study migration and in particular how to buy Fair Isle, in the Northern Isles, as a base for one of these observatories. Conder became director of the Royal Society for the Protection of Birds (RSPB). David Lack became director of the Edward Grey Institute for Field Ornithology at Oxford University, as a centre for training professional ornithologists.

Birds also changed their habits during the war. Black Redstarts found bombed-out London to their liking, and avocets moved into brackish lagoons at Minsmere in Suffolk, which had been flooded as a defence against invading tanks. The RSPB acquired Minsmere and nearby Havergate Island as reserves, which was to be the first stage in its growth to a mass membership organisation with a nationwide portfolio of reserves.

The ethology turn

Julian Huxley, who admired Selous, was to put his way of working to practical effect in developing the science of ethology. While Huxley published popular works that fit well within the nature writing genre, he also developed the special ways of describing behaviour that came to be associated with ethologists. Crist discusses how ethologists such as Tinbergen and Lorenz moved away from trying to understand an animal's experience of their world to develop a theoretical comprehension of their behaviours.

> With ethology, then, the depiction of animal life became epistemologically equivalent to that of the behaviour of inanimate phenomena. Just as there is no intrinsic meaning to a falling object, or a swinging pendulum, so an internal point of view is eradicated from animal life with the use of technical language, and the constitution of animals as 'natural objects,' is the effect of the technical idiom to animal life. (Crist, 1998: 61)

It is unlikely that these technical papers, with their specialised language and suppression of affect, would appeal to readers expecting non-fiction works to have some claim to being literature. This turn from literary modes of expression serves the professionalisation of science, but at the cost of placing knowledge about animals outside the discourse of a literary readership. The gap between the 'object' preferred by science and the 'subject' that allows for animals to have sentience and agency is a challenge for animal studies. Early ethology was particularly focused on behaviour that seemed to be instinctive or innate, that is, determined by inheritance and not by learning. Animal studies, on the other hand, is predisposed towards behaviour where the animal has agency, rather than being an automaton as imagined by Descartes. Even though in their technical papers the ethologists treated the animals that they studied as objects, they felt no need to abide by these conventions in all their works.

Both Tinbergen and Lorenz wrote very influential popular works in which the strict distance between the scientist (subject) and the animal (object) is bridged by the enthusiasm, affect and respect for the individual animals that they have studied. Later writers, including David Lack with *The Life of the Robin* (1943) and *Swifts in a Tower* (1956), and Jane Goodall with *In the Shadow of Man* (1971), made their fields of study accessible to the general reader. Lack has been criticised for his avoidance of statistics and, as we have seen, Goodall for becoming too close to the chimpanzees whose behaviour she was studying. Although going against the grain of scientific orthodoxy, these authors brought their readers closer to the nonhuman other. These works have played an important role in the development of animal studies by encouraging a wider audience to see the natural world differently and to share the joy to be found from watching animals closely enough to show their individual character and agency.

Stop and think

How does this way of seeing animals find its way into literary works? Can it inform the methodology of animal studies? After the discovery of the chemical structure of DNA in 1953, many professional biologists were drawn to the study of smaller and smaller components of the animal. Such a reductionist viewpoint makes it difficult to see the whole animal. Is it possible to have an animal studies reading when there are no individual animals in sight? How far does the continuing enthusiasm for amateur bird watching provide for a direct encounter between the human and the nonhuman that is expressed as the type of discourse in which an animal studies reading is possible?

Animals in the 'new nature writing'

The summer 2008 issue of *Granta* was dedicated to what it called the 'new nature writing'. In his editor's letter, Jason Cowley explained that in inviting submissions they wanted to get away from the old nature writing in 'the lyrical pastoral tradition of the romantic wanderer' in favour of 'voice driven narratives told in the first person, for the writer to be present in the story'. Such writing includes field reports, essays, memoirs and travelogues (Cowley, 2008: 10). While the first two decades of the twenty-first century saw an outflowing of writing in this genre, not everyone was happy. For Kathleen Jamie, even though she was a contributor to *Granta* 102, there was too much 'I' in the writing. In her *London Review of Books* review of Robert Macfarlane's *The Wild Places* (2007), titled 'A Lone Enraptured Male', she praises the 'lovely honeyed prose' and finds Macfarlane to be 'a delightful literary companion' (Jamie, 2008). However, there are no other voices and the focus on the author's affective state means that it is the author we behold and not the wild places. John Kinsella detests nature writing for its hypocrisy, for getting close to animals to soak up their natures and for the genre being a departmental party trick. Jamie and Kinsella are warning us to approach such writing with care. At its best, an animal studies reading will expose writers who pay too much attention to their own affective state and not enough to the agency and individuality of the nonhuman other. It will find a balance between these competing interests.

There are a number of important works in the new nature writing genre where animals are brought into sharper focus. These include Helen Macdonald's *H is for Hawk* (2014), Miriam Darlington's *Otter Country* (2012), Patrick Barkham's *The Butterfly Isles* (2010) and Mark Cocker's *Crow Country* (2007). All except Macdonald's book are on the wild side of the wild/domestic divide. Macdonald's hawk is a goshawk that she was training for falconry. The author is present in all of these and we share the tribulations and joy of finding sometimes elusive animals.

The new nature writing and the animals that are depicted are heavily influenced by the commitment in post-war conservation to the preservation of wild habitats and species. This philosophy was led by amateur naturalists and professional scientists with little interest in – and, in some cases, outright hostility to – the killing of animals for sport. In Britain, the first development of a plan for conserving nature is usually attributed to Charles Rothschild who founded the Society for the Promotion of Nature Reserves in 1912 (now The Wildlife Trusts). Rothschild was an entomologist concerned to preserve sites with high biodiversity, at a time when they were at risk from agriculture and development. In the post-Second World War period, there was an acceleration in the creation of nature reserves based on Rothschild's principles, both by amateur naturalists and government-sponsored scientific agencies.

In contrast, the much older North American conservation model was driven as much by hunting interests, anxious to secure a sustainable supply of quarry species, as by scientific study, or by the conservation of species for or their own sake. Theodore Roosevelt, who with John Muir, laid down the foundations of this model, was himself a hunter of big game in Africa and of other species in the American wilderness. With its focus on the individual rather than the species, contemporary animal studies could well avoid hunting narratives as being cruel. There are, however, creative non-fiction accounts of hunting that show as much empathy and concern for the welfare of the animals being pursued as there is in any text sheltering under the moral principles of the European conservation model.

Ian Niall, who was a prolific writer on the countryside of Scotland and Wales, had a particular interest in fishing and shooting. One of his best known books is *The Poacher's Handbook* (1950), in which his vivid descriptions have both literary merit and are true to nature on the individual behaviour of the mammals, fish and birds that were taken by poachers. He describes with disapproval the methods of some poachers that maim without killing, but saves his strongest condemnation for the industrial-scale poaching gangs that decimate the populations to below the level from which they could recover.

Animal studies readings in the time of environmental crisis will always challenge the reader. Rather than trying to develop a single integrated method, I am suggesting that each text should be subjected to successive readings from a variety of standpoints. We can get knowledge from scientists who deny the subjectivity of the animals they study and from literary figures, some of whom might hold abhorrent social convictions. What is required is that we read such texts critically to winnow out the true to nature parts of the narrative stripped of any assumptions that conflict with the principles of animal studies listed at the end of chapter 2. The following case study is an example of a writer trying to get close to the species he studies. Despite its position in the nature writing canon, reading the book from an animal studies viewpoint raises new questions.

Case study: J. A. Baker's *The Peregrine* and admission to the nature writing canon

In 2004 the *New York Review of Books* republished J. A. Baker's *The Peregrine*, which was originally published in 1967. Robert Macfarlane, who played a part in the republication of the book, brought it to the attention of the growing number of people interested in new ways of relating to nature. Kathleen Jamie and Mark Cocker, who also contributed to *Granta* 102, joined the chorus of praise for the book. For Cocker, *The Peregrine* is 'viewed by many as the gold standard for all nature writing' and 'a case could easily be made for its greatness by the standards of any literary genre' (Cocker, 2010: 4). Kathleen Jamie's interest was sparked when a pair of peregrines attempted to breed in the quarry that she could see from the window of the attic where she writes. 'His book is tremulous, overwrought, hungry. He writes like a falcon must see and so allows us to see, too' (Jamie, 2005: 43). The collection of Baker's papers at the University of Essex has enabled some of the mysteries about the man and his methods to be brought to light. Examining the manuscripts, Macfarlane found that Baker kept a page by page tally of metaphors, similes, adjectives and verbs. 'He had subjected his sentences to prosodic analysis, with stress and accent marks hovering above each syllable, as if scanning poetic meter' (Macfarlane, 2015: 153). The fulsome praise for its literary merits fulfils one criterion for creative prose in animal texts, but is the book also true to its subject matter? Does this fulsome praise rely on the assumption in liberal humanism that good literature is of timeless significance?

There were some questions at the time about the veracity of Baker's observations. Cocker gives the example that 'Baker was finding falcons in and around the Chelmer Valley, where few or no other observers managed to see them' (Cocker, 2010: 8). Sean Nixon, who has had access to the Baker archive, sets him firmly in the emerging bird-centred culture of nature from 1954 (Nixon, 2017: 205–26). He submitted records to the Essex Birdwatching Society, founded in 1949. The much older and more generalist Essex Field Club, founded in 1880 and still in existence, was part of the previous turn towards civic natural history often associated with the collection of specimens for museums.

Although Baker kept a diary of his observations, his practice of working alone made it difficult for others to verify some of the behaviour he saw. County recording societies had become increasingly nervous after a special issue of *British Birds,* published in 1962, suggested that fraud was implicated in some bird records for the area around Hastings from 1892–1930. While 29 species were deleted from the British record, subsequent analysis and new sightings have reinstated many of these records. Since then, all reputable recording bodies have had to develop robust procedures for validation (metadata such as species, where, when and who) and verification (identification supported by accurate field notes) of records. Baker was therefore submitting records against a new more stringent climate for their acceptance.

Cocker has remarked that Baker was 'absolutely fixated by peregrines' and over the ten years of observations, condensed into a single year in the book, he built up a knowledge of the birds that enabled him to find them when no others could. Derek Ratcliffe, whose eminence as an ornithologist matches the literary standing of the new nature writers, had no doubts. In his monograph on the species, he writes: 'we are indebted to J. A. Baker for the only detailed study of the wintering habits of the peregrine in lowland Britain. His story of infinitely patient watching and searching on the estuaries and arable lands of the Essex coast is told in his highly original book'

(Ratcliffe, 1993 [1980]: 132). This endorsement should be enough to meet the second requirement for animal studies prose, that it should be true to its subject. Critical attention to this work has mostly been in the context of the new nature writing. Could an animal studies reading add new insights?

The relationship Baker established to get close to his chosen species is of particular interest for literary animal studies. He developed a very specific field craft to be able to move through the landscape without upsetting the birds in their natural routine.

> To be recognised and accepted by the peregrine you must wear the same clothes, travel the same way, perform actions in the same order. Like all birds, it fears the unpredictable. Enter and leave the same fields at the same time each day, soothe the hawk from its wildness by a ritual of behaviour as invariable as its own. Hood the glare of the eyes, hide the white tremor of the hands, shade the stark reflecting face, assume the stillness of a tree. (Baker, 2005 [1967]: 13)

In this passage he describes the process of habituation by which a wild creature knows that the human is there, but also knows that there is no threat. Konrad Lorenz, wishing to ring (band) the jackdaws that he had habituated to accept him in his normal attire, went to the extreme of dressing up in a devil's costume to clamber over the roof of his home to reach their nests. The hope is that habituated animals will behave in the same way as they would if no human was present. For Baker, being ignored is not the same as being invisible. With poor eyesight himself, he understood that a peregrine would always be aware of his presence. The nature of the human–animal bond becomes one of mutual respect, allowing Baker to see behaviour that others had missed. It does, however, raise the question of whether he sees himself as a dispassionate observer recording facts about the peregrines as the objects of his study or as being involved in the peregrines' world even if they seem to ignore him.

At the time Baker was writing, there was pressure on naturalists to suppress feelings in pursuit of objectivity. However, it is clear that he wanted his book to stand both as literature and as a truthful account of peregrine behaviour. Initially for Macfarlane, '*The Peregrine* is not a book about watching a bird, it is about becoming a bird' (Macfarlane, Introduction to Baker, 2005: viii). Baker himself suggests that 'the hunter must become the thing he hunts' with sharpened vision and time measured by the pulse of blood (Baker, 2005: 13). To that end he approached his hunting with single-minded determination. 'Wherever he goes, this winter, I will follow him. I will share the fear, and the exaltation, and the boredom, of the hunting life. I will follow him till my predatory human shape no longer darkens in terror the shaken kaleidoscope of colour that stains the deep fovea of his brilliant eye' (Baker, 2005: 41).

He embraced the affect of the dedicated watcher for his chosen species. 'Everything I describe took place while I was watching it, but I do not believe that honest observation is enough, the emotions and behaviour of the watcher are also facts, and they must be truthfully recorded' (Baker, 2005: 14). Affect is inseparable from the pursuit of fact, for example, in this passage he identifies with the bird: 'I watched him with longing, as though he was reflecting down to me his brilliant vision of the land beyond the hill' (Baker, 2005: 140). Around the same time that Baker was writing *The Peregrine,* Jane Goodall was facing a similar conflict between detached observation and really getting to know her chimpanzees in Tanzania. By allowing human feeling to enter the narrative, both Baker and Goodall contributed, in their own way, to the animal turn. These ideas are now central to theory in animal studies.

Jamie Lorimer spent a summer with a skilled conservation scientist employed to count breeding corncrakes on a Scottish island. As with Baker and Goodall, this scientist had passionate interactions with the corncrakes, but such interactions are absent from the official breeding population statistics assembled remotely by the scientists overseeing the count. '[Lorimer] takes these as illustrative of the multitude of embodied and affective encounters between skilled humans, other species, and landscapes that underpin conservation' (Lorimer, 2015: 37). More directly, Donna Haraway was to stress the importance of kinship between species. Although her case studies relate mostly to companion animals, they could be extended to the feeling that scientists have for the animals they choose to study. It should, however, be understood that Baker's feeling for peregrines was not reciprocated. The best he could hope for was that their behaviour was not unduly influenced by his presence.

Peregrines elicit strong emotions in their watchers. Their distinctive way of hunting, in particular the spectacular fast dive or stoop, has attracted falconers and birdwatchers. For Baker 'the excitement of seeing a peregrine stoop cannot be defined by the use of statistics' (Baker, 2005: 21). I can vouch for this feeling, even when a peregrine was stooping on pigeons in my own loft, I felt this excitement before rushing round to see if any of my birds were missing.

One of his observations that others found hard to accept, was the tiercel (male) bird he saw catching and eating a worm (Baker, 2005: 152). This bird ambushed his prey from an apple tree. How Baker feels about this unusual behaviour takes him close to attributing human values to another species.

> For one tiercel peregrine there is the cloudless sky, the wide valley, the hills, the estuaries; twenty paradisal miles of hunting land, a million birds to choose from, ten thousand feet of warm and windy air to sail and soar upon. For the other tiercel, just as strong, with the same sharp bill and biting feet, there is only the quiet corner of an orchard, an acre of grass and apple trees, a few mice, a partridge perhaps, worms and then sleep. (Baker, 2005: 167)

Have other observers missed seeing this behaviour because they have been too focused on aerial pursuit? The strength of Baker's narrative is that he describes what he sees separately from how he feels, but in this passage does his use of language display a hint of anthropomorphism?

In a 2017 article, Macfarlane revisited his suggestion that the book is about Baker becoming a bird. Instead he suggested that it is about failing to become a bird. Baker wanted to live as the falcons do, but for Macfarlane, just as he seems to be getting close, he is aware of the limitations of his human body. 'Again and again, subject-object distance is almost closed – only to yawn open once more' (Macfarlane, 2017). If even someone as devoted as Baker cannot close this distance, does this mean that one of the most important goals of a posthuman reading can never be achieved? If, after Nagel, we can never know what it is like to be a bat, how much harder it must be to know about a bird? As discussed in chapter 1, Birkhead certainly feels that we should not abandon all hope of understanding bird behaviour. Patient and quiet observation is the first prerequisite, but the most important is to allow the bird to 'speak'. It is for this reason that Haraway celebrates the insights gained by ethologists. Baker certainly contributed records to the Essex Birdwatching Society, but another post-war development was the growth of ethology. Did he read Lorenz or Tinbergen?

This book is a rich narrative that can be read fruitfully in many different ways, as literature, as extinction study, as psychogeography, as environmental commentary and as natural history. Students of literary animal studies will find much to interest them, both in how Baker went about getting close to another species and in the emotions engendered when he was successful.

Stop and think

Consider why this book, first published in 1967, has enjoyed such critical acclaim in the twenty-first century. Was it Baker's specific aim to live like a bird that attracted those who were influenced by David Abram's *Becoming Animal: an earthly cosmology* (2011)? How far can the empathy he feels for the birds he studies bring him close enough to listen to what drives this top predator? Would this book have found favour if it had no literary qualities or alternatively if it was shown to have invented the facts?

Context in animal writing

Wolfe advises us to consider the biopolitical context for a text. Nixon notes that Baker was writing at a time when bird watching was becoming a more popular pastime, supported by new organisations such as the Essex Birdwatching Society. He also draws attention to the emerging understanding, particularly after Rachel Carson's *Silent Spring* (1962), that agricultural pesticides were having on the population ecology of even common species. Baker submitted records to the Essex Birdwatching Society and, as discussed above, his observations of the behaviour of peregrine falcons in winter were valued by professional ornithologists. Throughout the book he is conscious that, left unchecked, the pesticide 'rain' on the fields would lead to the extinction of peregrines in the near future. This book can therefore be read in the genre of extinction studies.

By the time *The Peregrine* was republished in 2014, new readers would be faced with a very different epistemological landscape. Baker's contemporary, Derek Ratcliffe, represented a further development in the second half of the twentieth century with the emergence of professional science-based ornithology, in which experts at the BTO collate and analyse data from amateur (but often very skilled) ornithologists across the country. Funding for these activities came from the new Nature Conservancy, which was both a research council and responsible for identifying national nature reserves. Ratcliffe, who was tasked by the BTO to research the breeding ecology of peregrines, was able to draw on an army of amateur birdwatchers to visit all known and possible breeding sites for these birds. This research identified the way persistent residues from these pesticides was concentrated up the food chain with fatal consequences for the breeding success of top predators such as the peregrine. That Baker was aware of these conclusions contributed to his pessimism that the Essex countryside might be without peregrines in the future.

For a contemporary reader the situation has changed: the particular pesticides implicated in the decline of the peregrine have been banned and the breeding population of peregrines has bounced back. These birds have been able to move into urban areas to feed on the plentiful supply of feral pigeons. Web cameras are focused on peregrine nests on cathedrals in cities enabling anyone who is so minded to watch the behaviour of adults and young at the nest. Observing winter behaviour would still be a challenge that calls for the sort of single-mindedness that Baker brought to his study over ten years. A modern birdwatcher on the Essex coast would now be faced with losses of other species, in particular waders such as lapwings and curlews, that Baker took for granted, but are now lost due to agricultural intensification and new pesticide challenges. The Nature Conservancy has gone through a number of reorganisations and name changes to split off its research functions and to organise into separate bodies for each of the countries that make up the United Kingdom. Amateur birdwatchers are now enrolled as 'citizen scientists', some trained to collect data in a structured way, others more casually.

There is no longer a need for a nature writer with an interest in animals to do their own research. They can draw on in-depth study by this army of observers and their professional scientist mentors, to place their own observations in context. Experts in animal behaviour may be happy to share their knowledge and take the aspiring writer into the field to see the species at first hand and to be schooled in the sort of field craft that Baker had to invent for himself. Creative non-fiction may therefore be from two converging groups: trained literary scholars and writers seeking out experts in field biology on the one hand, and trained biologists departing from their discipline to develop a literary style of writing. Both aim for the balance between literary merit and truth to nature in their prose.

A further change from when Baker wrote his book and its republication is the animal turn in literary studies. His feeling for the birds he was studying, and his desire to share with them the boredom as well as the excitement of the hunting life, could indicate an, albeit one-sided, empathy. From an animal studies viewpoint a reader would be drawn to that part of the text, but it is worth questioning whether kinship has to have at least some reciprocation from the other species. His wild peregrines were free to satisfy their own wants in contrast to a falconer's bird with a hood over its head and jesses (leather straps) on its legs so that its handler could restrain it. Books on falconry, such as Helen Macdonald's *H is for Hawk* (2014), can explore the growing bond of trust across species lines as the hawk, in her case a goshawk, grew to trust her, but at the cost of loss of agency and freedom in the nonhuman other. Although Baker's peregrines were free to ignore his presence they were very much at the mercy of humanity as they were gradually poisoned by the accumulation of agrochemicals.

The critical reception of *The Peregrine*

The critical reception of Baker's book illustrates how difficult it is to escape from the grasp of liberal humanism. Baker has attracted critics for his claim to live like the birds he studies, but as Macfarlane has concluded, this does not close the subject/object gap. In striving for a literary work, has Baker internalised the principles of liberal humanism, as Wolfe feared (Wolfe, 2010: 119)? He adopts a literary style but is still practising the skills of a field ornithologist developed by Selous, Nicholson and Fisher, as this way of looking at birds entered its rapid phase of expansion after the Second World War. Can we apply a posthuman reading to a work that was written long before the concept gained currency? The growth in professional ornithology, science-based nature conservation and recreational bird watching was dominated by the, mostly male, voices that came into their own after the Second World War. As Wolfe stresses the importance of understanding context, this male-dominated discourse was the background to his field work and writing. Does this dominance by men run the risk of crowding out female voices? This question is addressed in the next chapter.

Further reading

Braidotti, Rosi and Bignall, Simone (2018). *Posthuman Ecologies: complexity and process after Deleuze*. New York: Rowman & Littlefield.

References

Abberley, Will, Alt, Christina, Higgins, David, Harman, Graham and Marland, Pippa (2022) *Modern British Nature Writing, 1789–2020: Land Lines*. Cambridge: Cambridge University Press.

Baker, J. A. (2005 [1967]) *The Peregrine*. New York: New York Review of Books Classics.

Barry, Peter (2017) *Beginning Theory: An Introduction to Literary and Cultural Theory*. Manchester: Manchester University Press.

Birkhead, Tim (2022) *Birds and Us: A 12,000-Year History, From Cave Art to Conservation*. London: Viking.

Cocker, Mark (2010) 'Introduction' in J. A. Baker (ed.) *The Peregrine, the Hill of Summer and the Diaries*. London: Collins, pp. 4–15.

Cowley, Jason (2008) 'Editor's letter', *Granta* 102, Summer 2008, pp. 7–12.

Crist, Eileen (1998) 'The ethological constitution of animals as natural objects: the technical writings of Konrad Lorenz and Nikolaas Tinbergen', *Biology and Philosophy* 13, pp. 61–102.

Fisher, James (1945 [1941]) *Watching Birds*. London: Penguin.

Jamie, Kathleen (2005) *Findings*. London: Sort of Books.

Jamie, Kathleen (2008) 'A lone enraptured male: review of *The Wild Places* (2007) by Robert Macfarlane', *London Review of Books* 30:5, March 2008.

Kuklick, Henrika (2011) ''Personal equations: reflections on the history of fieldwork, with special reference to sociocultural anthropology', *Isis* 102:1, pp. 1–33.

Levine, George (2011) *Darwin the Writer*. Oxford: Oxford University Press.

Lorimer, Jamie (2015) *Wildlife in the Anthropocene: Conservation after Nature*. Minneapolis: University of Minnesota Press.

Macfarlane, Robert (2015) *Landmarks*. London: Penguin.

Macfarlane, Robert (2017) 'Violent spring: the nature book that predicted the future', *Guardian* 15 April.

Nice, Margaret Morse (1935) 'Edmund Selous: an appreciation, *Bird-Banding* 6:3, pp. 90–6.

Niemann, Derek (2012) *Birds in a Cage, Warburg, Germany, 1941: Four P.O.W. birdwatchers – The Unlikely Beginning of British Wildlife Conservation*. London: Short Books.

Nixon, Sean J. (2017) 'Vanishing peregrines: J. A. Baker, environmental crisis and bird-centred culture of nature, 1954–73', *Rural History* 28:2, pp. 205–26.

Ratcliffe, Derek (1993 [1980]) *The Peregrine Falcon*. Second edition. London: Poyser.

Selous, Edmund (1901) *Bird Watching*. London: J. M. Dent. (Full text on Project Gutenberg)

White, Gilbert (1987 [1789]) *The Natural History of Selborne*. London: Penguin.

Wolfe, Cary (2010) *What is Posthumanism?* Minneapolis: University of Minnesota Press.

4

Ecofeminism, intersectionality and animal studies in creative prose

Chapter 3 showed how hard it is to avoid being influenced by an internalised feeling of human exceptionalism, particularly when it is reinforced by the dominance of liberal humanism in the critical reading of literary texts. Was it also significant that the human–animal narratives that were formed during the growth of ornithology and bird watching after the Second World War were mainly authored by men? This chapter considers this issue from the viewpoint of ecological feminism. Are all human voices the same or should we also take account of gender, race, class and ability? The chapter also looks at how these different viewpoints might complicate or complement an animal studies reading of literary texts.

Ecofeminism and the human–nature dualism

That women might be seen as closer to nature than men has advantages and disadvantages. It might provide a way of closing the gap between human and nonhuman animals, but at the same time it risks women being belittled for being less than fully human. In her 1993 book, *Feminism and the Mastery of Nature,* Val Plumwood navigates through these conflicting issues in a phallocentric world:

> It is usually at the edges where the great tectonic plates of theory meet and shift that we find the most dramatic developments and upheavals. When four tectonic plates of liberation theory – those concerned with the oppressions of gender, race, class and nature – finally come together, the resulting tremors could shake the conceptual structures of oppression to their foundations. (Plumwood, 1993: 1)

It is Plumwood's addition of nature as a fourth category of analysis that extends feminist theory and brings her ideas within the scope of an animal studies reading (Plumwood, 1993: 2). As with animal studies, the first step is to break the dualism implicit in the Cartesian view of nature. It 'involves both affirming and reconceptualising the underside, nature'. For Plumwood, 'once nature is reconciled as capable of agency and intentionality the gulf between the conscious, mindful human sphere and the mindless, clockwork natural one disappears' (Plumwood, 1993: 5). Breaking down this dualism is central to Plumwood's approach to ecofeminism.

While all ecological feminist positions give a positive value to the supposed connection of women to nature, this has to overcome the negative cultural value this connection might have and the way it has been used in the west in the devaluation and oppression of women (Plumwood, 1993: 8, 11). Plumwood cites Rosemary Radford Ruether in her argument for these two factors to be taken into account: 'an ecological ethic must always be an ethic of ecojustice that recognises the interconnection of social domination and the domination of nature' (Plumwood, 1993: 18). There are traps for feminists in extracting themselves from their cultural devaluation on account of their being close to nature. Both rationality and nature have many meanings; further, those feminists who have endorsed the association between women and nature, may not have considered how this association is produced by exclusion (Plumwood, 1993: 20). It is evident that if we are to move forward with an animal studies reading, we have to consider the cultural barriers that might prevent us from taking a clear view of the nonhuman other.

An important objective in an animal studies reading of literary texts is to mitigate the exclusion of nonhumans from human interests. That women are also excluded, complicates this project.

> The framework of assumptions in which human/nature contrast has been formed in the west is one not only of *feminine* connectedness *with* and passivity towards nature, but also and complementarily one of exclusion and domination of the sphere of nature by a white, largely male elite, which I shall call the master model. But the assumptions in the master model are seen as such, because this model is taken for granted as the *human* model, while the feminine is seen as a deviation from it. (Plumwood, 1993: 22–3, original emphasis)

Because the concept of the human is heavily normative and based on assumptions of human exceptionalism, the linking of women with nature is seen to be insulting and degrading (Plumwood, 1993: 26). An animal studies reading that confronts human exceptionalism and accepts the moral standing of nonhuman animals carries with it an opportunity to correct any negative association of being close to nature regardless of gender. It is therefore necessary that 'women must be treated as just as fully human and as fully part of human culture as men' (Plumwood, 1993: 36). This chapter listens closely to women when they write about animals. In focusing mainly on female authors in this chapter, I have attempted to confront any assumptions that might be hidden in my unconscious.

By rejecting any dualism between nature and culture, Plumwood sees ecological feminism as an integrative project. Women do not have to accept an ancient identity in which they are seen as closer to nature, nor do they have to endorse the dominant master model. By attending to dualism:

> Women must be just as fully human and as fully part of human culture as men. But both men and women must challenge the dualised conception of human identity and develop an alternative culture which fully recognises *human* identity as continuous with, not alien from, nature. (Plumwood, 1993: 36, original emphasis)

This approach encapsulates the driving ambition of animal studies. Despite her challenge to the dominance of men in discourse, Plumwood found herself inhibited in some of her own writing by this very exclusion.

In 1985, while canoeing in Northern Australia, she was attacked by a salt-water crocodile and taken underwater on three death rolls. Severely injured she managed to escape and seek rescue. Surviving such an attack is rare and she found herself overwhelmed by the press interest and its distortion of how she felt. 'I had survived the crocodile attack, but not the cultural drive to represent it in terms of the masculinist monster myth: the master narrative' (Plumwood, 2008). It was to be ten years before she 'could repossess her story and write about it in [her] own terms'. This confrontation with myth and human exceptionalism has led to some of Plumwood's most important writing about the human–animal bond and how we see death. She was working on a book developing her ideas when she died in 2008. This unfinished work was gathered together posthumously with other essays in *The Eye of the Crocodile* (2012). Thinking about ourselves as food confronts all ideas that we are the masters of nature. By challenging the master narrative, Plumwood shows how a female voice can add depth to our understanding of nonhuman animals and our relationship with them. The following sections of this chapter attempt to listen to female voices, some of which have been belittled or silenced, as they find a way to break down the barrier between humans and nature.

Women and the natural world

Although women's voices have often been unheard or marginalised, they have made important contributions to thinking about our relationship to the natural world. Sylvia Bowerbank shows how women in early modern England were able to write with and against the men that dominated scientific thought. She cites Susan Griffin's invention of ecological woman as a counterpart to scientific man. 'Griffin creates a shrewd rhapsody, thus conceiving the art of ecological woman as radiant and resistant, while assigning dry technique to scientific man' (Bowerbank, 2004: 2). While acknowledging that ecofeminism can be problematic, given the way that women's closeness to nature has been seen as grounds for oppressing both women and nature, it also has the 'positive potential to motivate women to intervene as stake-holders in public environmental debates' (Bowerbank, 2004: 2–3). Although early modern women were excluded from the professional pursuit of science as a way of knowing nature, they were allowed to study it as an example of God's wisdom.

Among the women who have made a mark in bringing us closer to nature, Bowerbank considers Margaret Cavendish, whose writings 'advance a sympathetic defence of animals and trees, thus anticipating the new attitudes that became common by the end of the eighteenth century' (Bowerbank, 2004: 53–4, citing Keith Thomas). Bowerbank sets her discussion of 'the radical logic of Cavendish's ideas about nature, in the context of shifts in attitudes and values, for example, during the transition of Sherwood Forest as this royal forest was appropriated by people and their animals (Bowerbank, 2004: 54). In her poem 'A dialogue between an Oake and a Man cutting him downe', Cavendish has the oak asking the man to remember all the ecological blessings that the tree brings to him, but the man counters with the opportunity for the oak to become a great ship or a stately house (Bowerbank, 2004: 61). It is evident that her sympathies are with nature.

Anna Seward, through her associations with Erasmus Darwin in the Lichfield Botanical Society and with the men in the closely related Lunar Society of Birmingham, had a privileged view of the male-dominated fields of science and industry. For Bowerbank it is her defence of the natural world in such places as Colebrooke Dale (161–87) that is significant, but she also played a role in opening up the study of botany for women. Seward collaborated with Darwin in bringing the Linnaean system of taxonomy to an audience that was literate in English, but without a classical education to read it in the original Latin. One problem for women was that Linnaeus had based his classification of plants on their sexual organs. Seward declined to write some botanical verses for Darwin, because 'the plan was not strictly proper for the female pen' (cited by George, 2014: 686). Despite this problem, Darwin's work was widely read by women who based their own writing on the Linnaean scheme, while avoiding overt discussion of the sex lives of plants.

> For a brief period, before reaction set in, the botanical texts examined here opened up – though not without ambivalence – a space for female radicalism. Texts such as Seward's have been ignored by scientists because of their literary format and overlooked by literary scholars because of their scientific content. (George, 2014: 691)

For George 'the sexuality of plants uncovered by Linnaeus is a paradigmatic illustration of how societal forces can simultaneously both constrict and stimulate women's involvement in science' (George, 2014: 691). This window of opportunity was to close in the nineteenth century as writers such as Ruskin regarded the study of botany as very unsuitable for women.

Female primatologists who gave us a new understanding of animals

We saw in chapter 1 how Jane Goodall and other primatologists transformed our understanding of the great apes in a way that challenged the assumptions about human exceptionalism. Goodall and others who studied primates also challenged the assumption that only men could do that type of science. Anthropologist Louis Leakey's belief that women were best suited to getting close to these animals in the wild made it possible for Goodall to study chimpanzees, and Dian Fossey to study gorillas in Africa (Jahme, 2000: 47–8). He also helped Biruté Galdikas to research orangutans in Borneo. Goodall started her research with no formal academic qualifications, and is one of the few people to be awarded a PhD without having a first degree. Fossey had a degree when she started, but that was in occupational therapy. Galdikas, who was inspired by Goodall, had a more conventional academic background, with a bachelor's degree in psychology and zoology, and a masters in anthropology. Leakey was prepared to take a chance with these three women and obtained funding for their research, which would have been impossible through the normal route for postgraduate funding that would have favoured academic qualifications over the personality traits needed to build relationships across species lines.

The success women have had in primatology might seem to reinforce the idea that they are innately closer to nature. Carole Jahme offers an alternative explanation: 'that men, generally, are suspiciously hasty to finish their theses and return to the safe man-made environments of university tenure' (Jahme, 2000: 3). They do not form the same close attachment to the individuals in their study population, which it makes it easier to leave them behind when they return to their academic posts. These women, a long way from home, were able to ignore some of the conventions of a science dominated by men, but they still brought with them western cultural norms. These include the assumption, in both the European and North American conservation models, that allowing a species to progress toward extinction is a very bad thing. All three women were challenged on the ground – with war, impoverished people harvesting chimpanzees as bush meat, and colonial exploitation of forest resources leaving their chosen species in an ever decreasing and fragmented habitat. All ideas need to be tested for cultural bias, but we owe a considerable debt to these brave women who have done so much to break the subject/object boundary between humans and animals.

Len Howard's research in Bird Cottage

A female naturalist who shared J. A. Baker's obsession with a single group of birds, Gwendolen (Len) Howard published two books, *Birds as Individuals* in 1952 and *Living with Birds* in 1956. These books were based on observations made in 1938 of the birds, in particular great tits, that cohabited with her in her cottage in Sussex. Howard grew up with a love of birds and the natural world and was, in a sense, part of the growth of bird watching discussed in chapter 3. The books were best sellers in their day, but unlike Baker's *The Peregrine*, they have not been championed by any of Jamie's lone enraptured males that have been so enthusiastic about Baker's work, and both her books are out of print. There could be a number of reasons for these books to be excluded from the nature writing canon. Although Baker was a loner, he contributed his findings to the Essex Birdwatching Society and was therefore trusted as an observer. Howard was a much more unusual observer. Trained as a classical musician, she had an early career as an orchestra violinist, but once she retreated to her cottage in Sussex she became a recluse. Her chosen study method, which was to allow garden birds into her house, enabled her to gain their trust but came at the expense of severely restricting visitors.

Her musical ear allowed her to discern differences between the individual songs of these birds, and to relate that to how they behaved. Her intimacy with the individual birds meant that she could recognise them as individuals and understand how they differed in behaviour. These skills are not easily replicable or verifiable; her writing was well received in generalist natural history and countryside magazines, but not in scientific journals. Howard was particularly critical of behaviourist research where birds were studied in captivity; she stressed that the birds she was watching were free to come and go. If they took part in her learning experiments, it was with their consent.

While both her books are out of print, her work has not been completely ignored. Dutch philosopher Eva Meijer has recounted her story as a novel, but with anecdotes about a favourite great tit drawn from Howard's own writing. The Dutch version of this book, *Het Vogelhuis* (2016), was translated into English as *Bird Cottage*

(2018). It is the English version that is discussed here, with Howard herself as the narrator. This book fills in the details around what is known about her upbringing and life, and imagines for us what she was thinking as she built a close relationship with birds that were wild, in that they were free to come and go, but which had formed a close reciprocated bond with Howard. Her most important contribution is to show that the birds were intelligent, adaptive and possessed of individual personalities. If, for Macfarlane, Baker was unable to close the subject/object gap with his peregrines, could it be that Howard had found a way to grant the great tits subject status?

This question is addressed by Eileen Crist who suggests that Howard and the birds she was intimate with were co-creators of the knowledge that she gained from such encounters (Crist, 2006: 181). The birds were altered by this close relationship, but so was Howard. For Crist the method of studying 'transcends the divide between inside and outside her home' to create a space where there is no clear-cut division between wild and tame.

> This space, I will argue, became the field of thick reciprocity that philosopher Martin Buber (1996) called the 'I-and-Thou'. Within the I–Thou specific individuals – with all their personality characteristics, peculiarities, and emotional-cognitive make-up – genuinely meet and transform one another. (Crist, 2006: 182)

It was Howard's practice to record her narratives as anecdotes, or as Crist has it as vignettes, recording what she saw and understood from observing particular birds. These vignettes of the life experiences of an individual bird show that it 'can be more complex and surprising than we would be led to expect through knowledge of the standard behaviour of the species' (Crist, 2006: 184). Crist contrasts the I–Thou method used by Howard to the I–It mode of relating used in institutionalised science. That method, where behaviour is not altered by the relationship between the scientist and the animal, gives a certain objectivity, but at the cost of reinstating the subject/object gap. In classifying behaviours abstractly as belonging to a species rather than an individual, the scientists aim to be able to demonstrate that the behaviour is determined by genetic inheritance, rather than social interaction and learning. Howard's way of relating to each bird means that 'there is not a single dimension of being that does not bear the unique fingerprint of the individual bird' (Crist, 2006: 189).

This intimacy and the insight that follows from it directed Howard to the kinds of observations that were the building blocks of the knowledge that she created. 'The full experience of intimacy emerges only in the reciprocity of I–Thou, wherein each regards the other as the subject with a distinct existence autonomous of, and as rich and deep as, one's own' (Crist, 2006: 189). Although the use of anecdote had fallen into disrepute for unreliable stories about animal intelligence, Crist suggests that anecdotal evidence is valid when Howard is at pains 'to show not how intelligent birds are, but how they differ in their predilections' (Crist, 2006: 191). The category of tame-wild is missing from our experience of wild nature. It confronts the dualism between domesticated and wild, for a category where birds are wild in that they are free to express their wild natures, but tame in their trust of Howard. 'There is a deep message in Howard's Bird Cottage about humanity's potential connection with the wild: we will not hear that lesson if we regard her story as eccentric and view its telling anecdotally as a case study' (Crist, 2006: 92–3). From the viewpoint of literary animal studies, the claim that Howard has bridged the subject/object gap is one that we should examine with a very open mind.

The naturalists' tradition of studying birds in the wild, pioneered by Selous and others, informed Howard's approach to her own studies. Her contribution to institutional science was, however, marginal. Crist suggests that Howard may herself have played a part in this obscurity by not citing works and debates about birds that preceded her own. 'Combined with the fact that she was a musicologist and a woman, her non-engagement with people and texts in her writings conspired to virtually erase her contribution to behavioural studies during her own lifetime' (Crist, 2006: 202). Classical ethology was emerging between the 1930s and 1950s, but the preoccupation of scientists such as Konrad Lorenz and Niko Tinbergen was to emphasise the importance of instinct, when compared with comparative psychology, which emphasised learning and behaviour modification (Crist, 2006: 202–3). Not mentioned by Crist, the anecdotal evidence of great tit behaviour and individuality was also swamped by what was to become a long-running study of great tits in the wild, at the very centre of the scientific establishment.

Before the Second World War, David Lack had carried out pioneering studies of the individual behaviour of the robin. His book *The Life of the Robin,* originally published in 1943 and still in print, has inspired generations of naturalists, myself included. Lack captured robins to fit them with combinations of colour rings, so that he could identify them as individuals. Apart from the rude shock of being caught and handled, these birds returned to the wild so that he could observe them from a distance. Robins can be quite tame, as any gardener who has dug a vegetable garden with know. Viscount Grey of Falloden (Edward Grey) was photographed with a robin perched on his hat. Lack's experience with this species led him to conclude that these studies could not be scaled up. The nests were difficult to find and the territorial behaviour of robins limited the size of the population that could be studied. When Lack became director of the Edward Grey Institute for Field Ornithology at Oxford University, an opportunity presented itself in the gift to the university of Wytham Woods on the outskirts of the city. Great tits and other tit species readily nested in boxes erected around the woods. Inspired by pioneering work on the great tit in the Netherlands, David Lack, together with John Gibb, set up a study based on 100 nest boxes erected in part of the wood. There are now over 1000 boxes that are visited by researchers throughout the breeding season (wythamtits.com, accessed 11 May 2025). The birds and their offspring are individually marked, enabling researchers to follow their fortunes and behaviours as individuals. By the time the project celebrated its 75 year anniversary in 2022, some 70 doctorates had been completed on aspects of their breeding biology, ecology and behaviour.

There are many research papers to choose from, but I have selected one that addresses these birds as individuals. This paper suggests that male great tits assort by personality during the breeding season (Johnson et al., 2017. These researchers grant the individuals agency and their own personality, but their approach differs from Howard's I–Thou relationship. To assess their personality individuals were caught in mist nets and taken to the laboratory. After being kept in the aviary overnight they were released in a novel environment with five perches. The frequency and location of their movements was recorded on a hand-held computer and the subsequent data was analysed to rank the birds on a shy-bold scale. The birds were then observed in the field. From this work, the authors of this paper concluded that males are more likely to breed closer to another male with the same behavioural phenotype (Johnson et al., 2017: 7). Note that phenotype refers to the behaviour and other characters that an individual acquires through contact with its environment, as opposed to genotype, which are those characters that are genetically determined. The shyer males prefer the proximity of other shy males, and the bold prefer others to be bold. This research has a scope and repeatability that would have been challenging for Howard. By standardising the method, the researchers had a claim for objectivity, while Howard would have depended on her own insight into each individual's behaviour.

Women are well represented in the current team working on this project and in this paper four of the seven authors are female. Lack and Gibb chose their study species well. Great tits have continued to breed in the wood, while other breeding birds have been in sharp decline. Unlike the female primate researchers spending years isolated in Africa or Borneo, the woods can be reached by a short bicycle ride from the university. Compared with chimpanzees, great tits have a short lifespan that fits within the study time for doctoral research. In addition to the work on tits, other researchers in these woods are studying invertebrates, mammals and other avian species. The vast data bank from all these studies adds to the power of a collegiate approach to research. More evidence would be needed to see if women still feel that their contribution to the production of knowledge is marginalised even when the practical barriers have been lowered.

Stop and think

Plumwood introduced the idea that the liberation of women and animals was equally as important as that on based on race or class. Singer had already argued for the liberation of animals, and second-wave feminists sought alliances with other liberation movements. The master model was developed by the men who dominated science and society until well into the twentieth century, although in Britain the male scientists in the Birmingham-based Lunar Society had to escape from the primacy given in the old universities to a classical education, and to the marginalisation of those outside the Church of England. That women had to make their contribution outside the established hierarchies gave them an opportunity to make original contributions to thinking, from early modern times, and through the work of the female primatologists. Len Howard was an outsider as a woman and as a classically trained musician. Has this outsider status allowed her to bridge the subject/object gap that seemed to be beyond the authors in chapter 3? By coproducing her research with her animal partners, does she get closer to understanding what they want?

Identity and the animal other

The presence of the author in a narrative may be helpful in an animal studies reading, except where there is a risk that the human perspective becomes so dominant as to overshadow the story of the nonhuman others. Baker treated his own emotions as facts that should be recorded alongside his observations of peregrine behaviour. After Latour, we know that affect is ever present in scientific study, and from Lorimer that the kinship that field naturalists feel for the animals they study is very real, even when all feelings are written out of the final 'factual' scientific report. This section considers texts in which the author is conscious of how their feelings towards other species could illuminate or obscure the nonhuman others in a story. As animal studies has gained ground in literary studies, twenty-first-century authors often take time to question how affect predisposes them to consider nonhuman animals, but at the same time makes them wary of how they handle this self-knowledge in the narrative.

Jasmine Donahaye's *Birdsplaining: A Natural History* (2023) is a hybrid example of creative non-fiction. This book is part memoir, part examination of the challenges faced by a writer in interpreting and narrating her experience of the nonhuman world. Structured around her life-long interest in birds, she pushes against the dominance of men in defining how birds should be watched and against how the men take the lead in many wildlife encounters. Further, she feels othered in the Welsh countryside because of her Middle-Eastern heritage. This issue is considered further in chapter 8. What concerns us most here is the critical way she questions her own experience of the natural world:

> No matter what I see in them, I know that birds are sovereign, autonomous, not subject to the projects of my small needs and anxieties. The natural world is not glorious, a respite, but a matter of implacable drives. Still I read it for signs as I have always done – as some thirty years ago when a cloud of tortoiseshell butterflies emerged from a patch of nettles on a late September day, the morning I was to leave with a man I hardly new. What was that a sign of – the cliché of freedom that I was about to loose, or a mad, hopeless dash towards frost? (Donahaye, 2023: 7)

The first of these options sees the natural world as being mainly relevant to provide signs and metaphors that can reinforce or even trigger an emotional response in the person experiencing such an event. The second is to fall back on Darwin and Tinbergen in seeing all animal behaviour as driven by instinct.

In common with Howard, Donahaye grew up in a home with field guides, which she spent hours poring over as a child. Finding a second-hand copy of the Collins Field Guide to the *Birds of Britain and Europe* in a bookshop takes her back to that childhood. Although writing in the twenty-first century, she learned her birdwatching from the men who took up the challenge in James Fisher's *Watching Birds*. The copy she purchased, which was first published in 1954, made use of the identification system developed by American artist Roger Tory Peterson. This system uses pointers to highlight the important features that distinguish one species from another, such as eye stripes or wing bars. It was for watchers, not those who had the bird in the hand.

The male authors seemed to her to place greater emphasis on the male birds than on the female, which was usually shown behind the male. Some artists were conscious of this apparent bias. Robert Gillmor, who specialised in linocut images, gave the example of the drake eider whose distinctive black, green and white plumage made them 'walking linocuts' whereas 'Female eiders are also very attractive, but in a quite different way to the dapper drakes. Their richly streaked and mottled sepias and browns are fine camouflaged outfits when sitting on fifteen eggs but are not as linocut friendly as [the drakes]' (Gillmor, 2006: 24). The Peterson method of identifying birds would also work better with male birds, rather than their better camouflaged mates. Donahaye finds it difficult to 'see equal value in [her] own life, or any woman's life when viewed through such familiar and easily recognisable patterns. Those patterns, laid down so early on, were echoed and reinforced by representations of sexual difference every time I opened a bird book' (Donahaye, 2023: 22). There is no respite even when out in the field.

She describes searching the Dyfi estuary in Wales for nightjars, the charismatic species that was to change the way that Selous looked at birds, and that was J. A. Baker's favourite species before he switched to peregrines. On her search for nightjars with a single companion, she hears their distinctive churring call only to find that it comes from someone's MP3 player, as she is greeted by a man who seems to have taken ownership of the place and its explanation. Walking on she does eventually see and hear these birds without the need for a helpful, but unwanted interpretation from a man.

The term 'birdsplaining' is derived from Rebecca Solnit's (2014) *Men Explain Things to Me*, which easily transfers to the world of bird watching where self-appointed experts, often men, take it upon themselves to get between the person and their direct experience of the natural world. She prefers her experience of nature not to be curated. Her experience was echoed by George Raeburn, one of the bird-watcher prisoners enlisted in Buxton's redstart study, in an article for *The Magazine* [of the RSPB] 'Bird-watching made difficult'. This humorous piece identified the 'pundits' as 'the Olympians of ornithology who are apt to pour from the Parnassus of their knowledge douches of exceptionally cold water upon the more imaginative discoveries of the keen young observer'. In particular:

> The female yellowhammer is a very sinister foe. It is a common bird. It is unlike its husband. Its plumage varies with the seasons, it resembles many other rarer species. Thus it is one of the trump

> cards held by the Pundits, and the aspiring observer will find it a hard task, in his early days, to identify any bird, other than a crow, which might not equally well be a female yellowhammer. (Cited by Niemann, 2013 157)

In this piece we see the arrogance of those who have set themselves up as pundits and the difficulty in identifying the species of many female birds. In this context it is all the more necessary that difficult-to-identify females were brought to the fore in the field guides that Donahaye grew up with.

Since 2009, there have been a pair of ospreys nesting in the Dyfi valley in mid-Wales. There are three ways to see these ospreys during the breeding season: the armchair way from anywhere in the world by logging onto the webcam that provides intimate views of the nest and the nearby perch; the curated way by visiting the nature reserve where a walk across the bog on a boardwalk brings you to an raised observatory, staffed by enthusiastic volunteers, to watch from afar, perhaps by looking down someone's telescope; or the opportunistic way from the Shrewsbury to Aberystwyth train, where as it slows for Dyfi junction, there are clear views of the nest. It is this last that Donahaye prefers, joining those in the know by switching seats as the train pulls out of Shrewsbury to be on the right side for the best view.

On another walk at dusk to look for nightjars, she was dismayed to meet a couple with a child and dog, which seemed to put paid to her chance of hearing nightjars, but suddenly one began: '*unheimlich*, I thought, afterwards – reaching for a word that has no strict equivalent in English: eerie, uncanny, but really meaning the familiar made other' (Donahaye, 2023: 88). Once it had started churring it continued, with others joining in, then she was startled by a 'strange, frightening clacking sound' and feared that someone was near her. Later, hearing the sound again she realised that it was the bird clapping its wings above its back as it hovered just three feet away from her (Donahaye, 2023: 89). For Donahaye 'there was no other bird that [she] had seen that made her so full of delight and so ill at ease' (Donahaye, 2023: 89). She gives some thought to why that should be – was it seeing them at dusk, was it the mythology that had gathered around this species, or perhaps a predisposition to any feel ill at ease with any encounters with the other. Finding this feeling common among birdwatchers reinforced her own experience.

We have seen from Lorimer that affect is a common reaction to encounters with the wild; his research on that other night-time caller, the corncrake, has shown how important affect can be. That a bird hovers so close to her shows that she was mindful of the field craft to keep still and quiet in the hope of such a close encounter. It feels intimate, but is that feeling reciprocated? According to the instructions on how to behave around nightjars, the birds will not see you if you remain quite still. If so, that is not a mutual encounter, and certainly not the I–Thou spoken of by Crist. Drawing the birds close by playing their call on an MP3 player, or waving a white handkerchief to mimic the white wing flashes of another bird, has birds respond to the deception, but not in a mutually respectful way. The bird has to divert from hunting to see off a presumed intruder of its own species. But as J. A. Baker always understood that the peregrines could see him, perhaps any human presence in the landscape creates a disturbance. For example, could it be that by her presence, Donahaye had disturbed moths into flight which had brought the nightjar in close. Not mentioned in her discussion is that the nightjar's natural habitat: heathland has declined by 85 per cent in the last 150 years in lowland Britain, through more intensive grazing and the planting of conifers. The woodland where Donahaye looked for her birds was recently clear felled, which mimics heathland.

Her preference for seeing things herself rather than having them shown to her makes sense in an animal studies reading of her book. In reading a text of this sort there is a risk that we pay too much attention to the writer's introspection about their identity and not enough to the nonhuman other. While Donahaye bristles at having birds explained to her by a man, she sometimes feels further othered in the field because she is conscious of her brown skin (Donahaye, 2023: 78).

Donahaye specifically rejects any reading that would link the othering of nonhuman species, with the implicit misogyny in being talked down to as a woman, or with her sensitivity to being a brown person in the countryside. As a professor of creative writing, she is more interested in the discussion of these issues in literary criticism.

An animal studies reading already has to reconcile the many different strands that have been pulled together under that heading, without further complicating it with intersections that might draw attention further away from the matter in hand: that is, the agency, individuality and moral worth of the nonhuman animal.

Perhaps one way to read this book is to consider issues relating to identity in one reading and then to do a second reading in which the birds and other animals are brought to the fore. The part of the book where she speaks of the animals that make their home in the permeable structure of her Welsh cottage is open to such a reading. Within limits she allows these animals to do what they want. In this book, where Donahaye is concerned with her own feelings and identity, she does not generalise these into a collective identity politics. It is at this interface between herself and the nonhuman other, even when she is professing that 'birds explain nothing to me', that other humans can get in the way. The same passages can therefore be read either as illustrating the affect that animals have on her or to show how she repays the freedom from another human controlling the narrative, to allow the animals to speak for themselves.

Stop and think

Even in the twenty-first century, Donahaye has to make an effort to avoid the master narrative, in this case when self-appointed 'pundits' insist on curating her experience of the natural world. While Howard saw herself as a researcher who wrote to make her ideas better known, Donahaye is a creative writer whose chosen subject is the natural world and her experience of it as a brown woman. Her own reaction, as with the nightjar, can be just as intense as Howard's reaction to the great tits. Does the fact that this interaction is with an individual bird, but is not with knowing how its personality differs from others in its species, reduce the validity of her insights? On the other hand, Howard was isolated from the mainstream in both creative non-fiction and animal behaviour. Is it helpful that Donahaye is writing from within the mainstream of creative non-fiction when she is discussing birds and other animals? Further, is it helpful that her work is both accessible and offers a point of departure for an animal studies approach for students of literary studies?

Intersectionality of gender and animals with other oppressed groups

Around the same time that Plumwood was writing on ecofeminism, two other women were publishing ideas that were to have wide implications across the academy. Judith Butler (1990) introduced the idea that gender identity is constructed through discourse, rather than genetically determined from birth. Plumwood was aware of Butler's contribution, but in her 1993 book, was reluctant to embrace it, feeling that the dissolution and repudiation of gender identity is problematic.

> The fracturing of binaries (Butler 1990) is not sufficient for escaping the deep structures of colonisation. The dissolution of gender identity through the stabilisation and the definitive act of parody recommended by the post-structuralists (Butler, 1990: 142) amounts to the formation of anti-identities that become further identities. But these identities are not independent. They are still defined essentially in relation to the objects of parody which originate in the problematic of colonisation. Such an approach not only continues to tie the subject to the master, but still has to face the problem of allowing for a multiplicity of responses to traditional gender identity. (Plumwood, 1993: 63)

From the context of second wave feminism, it is perhaps understandable that Plumwood felt that such proliferation of identities risked diluting her main message about the dualisms between men and women, and human and nonhuman animals. Her contribution to thinking is still valuable, although all those working within the current academic environment will have to cope with a multiplicity of claims of oppression based on performative identities.

Another woman who has a continuing influence on academic thinking was Kimberlé Crenshaw. At first sight she would seem to have much in common with Plumwood, although her paper is not cited in *Feminism and the Mastery of Nature*. Whereas Plumwood used the analogy of the great tectonic plates of liberation theory meeting and shifting to impact on the oppressions of gender, race, class and nature, Crenshaw (1989) introduced the concept of 'intersection' between race and sex. This landmark paper was specifically concerned with the marginalisation of Black women in feminist theory. 'Because the intersection experience is greater than the sum of racism and sexism, any analysis that does not take intersectionality into account cannot sufficiently address the particular manner in which Black women are subordinated' (Crenshaw, 1989: 140). This original paper was concerned with theory and the legal framework of oppression on the two variables of race and sex. The idea has since been extended to include animals. Further examples of intersectionality with animal rights include Kim (2015), Taylor (2017) and Jackson (2020).

In *Birdsplaining*, Donahaye feels subject to a master narrative that, at the very least, talks over her own experience of animals in the wild, but with the added complication of a real or perceived xenophobia. 'In Britain if you are brown in a rural place, you're always seen as being from somewhere else' (Donahaye, 2023: 78). In rural Wales, where she currently lives, this experience is complicated by the feeling among the Indigenous population, that Wales has been colonised by the English, so that even those passing as white might feel excluded, with the added exposure for a person whose brownness advertises herself as other. By persisting in her openness to the natural world and with a measure of serendipity that sometimes comes to those who are receptive, she is able to get past these barriers to explore how she responds to animals when they come close to her. One challenge for a beginner in animal studies is that the heavy burden of theory can inhibit the affect that is possible when we reach towards achieving some sort of kinship with other animals.

Intersectionality has been embraced by those who advance critical animal studies in which the scholar is also an activist. Critical animal studies, which was discussed in chapter 2, draws on the animal liberation of Singer as embodied in the activities of the Animal Liberation Front, which is grounded in anarchism and direct action (Colling, 2019: xii). While Plumwood could list the four main streams of liberation theory, the growth of identity has introduced many other classes of oppressed people. The collection of essays in Nocella and George (2019) covers queerness, disability, class, race, gender and decolonizing, each of which has subdivisions as they impact on animal rights. These essays are mainly from a social science perspective, but creative writers have also written about how their identity and capacities can colour their experience of the natural world, and the meanings they co-create from these interactions.

A case in point is Sabrina Imbler (they/their), a mixed Chinese and white non-binary writer, whose *My Life in Sea Creatures* explores an ever stranger range of marine animals at the same time as they are trying to make sense of their own identity. As with Donahaye, they are preoccupied with what their race means and how they should feel about it (Imbler, 2022: 149). On one occasion they come across huge numbers of small gelatinous blobs that might have been salps (also known as sea squirts), which are fantastical creatures. Some glow in the dark; in water they exist as pulsating chains.

> Many chains can grow as long as 20 feet, drifting through the ocean like giant quartzite bracelets. This is to say that individual identity is confusing for a salp, creatures for whom the notion of selfhood exists in the plural. For a salp, home is the rest of its salp. (Imbler, 2022: 174)

Imbler intersperses musing about the salp and other sea creatures with writing about their own identity, in particular in the context of swarming for the annual Dyke March in New York City and at the gay haven on Riis beach. Although they have not made a positive identification that these blobs are salps, they are drawn into the strangeness of their way of living, inspiring thought about how the convivial collective on the beach might emulate them. 'I want all of us, teeming masses, swirling riot, heaped atop one another until we become something more than summer, more than life' (Imbler, 2022: 193). As their narrative moves towards its conclusion it is the cuttlefish that engages their attention.

As with Donahaye, Imber notes that scientists at first concentrated their attention on the male, but the female is just as interesting. 'Cuttlefish are creatures born to morph' (Imbler, 2022: 201). When a female meets another female, milky white splotches appear across its head, arms and mantle. '[Scientists] suggested the splotch could be a way of preventing attacks from other cuttlefish, a physical affirmation of safety and sameness, like the gay nod. I see it as a kind of love language. If you splotch, I splotch' (Imbler, 2022: 205). By writing separately about the cuttlefish and about their own acceptance of a binary identity, Imbler allows the animal to have agency. There is no mutual kinship established between the human and nonhuman individuals, but what is essential is that the phallocentric assumptions of much science are challenged to allow the distinctive behaviour of the female to be seen, even if poorly understood. Although their book is about a human finding their identity and taking comfort from the many varied ways of living adopted by other species, it does not project human desires and values onto those species.

Disability, the body and corporality of animals

Another ecofeminist writer and critic has written of her disability and getting along with a body in which pain is never ending. Polly Atkin (2023), in *Some of Us Just Fall: On Nature and Not Getting Better*, writes mainly about disability, which for many years remained undiagnosed and, worse still, being told there was nothing wrong with her. Diagnosis, when it came, was a relief; although the pain was still there at least she could make sense of it. 'Hypermobile Ehlers-Danlos syndrome is characterised by hypermobile joints that shift in and out of place and by velvety, fragile skin' (Atkin, 2023: 87). This condition is genetic and therefore a character of the material body; it is not socially constructed, despite some doctors suggesting that it was all in her mind. It places limitations on what she can do and conditions her response to nature. During lockdown for the COVID-19 pandemic, she and her partner were living in Grasmere. On their evening walks they looked for frogs in the duck pond, and in wet months for a heron.

With so few people about during lockdown, they 'rarely met other people, only animals, insects, amphibians, birds' (Atkin, 2023: 169). She also swims in the lake, which moves her muscles and joints gently, but does not cure her. It lets her feel joy, but does not erase the pain (Atkin, 2023: 202). There is not a strong current of ecofeminism in this book, although she shares Jamie's objection to the lone enraptured male for being necessarily 'bright, healthy and highly educated' (Atkin, 2023: 211, citing Jamie, 2008). Stacy Alaimo also 'recognises it is "the abled, hyperfit body" that dominates environmental writing and thinking' (Atkin, 2023: 211). Atkin does not have a romantic view of nature: although she laughs when a family of treecreepers play above her partner's head while she swims, she knows from *Springwatch* that the woodpeckers she sees in the spring will eat the treecreeper's babies. 'This is nature' (Atkin, 2023: 221). Following Wordsworth she looks to nature as her teacher, but does not expect it to be her healthcare system. She feels a flush of kinship when she senses the eyes of the deer and sees them acknowledge her in the shifting of their muscles, even when they don't run. 'I think of my own wild body, its refusal of my claims to autonomy. Its refusal of any beast else's authority. And I try to kindle the same fellow feeling in our shared heart' (Atkin, 2023: 284). It is evident that oppression can take many forms, sometimes two categories of oppression can work together, at other times one aspect will dominate. Atkin is a nature writer with ecofeminist leanings, but here it is the ever-present pain from her disability that presses to the fore.

Intersectionality brings new classes of oppression that complicate any narrative about the human–nonhuman bond. Some readings will be sufficient if they concentrate on one class of oppression. There is a risk, however, that in spending so much time complicating the human side of the cross-species relationship we simplify the circumstances of other animals. As a general rule in animal studies, animals should be allowed to have at least as complicated a life as their human counterparts. They are just as likely to have conflict between the sexes, different ways of expressing their sexuality, and genetic mutations that alter their capabilities and potential.

Coping with complexity in the Chthulucene

For Haraway, new thinking is required to come to terms with the challenges of the contemporary age. 'What happens when human exceptionalism and bounded individualism, those old saws of Western philosophy and political economics, become unthinkable in the best sciences, whether natural or social? Seriously unthinkable: not available to think with' (Haraway, 2016: 30). Haraway is challenging the concept of a bounded autonomous self that can be consulted for answers to equations that arise through life. The terms associated with this self are agency, autonomy, fulfilment and choice. See also Becker and Marecek (2008) 'Dreaming the American dream: individualism and positive psychology'. Haraway is especially impatient with responses she hears to the Anthropocene and to the Capitalocene, one is a comic faith in technofixes and the other is that it is now too late to do anything (Haraway, 2016: 3). She invokes the idea of string figures as an aid to speculative thinking. Although string figures as a concept is used by physicists to challenge conventional ideas about the basis of matter, Haraway uses it more from the practice of making patterns with cats' cradles of string in which the pattern is held in the hands and passed backwards and forwards, as a means of staying with the trouble in multispecies worlds (Haraway, 2016: 12). She plays with the abbreviation SF to link science fiction, speculative fabulation, string figures, speculative feminism, science fact [and] so far (Haraway, 2016: 2). For her 'this material semiotics is always situated, someplace and not noplace, entangled and worldly' (Haraway, 2016: 4). In common with Charles Darwin, she finds pigeons good to think with and illustrates these ideas by exploring the racing pigeons of California. In particular, how contact with things and other living beings renders human beings as capable. How pigeon fanciers engage with their birds to understand their ways of knowing and their social practices (Haraway, 2016: 19). Haraway's approach to living with companion species is, then, messy, but above all it requires the human partner to listen closely to their individual and social needs.

Following from her challenge to individualism, Haraway questions the concept of autopoiesis, in which an individual is capable of sustaining itself by creating its own parts, advancing instead a sympoiesis, in which information and control are distributed among components. In practice these are 'collectively-producing systems that do not have self-defined spatial or temporal boundaries'. This idea makes sense when neither biology nor philosophy supports the notion of independent organisms in environments (Haraway, 2016:

33). Citing Despret, she shows that what ornithological 'scientists actually do in the field affects the ways that "animals see the scientists seeing them" and therefore how they respond' (Haraway, 2016: 128). In doing it together, the scientists and the birds become-with each other. The narrative that emerges is therefore co-produced.

Haraway situates this messy, more organic way of thinking within an era she calls the Chthulucene. While not altogether abandoning the concepts of the Anthropocene and the Capitalocene, which give too much emphasis to the human, Haraway favours tentacular thinking, from an analogy with a spider, whose 'many appendages make string figures; they entwine me in poiesis' (Haraway, 2016: 31). For Haraway:

> Unlike the dominant dramas of Anthropocene and the Capitalocene discourse, human beings are not the only important actors in the Chthulucene, with all other beings able simply to react. The order is reunited: human beings are with and of the earth, and the biotic and abiotic powers of this earth are the main story. (Haraway, 2016: 55)

In *Staying with the Trouble,* Haraway looks past posthumanism to an altogether messier future. Firmly grounded in ecofeminism and rejection of masculinist models of control, this joyous book prepares us to come to terms with our connectedness to all living beings and to inanimate matter in our shared world. In the next chapter we consider how Bruno Latour, who Haraway regards as a partner in science studies, anthropology and story-telling (Haraway, 2016: 5), addresses the complexity in such a world.

Further reading

Becker, Dana and Marecek, Jeanne (2008) 'Dreaming the American dream: individualism and positive psychology', *Social and Personality Psychology* 2:5, pp. 1767–80.

Braidotti, Rosi (2021) *Posthuman Feminism*. Cambridge: Polity.

Jackson, Zakiyyah Iman (2020) *Becoming Human: matter and meaning in an antiblack world*. New York: NYU Press.

Kim, Claire Jean (2015) *Dangerous Crossings: race, species and nature, in a multicultural age*. Cambridge: Cambridge University Press.

Taylor, Nik and Twine, Richard (eds) (2014) *The Rise of Critical Animal Studies: From the Margins to the Centre*. London and New York: Routledge.

Taylor, Sanaura (2017) *Beasts of Burden: animal and disability liberation*. New York: The New Press.

References

Atkin, Polly (2023) *Some of Us Just Fall: On Nature and Not Getting Better*. London: Sceptre.

Bowerbank, Sylvia (2004) *Speaking for Nature: Women and the Ecologies of Early Modern England*. Baltimore and London: Johns Hopkins University Press.

Butler, Judith (1990) *Gender Trouble: Feminism and the Subversion of Identity*. London and New York: Routledge.

Colling, Sarah (2019) 'Foreword' in Anthony J. Nocella II and Amber E. George (eds) *Intersectionality of Critical Animal Studies: A Historical Collection*. New York: Peter Lang Publishing, pp. xiii–xvi.

Crenshaw, Kimberlé (1989) 'Demarginalizing the intersection between race and sex: a black feminist critique of antidiscrimination doctrine, feminist theory and antiracist policies', *The University of Chicago Legal Forum*.

Crist, Eileen (2006) '"Walking on my page": intimacy and insight in Len Howard's cottage of birds', *Ethology and Ethnology: The Coming Synthesis. Social Science Information* (45:2) pp. 179–208.

Donahaye, Jasmine (2023) *Birdsplaining: A Natural History*. Aberystwyth: New Welsh Review.

George, Sam (2014) 'Carl Linnaeus, Erasmus Darwin and Anna Seward: botanical poetry and female education', *Science & Education* 23, pp. 673–94.

Gillmor, Robert (2006) *Cutting Away: The Linocuts of Robert Gillmor*. Peterborough: Langford Press.

Haraway, Donna J. (2016) *Staying with the Trouble: Making Kin in the Chthulucene*. Durham, NC and London.

Imbler, Sabrina (2022) *My Life in Sea Creatures*. London: Chatto & Windus.

Jahme, Carole (2000) *Beauty and the Beast: Women, Ape and Evolution*. London: Virago.

Johnson, Katerina V.-A., Aplin, Lucy M., Cole, Ella F., Farine, Damian R., Firth, Josh A., Patrick, Samantha C. and Sheldon, Ben C. (2017) 'Male great tits assort by personality during the breeding season', *Animal Behaviour* 129, pp. 21–32.

Meijer, Eva (2018) *Bird Cottage*, translated by Antoinette Fawcett. London: Pushkin Press.

Niemann, Derek (2013) *Birds in a Cage, Warburg, Germany, 1941: Four P.O.W. birdwatchers – the Unlikely Beginning of British Wildlife Conservation*. London: Short Books.

Nocella, Anthony J. II and George, Amber E. (eds) (2019) *Intersectionality of Critical Animal Studies: A Historical Collection*. New York: Peter Lang Publishing.

Plumwood, Val (1993) *Feminism and the Mastery of Nature*. London and New York: Routledge.

Plumwood, Val (2008) www.valplumwood.files.wordpress.com/2008/03/being-prey.doc, accessed 12 June 2025.

Plumwood, Val (2012) *The Eye of the Crocodile*, edited by Lorraine Shannon. Canberra: Australian National University E Press.

5

Bruno Latour and actor–network theory in animal studies

This chapter takes a different approach to posthuman readings. Rather than drawing on the philosophical analysis of Wolfe and Braidotti, and the ecofeminism of Plumwood and Donahaye, it assesses the scope for using the actor–network theory (ANT) developed by Bruno Latour to understand the interface between humans and other animal species. Latour developed the concept of ANT in recognition that society is not distinct from nature. His insistence that nonhuman actors, actants in his usage, should be admitted to the study of society, makes ANT potentially useful in literary animal studies. For Latour 'ANT is the sociology of associations that are continually being made and re-made' (Latour, 2005: 35). The attraction for students of animal studies is that it provides a way to break down the nature/culture divide by calling into question the utility of the terms 'Society' and 'Nature' (Latour, 2005: 110). Any critical approach that has ambitions to be posthuman has to confront the restrictions where 'Nature assembles non-humans apart from the humans; society collects humans apart from non-humans' (Latour, 2005: 164). How far are these ideas useful in a critical reading of animal texts?

Latour's introduction to ANT contests the traditional way of thinking about society as a stable set of associations. For Latour 'If you stop making and remaking groups, you stop having groups' (Latour, 2005: 35). Although his primary aim is to 'reassemble the social', his admission of nonhumans to be actants, and to have agency in human associations, is a springboard for advancing these ideas into an animal studies reading of literary texts. In this chapter I summarise his arguments and then see how they might be useful when reading animals in creative non-fiction.

Latour's concept broadens sociology to include nonhuman actants. It therefore crosses boundaries such as that between ethology (the study of animal behaviour) and ethnology (the study of human behaviour). The networks in ANT are ephemeral, as they are only relevant when the actant is directly influencing the behaviour of another entity. Although Latour has applied this approach to the interactions between human and nonhuman actants, he stresses that it is not another social theory, rather it is his attempt to escape the 'tyranny of social theories' (Latour, 1996: 372). In this chapter I have selected two themes that challenge some of the similar artificial barriers as those between nature and society. The first is the reintroduction in the twenty-first century of beavers to the British countryside after an absence of several centuries. The second is the place of livestock farming in rural England. The animals in the latter are domesticated, but those in the former are wild, albeit tightly managed during this reintroduction phase. The categories 'wild' and 'domesticated', problematic in themselves, are challenged by ANT. In animal studies these categories are important because in law we have a duty of care to the individual animal if it is domesticated, whereas wild animals are mostly to be left to get on with the business of living and dying, often from starvation, with human concern more at the species level than for the individuals. Both 'wild' and 'domesticated' are human constructs that condition the human actant in its relations across the species divide. Through artificial selection of domesticated animals, human pressure has changed the phenotype of many breeds of domesticated animals to the extent that it is no longer clear how these animals have evolved from their wild ancestors. This change has not all been one way, with human society also changing in response to animal actants.

Both beavers and domesticated livestock have had a cultural presence for millennia. How far does this backstory colour how we read contemporary accounts of rewilding with beavers or the pastoral practices of modern farmers? Can these ancient texts become actants that influence us when we read about these animals? Latour's approach to posthumanism is particularly relevant in creative non-fiction that draws its knowledge from close contact with animals by farmers, naturalists and practitioners of science-based nature conservation.

How far are these ideas useful in a critical reading of animal texts? The aim is to put ANT to work rather than just mention it in passing. Echoing Latour's idea that entities that are not acting are not actants, mentioning a theoretical concept without showing how it might be useful adds nothing to a critical reading. These issues will be examined as we address two key texts: 'Rodents of an unusual size' in Amy Jane Beer's *The Flow: Rivers, Water and Wildness* (2022) and James Rebank's *English Pastoral: An Inheritance* (2020).

Affect, ecology and beavers

Bruno Latour sets the scene for a chapter in his introduction to ANT, as follows: 'An office at the London School of Economics on a dark Tuesday evening in February before moving upstairs to the *Beaver* for a pint. A quiet but insistent knock is heard. A student peers into the office' (Latour, 2005: 141). The rest of Latour's chapter is a dialogue between the student and the professor about the use of ANT in their thesis. While the student is looking for a clear method, Latour is trying to instil a way of thinking. The aim in this chapter is to show how this way of thinking, which goes beyond a mere nod in the direction of ANT (useful only where a single sentence mention scores a point in a marking scheme), can inform a reading of animals in literary texts

The *Beaver* was at that time a place where students and staff could meet informally; it was named after the beaver on the LSE coat of arms. The beaver was chosen for this emblem in 1922 by Edwin Cannan, Professor of Political Economy, together with a committee of staff and students, for its attributes as a hardworking and industrious yet sociable animal. It was hoped that LSE students would approach their studies in a similar way. I have taken the presence of the beaver in this anecdote as an excuse to select a chapter on the beaver for the first topic for discussion. Latour did not develop this association himself, but he was aware of the reputation of beavers as 'ecosystem engineers'.

> Beavers, birds, ants and termites are not the only ones who bend the environment around them to make it more favourable; so too do trees, mushrooms, algae, bacteria, and viruses. Is there a risk of anthropomorphism here? Of course; this is even what makes the reasoning so

> clever: the capacity of humans to rearrange everything around themselves is a *general property of living things.* (Latour, 2017: 99, original emphasis)

Beavers, then, can be actants in a network that has human and nonhuman elements, and we must always be aware that whatever the beavers do, humans may well bend it around their own needs.

In this case study, the intention is to walk with Latour to establish how useful ANT might be in a critical study of the beaver in prose nature writing. Beavers became extinct in England in the twelfth century and in Scotland in the seventeenth century. Following official and unofficial releases of Eurasian beavers in the twenty-first century, it is now possible to see beavers in both England and Scotland. This has stimulated an interest among nature writers and poets. The official release to the wild was said to be 'science-led', as was, to a lesser extent, the decision about whether unofficial beavers, which have escaped from enclosures or have been released clandestinely as an act of 'guerrilla rewilding', could be allowed to stay. The scientific discourse around beavers as the background to creative responses to their reintroduction opens the way for the insights that Latour brings from science. While the sociology of science is complex, the influence that science has on nature writing, and in turn the part that literature plays in bringing beavers into public discourse, is an issue to explore when reading a text.

Beavers are the second largest aquatic rodents after the South American capybara (*Hydrochorus hydrochoraeris*). There are two species, both from the northern hemisphere: the North American beaver (*Castor canadensis*) and the European beaver (*C. fiber*), which look alike and have similar behaviour. Since ancient times, both species have been seen by humans as prey hunted for meat, fur and an excretion from the castor gland known as castoreum. The fur and the castoreum were valuable commodities that were traded in the Roman Empire, later by the Hanseatic League, and then by Dutch and British interests in North America. While fur and castoreum were the principal commodities traded, narratives about these creatures also flowed along the trade routes. These stories have enhanced the beaver's mythical status and sometimes reinforced very inaccurate accounts of its behaviour.

Beavers are social animals living in family groups of the parents and two generations of offspring. They are also territorial. Beavers' reputation for collaboration, ingenuity and industriousness was attractive to Enlightenment thinkers as examples of how a utopia could work. Rafael Landívar's Neo-Latin poem *Rusticatio Mexicana* (1782) includes at book six a discussion of beavers. Kerson develops the theme that this book suggests 'a kind of utopian society, expressed poetically and metaphorically in terms of the community of beavers' (Kerson, 2000: 14). He cites another author who regards beaver society as a 'perfect republic' (Kerson, 2000: 16). Taking such stories as true to nature, risks the reputation of authors who rely on written sources, rather than seeing the behaviour for themselves. In this respect it is interesting to contrast two versions of Thomas Bewick's *History of Quadrupeds.* In the version published in 1804 he repeats the story of how they collaborate by dividing their labours:

> To this purpose, a community of two or three hundred assemble together: an overseer is chosen, whose orders are punctually obeyed; and by striking the water with his tail, gives the signal where the united force of numbers is necessary to be applied, in order to strengthen and support the fabric; or at the approach of an enemy, to apprize the society their danger. (Bewick, 1804: 417–18)

In the revision to the book for publication in 1834 he was able to draw on first-hand reports, based on the Canadian species, from an agent of the Hudson's Bay Company:

> He treats as fable accounts of them assembling in large bodies, for the purpose of erecting large towns and cities, and commonwealths, and of finishing their houses in different stories and apartments, in the neat manner ascribed to them. (Bewick, 1834: 258)

Even as the physical sight of beavers became rare, they were not forgotten in literature and culture.

Beavers in British nature writing

Beavers have a long presence in English literature, even though they have been extinct in Great Britain for the last three or four centuries. Their reintroduction as part of various rewilding schemes has excited twenty-first-century nature writers. For this example I have selected an essay, 'Rodents of unusual size', in Amy-Jane Beer's *The Flow* (2022). Is there any merit in reading this work with and against Latour's ideas about ANT? Beer begins the essay with a description of the sensory experience of hearing and then seeing beavers at work. After centuries of absence, beavers have been remarkably quick to settle in the British countryside. What is familiar for the beavers is strange and exciting for the humans who encounter them. They are not easy to see; on this occasion Beer is taken to a Cornish valley where they have been released within an enclosure. Approaching in the dark it is the sound of them gnawing that impresses with its loudness, then a splash as it enters the water. Using a red-light torch she sees the shape of the animal swimming as 'a low, humped form, an island on the move' (Beer, 2022: 346). The lyrical experience of beavers with the associated affect felt for the animals themselves, and for the joy at the reversal of what looked to be a decline towards extinction, is very much the domain of nature writing. ANT bridges the gap between the science of rewilding and the human affects that are engendered by the encounter of these species in the wild, albeit often enclosed.

For Latour, ANT is an extension of tools available to social science. It has to cope with two contradictory demands, that sociologists do not limit themselves to social ties, but on the other hand they don't have to become specialised technologists to admit nonhuman and non-animate objects as having a social impact. He offers as a solution the adoption of 'a new definition of the social as a fluid visible *only* when new associations are being made' (Latour, 2005: 79, original emphasis). The beaver's management of the hydrology is visible and in many cases has a social outcome, particularly if the risks of flood and drought are mitigated and if the loss of biodiversity is reversed. In this sense biodiversity has both a pleasing affect on humans and, by reference to ANT, complicates the relationships between an extended cast of actants in a network that is necessary for the survival of all life, including that of humans. Beer's attention is drawn to water as the medium through which she has paddled her kayak and in which she has swum. In much of this collection of essays, water is an object to be reckoned with and is central to the new associations that are made in such activities. For Latour (2005: 79) such objects 'by their very nature of their connection with humans, quickly shift from being mediators to being intermediaries, counting for one or nothing, no matter how internally complicated they might be'. Literature has a part to play in such networks.

Trained as a zoologist, Beer became a science journalist and writer. She helped to found New Networks for Nature, which each year until 2024 convened a cross-disciplinary conference at which ideas were exchanged and people were able to make personal connections outside their own disciplines. From a literary point of view, this gives writers access to scientists who have in-depth knowledge of animals, their ecology and their environmental impact. While beavers are of interest to the scientific community, there is another network of enthusiasts for rewilding who are part of an international community with the practical expertise to obtain, quarantine, breed in captivity and release beavers. Derek Gow was campaigning for beavers long before they were officially released, and has an even longer association with other rewilding initiatives. He has written of his experience in *Bringing Back the Beaver* (2020). Beer has known him for twenty years and has written of his various 'adventures in conservation and animal husbandry' (Beer, 2022: 346). Without such pressure it is likely that, even with beavers being listed for reintroduction in the 1992 EU Habitats and Species Directive, progress would have been much slower. The official network of scientists and administrators that carry out government environment policy is remarkably slow to react. Latour directs us towards the dynamic, ever changing networks of people, animals and other objects that lie outside formal structures.

Without the informal network of enthusiasts and informed writers such as Gow, the official 2008 Scottish Beaver Trial in Knapdale, Argyll might still be being discussed. This trial was sponsored by Scottish Natural Heritage (now NatureScot), the Royal Zoological Society of Scotland and the Forestry Commission (now Scottish Forestry and Land), backed up by an impressive array of scientific studies overseen by universities. In practice, it is the individuals seconded to the joint team that establish the relationships in the fluid and changing networks that progress the trial. Each of these individuals will have their own networks of contacts built up over their career, which may or may not be reactivated during the trial. While Latour would have been very interested in the social science of how all these networks collaborate, he cautions that 'Scientific practice is too hard to be cracked by ordinary social theory and a new one has to be devised which can be used to throw a light on "softer" topics as well' (Latour, 2005: 96). The enthusiasm of people like Derek Gow and the witness of writers such as Beer confront the idea that once the science is known, decisions in a modern society are made rationally. In her essay Beer highlights that the success of this trial was contingent on strong leadership in the field by a 'dogged beaver advocate, Roisin Campbell-Palmer, and [on being] supplied with beavers imported by Derek' (Beer, 2022: 347). This support continues through the ranger service provide by the Heart of Argyll Wildlife Organisation. These people and their fluid associations were all actants that had direct consequences for the beavers as individuals. ANT becomes even more useful when the focus turns to the animals themselves.

Beer calls on the ecologist's concept of 'keystone species' for the increase in biodiversity that is made possible by these works. Without the beaver, humans in many other wetland rewilding projects would have had to bring in diggers to achieve the same effect. As it bends the environment to meet its own needs, the beaver is an actant in a network of other species that benefit from the hydrological effects from damming streams and digging canals, and habitat creation by felling trees. The effect these works have on biodiversity qualify the beaver as a keystone species in ecological narratives. The keystone in building is the stone that holds all the others, in say a bridge, in place. This does perhaps give the beaver's contribution a rather static feel, but ANT will encourage us to see it as constantly changing: as trees are felled, canals are dug, sediment fills the lakes and trees regrow.

Beer was introduced to beavers through her network of human contacts, but ANT allows us to consider a beaver-centred network. While ecology uses shorthand descriptions such as 'ecosystem engineer' and 'keystone species', a beaver-centred network would also have to consider humans as actants who translocate them, mitigate undesirable flooding and respond to their presence with affect. As was the case when beavers appeared on the River Otter in Devon, affect becomes amplified in the social space, to become evident as community resistance to their removal. It is this interplay between nature and society that gives ANT a way of looking at the fluid networks in play, which is wider than traditional models of both ecology and of social sciences.

At this stage in their reintroduction, the beaver population is growing as individuals move into new territories. The elaborate structure of lodges, dams and canals is protection against the predators that beavers have coevolved with, in particular the grey wolf. Beaver kits can also be killed by otters or pine martens, but there is not sufficient top-down pressure from predators to stop the population expanding. Humans have taken over the role of predator in this network, with translocation and lethal control (killing) to mitigate any potential damage to crops or human habitation. At the time of writing, lethal control of unwanted beavers has given way to rehoming the animals to places where they are wanted. ANT stresses the fluid nature of the network and there will be a time where, in the absence of a natural predator, lethal control will once more be necessary. Talking about this issue to one conservation manager, Beer (2022: 358) was surprised that he looked forward to the day when beavers were so numerous that children would go to school wearing beaver fur gilets. Why was Beer taken aback by this idea? As a biologist she would have known that herbivore populations will either be controlled by top-down pressure from carnivores or by bottom up pressure from starvation.

That water is the most important actant in this network, aligns with Latour's inclusion of non-animate bodies as actants. Beer cites the view that it is the sound of running water that drives the beaver to repair dams or raise their level. She does allow them individuality and agency, for example, when observing the individuality of a pair of beavers being released to an enclosure near her Yorkshire home (Beer, 2022: 350). Also beavers have a social life in family groups and in defence of their territory. Any essentialist reading of beaver behaviour as wholly instinctive would be both misleading and against the spirit of an animal studies reading. Water is an actant in the network, as are trees that have coevolved with beavers to recover after felling. Did beavers teach humans how to harvest these trees sustainably in coppice rotations? Many species depend on the open and edge habitats that beavers create. 'The potential at landscape scale is enough to make hydrologists and ecologists dance' (Beer, 2022: 349). The beaver's impact on species diversity is in part a result of opening up the canopy to allow the flora of the field layer and associated insects to flourish. Insects associated with dead wood also take advantage of fallen trees and the structure of the lodge itself.

The beaver is credited with delivering ecosystem services through local effects on hydrology and ecosystems and through the wider significance at catchment and global level. Biodiversity increases as beavers modify their immediate surroundings. Flood alleviation and drought prevention operate at a catchment level, but carbon sequestration plays a useful part in reducing the release of greenhouse gases to the atmosphere. Latour does, however, caution against trying to integrate feedback loops at the local level with the global feedback mechanisms discussed in the Gaia model. 'The hard lesson of actor-network theory, according to which there is no reason to confuse a *well-connected* locality with the utopia of the Globe, holds true for all associations of living beings' (Latour, 2017: 136, original emphasis). Beavers' contribution to carbon sequestration in the wetland might help remove carbon dioxide from the atmosphere, although wetlands also release methane, a powerful greenhouse gas, to the atmosphere. An ANT based on the actants around the beaver, while a useful source of insights at that level, cannot be joined up in any meaningful way to the immensely complex systems that control the global climate.

The main effect of including an ANT perspective in a reading of this essay is that it directs us to consider and question how the beaver, together with water, acts on the environment and biodiversity, and how these impacts in turn are actants on the sociological response to the presence of beavers. Concepts such as keystone species and ecosystem services need to be unpacked in terms of the body of actants and effects. It stops us from getting too closely involved in the machinations of science-based nature conservation, by admitting that social networks have played a major role in making the practical arrangements and providing local support, particularly on the River Otter in Devon, where such engagement prevented officialdom from removing the beavers that had become established there.

Stop and think

How does this example of writing about the reintroduction of beavers give these animals a voice? Contrast the development of affect for beavers in the River Otter with the more formal and risk averse approach of the official conservation agencies. Is this an example where the nature and culture have reinforced each other to favour allowing the beavers to remain? Is it an example of the shifting and ephemeral links that Latour had in mind for ANT? Does nature writing play an active part in such informal networks? Think about how bringing writers into conversation with ecologists, as in the New Networks for Nature, facilitates writers to see beavers at first hand and also ensures that myths are exposed to reality. Is there a risk that the resulting text can replace myth with the dominant paradigm in the current scientific consensus?

Latour is a social scientist rather than a literary critic, but his insights can help in a critical reading of animal oriented texts and in the case of the beaver these texts have helped make this rodent a popular actant in the rewilding movement. The texts considered in this chapter are from creative non-fiction works but, as will be discussed in later chapters, fiction and poetry also have a part to play. 'The resource of fiction can bring – through counterfactual history, thought experiments, and "scientifiction" – the solid objects of today into fluid states where the connections with humans make sense'. (Latour, 2005: 82) This example explores how prose writing can bring the unseen impact of nonhuman objects into our understanding.

How wild animals and domesticated animals differ in animal studies

The beavers in the Scottish Beaver Trial and in other schemes where they have been released to enclosures have been closely monitored. Despite this management, they are as wild as those that have established themselves by escape or clandestine release. As herbivores that deliver environmental benefits, they have generated considerable excitement in the rewilding movement. As discussed in chapter 1, the distinction between wild and domestic is both open to interpretation and can complicate an animal studies reading. The next section considers how ANT might approach the reading of texts where animals have been domesticated.

Wild animals and wilderness are heavily over-represented in the new nature writing, and in those texts from earlier times that are valued today. The emphasis on cross-species kinship in the animal turn brings companion animals into focus, but for the main part, farm animals and assorted alien, feral, pest and other undesirables are left out. Early nature writing tended to make a fetish of the wild. John Muir, in particular, praised the wild bighorn sheep as 'elegant and graceful as a deer', while being full of scorn for their domesticated counterparts and the shepherds who tended them (Muir, 1894: chapter XIV: n.p.). Mary Austin in *The Flock* (1906) was critical of Muir for not taking the testimony of the shepherds into account when rangelands were taken into national parks. She acknowledges that sheep can cause overgrazing and that shepherds sometimes practised ill-advised burning, but these excesses can be managed. Austin is very much writing against the grain of traditional wilderness worship (Nelson, 2000: 18). Depending on which of the propositions at the end of chapter 2 are brought into play, an animal studies reading will bring with it a set of moral values that will sometimes be in accord with those of the writer of a non-fiction text, but for other texts there may be dissonance. Such dissonance may be critical to the reading or it may be necessary, for example, to set aside reprehensible attitudes known to be held by a writer, so that we can winnow out examples where the nonhuman other is allowed agency and is treated as an individual without an overlay of human exceptionalism.

Domesticated animals as actants have a direct influence on how humans relate to one another, and on how the lives of animals are intertwined with those of the humans who are tasked with their care. The keepers of domesticated animals have a moral and legal responsibility to care for the welfare of each individual animal. Many also care about the future of the distinctive breeds created by social and environmental pressure over many centuries. The benefits of maintaining the biodiversity of wild animals across and within species is seen as a 'good thing', even as year by year more species move to extinction. There is scope for disagreement between those that champion wild biodiversity and those who seek to preserve the diversity in heritage breeds of livestock. The way that these sometimes opposing positions are constructed is also of interest in an ANT approach to human–animal studies.

Professionals in this relationship with domesticated species will take on roles that construct their identities as farmers, shepherds, handlers, veterinary surgeons, auctioneers and slaughterers. Despite the advance of urban living, these identities still have meaning to those who are in direct contact with animals. Latour brings the insight that these relationships are constantly changing and there will be some times where a person is not relating at least directly to a nonhuman actant. The next section considers how ANT might add to our understanding of recent developments in writing on pastoralism.

Animals in pastoral agriculture

The backstory for domesticated livestock and the culture of farming has an equally long history as that of beavers. I have used the term 'pastoral' as encompassing these practices and the narratives that flow from them, but this can have different meanings depending on the context. In literature it is the leisure, song and culture of the shepherds celebrated in Virgil's *Eclogues* and Lucretius's *Idylls* that is the cultural inheritance of the pastoral style of writing, which sometimes forgets that there are no shepherds without sheep. An animal studies reading of some of these texts will have to search for the sheep or cows between the lines. ANT can help break away from what is a very humanistic standpoint, by questioning what part the animals have played in the making of music, when the demands that animals have on their keepers if they are to live and thrive slacken enough to allow an appearance of leisure;, and what other aspects of being about animals allows for such a bucolic scene.

While those who look back to classical literature will regard Virgil's *Georgics* as being the place for the discussion of the practical aspects of animal keeping, the term 'pastoral' is used in geography to cover any way of using land by raising livestock. Under this heading there are many different ways of relating to the animals. It has to cover nomadic people who travel with their animals over vast areas; those practising transhumance where animals are moved, sometimes over large distances to high pastures for summer grazing; those where the animals are housed over winter in barns or byres attached to the family home; those where animals are sold as stores on weaning to be kept on richer pastures until ready for market, and those where they are 'finished' on the farm where they were born. Each of these systems provides different opportunities for interacting with these animals, and for both people and animals as actants to have a distinct effect on each other. The scale of the enterprise is also an important factor, from a tiny flock or herd in subsistence farming, to many thousands in industrialised feedlots. The degree to which farmers have sentimental feelings towards their charges or regard the whole thing as an instrumental relationship is another variable that has to be taken into account. In all of these systems the relationship between the humans and nonhumans will be constantly being made and remade. ANT requires us to recognise the dynamic nature of these relationships, which might not fit into predetermined classification systems such as pastoral or georgic.

The domesticated animals of today have developed over millennia where natural selection has adapted sheep to their land, and where human preferences – economic and aesthetic – have had the effect of artificial selection. Looking through the young at the end of the breeding season to decide which females to keep for breeding, and which males to be offered for sale for breeding on other farms, is an important ritual in which the individual qualities of the animal are assessed. These choices may well not be entirely rational – personal preferences can influence the choice. For my part I still look with admiration at the selection a local farmer makes from his Cheviot ewe lambs, which will enter the breeding flock next year. A well-chosen batch will have a uniform look, which will present well at the livestock show, where the similarity of say five lambs is a judging factor. The farmer as actant makes decisions that have life or death consequences for the animals. A similar routine will assess which of the older animals should be retired or more likely culled.

Pastoralism in the twenty-first century

In *English Pastoral: An Inheritance* (2020), James Rebanks describes a system that would have been recognised by Wordsworth. The book is part personal memoir and part discussion of how farming can be sustainable in the twenty-first century. It can be read as non-fiction prose, but it is his thoughtful insights into the relationships farmers have with their animals which adds to the more theoretical approach to human–animal studies that concerns us here. Rebanks' flock of 500 Herdwick ewes are hefted to their common grazing on the fells, where each flock keeps more or less to its own part of the fell, in an arrangement that Wordsworth regarded as a perfect republic of shepherds. Herdwick sheep are an ancient breed that is adapted to the environment of the Cumbrian fells. In the winter they are brought to lower ground where they can be mated with carefully chosen rams to preserve the characteristics of the breed, and perhaps improve the overall quality of the flock. Despite an appearance of timelessness, the Rebanks family has gone through considerable turmoil to reach its current position. Severe financial pressures and foot-and-mouth disease have put the system under strain. Latour's insight that social systems are dynamic, and affected equally by environmental pressures, is particularly relevant here. The traditional ways of farming are still subject to market pressures, from the supermarkets squeezing suppliers to provide cheaper food, and from the collapse in the price paid for wool to the point where it doesn't cover the costs of shearing. Rebanks, who also has a herd of Belted Galloway beef-suckler cows, is forced to find alternative sources of income away from the farm. In previous generations this farm would have given the farmer a good living. Perhaps a good place to start with a human–animal studies reading informed by ANT is to pose the question: why does he feel the need to farm this way?

Knowing animals as individuals is one of the major differences between rewilding, where the reward is seeing a healthy and diverse wild population, and agriculture, where the special needs of each individual are taken into account. This difference is formalised in the animal welfare rules that apply to farmed animals, where only explicit acts of cruelty towards individual wild animals will attract censure. Recalling Rebanks' own grandfather:

> He would simply gaze at his cows or sheep for what felt like ages, leaning over a gate. As a result he knew them all as individuals. He could spot when they behave differently because something was wrong,

> when they were coming into season or were about to give birth. He believed that a good farmer was patient and used his, or her, eyes and ears, and nose and touch. Doing things well was his goal, not doing things quickly or with the least effort. (Rebanks, 2020: 28)

It was largely from his grandfather that Rebanks learned what it took to be a farmer. This was his inheritance. The bond of affect, for instance when watching a mare foaling (Rebanks, 2020: 77–8), sustains the sometimes lonely life of a farmer who spends more time with his animals than he has contact with the wider community. As I write this I am in my study in what was the byre of the traditional house. Rebanks' grandfather told him that in the traditional long-houses the heat generated in the byre and from the piles of muck was a valuable commodity, which kept the house warm through the winter (Rebanks, 2020: 79). These stories illustrate the complexity, fluidity and mutual supportiveness of the relationship that farmers and their families have with their animals. These are all features that Latour ascribes to human–animal–other relationships in ANT.

That farmers have strong feelings of affect for their animals cannot be denied. What has to be addressed is how they can then bear to send them for slaughter. Rebanks' grandfather, who could be tender with new-born lambs, could also be 'tough and almost a cruel man'. 'For him death and killing were simply part of his life' (Rebanks, 2020: 36). Killing would be done swiftly, respectfully but without emotion. Animals going to slaughter tomorrow would be treated with every effort to keep them alive today. 'He existed in nature, as an actor on the stage, always struggling to hold his ground. A risen ape, not a fallen angel (Rebanks, 2020: 36). This description of his grandfather fits closely into an ANT reading. A commitment to preserving a healthy and biodiverse flock of Herdwick sheep, rather than see this unique breed becoming extinct, which supports the actor–networks in the hill farming system, is only sustainable if a harvest is taken. ANT gives us no answers to the moral dilemma around the eating of meat; it does, however, ask us to explore the complexity of all the alternative ways of living in the iconic landscape of the romantic poets.

Economic pressures drove his father to follow the market by introducing modern 'improved breeds' of sheep and cattle, which grew quicker and had more valuable carcasses. These had to be kept at higher stocking levels with more reliance on bought-in feed. They were not as hardy as the native Cumbrian breeds and losing just a few each season could eliminate the profit. More subtle was the change in the relationship farmers had with their animals:

> Our farm animals had never been pets, and we were rarely sentimental about them, but there was a lot of care involved and a kind of intimacy that vanished as things got bigger and more industrial. The farm animals' characters were well known to us: they all had backstories. To earn the title 'stockman', or 'stockwoman' we were expected to have an encyclopaedic knowledge of all our cows and ewes. But on the modern farm something had changed: it wasn't necessarily that the animals were ill treated, I didn't see much of that, but more that they had become just units of production. (Rebanks, 2020: 128)

In traditional methods, sheep or cows were either allowed to move themselves around the farm, helping themselves to a wide range of plants, or were herded by shepherds or cowherds to move away from any fields that had been heavily dunged. In contrast, intensive methods of farming left the animals dirty, stressed and diseased, depending on medicines including antibiotics, wormers, hormones and vaccines to cure these problems (Rebanks, 2020: 131). These 'modern' methods also impacted society, as farms employed fewer workers and the social life of the villages collapsed. The complex and shifting relationships between actants in the move to 'modern' breeds changed the social makeup of the community and the relationships that farmers had with their animals. ANT can help us to understand the insidious accumulation of effects these changes have, and how dynamic the network is. Having taken on a flock of hardy Herdwick sheep and Belted Galloway cows, Rebanks had to set about making his farm sustainable, both as a living for his family and to make the farm less reliant on bought-in feed, fertiliser and medicines. To do this he has had to look beyond the immediate relationships with his stock. Rephrasing his approach in the language of ANT, he had to establish how actants that had been overlooked in the rush to modernisation were important players in the actor–network.

Aside from the change in breeds of livestock, late-twentieth-century modernisation relied on ever increasing inputs of artificial fertiliser with the associated risk of run-off polluting streams and rivers, and the gradual decline in the quality of the soil. A neighbour of his father who had farmed with traditional breeds, rotational crops and spreading straw-based muck rather than artificial fertiliser was regarded as backward by the modernising farmers of the neighbourhood. When he died, one of the farmers who took on his land sent soil to be analysed to see how much lime and fertiliser he should apply. The answer came back that the 'soil was healthy. It needed nothing. It was full of earthworms, rich and fertile' (Rebanks, 2020: 144). The modern methods had ignored important actants that ANT would require us to seek out. Earthworms are as important to the farm as the cows and sheep. The decomposing pathway with actants, which include springtails, bacteria and fungi, break down the manure to release the nutrients for recycling and to incorporate the humus into the soil. ANT takes us a long way from a human–animal reading that is only populated with animals known to be sentient, to complicate the narrative by engaging with all these other animate and inanimate entities that are needed for a sustainable life.

Having the right breeds of sheep and cattle for the land is necessary, but not sufficient, to guarantee its long-term health. Rebanks has worked with an ecologist to understand the science that earlier farmers took for granted. The simplest technique was to dig out six-inch squares of soil to count the worms as an indicator of how healthy the soil is. Admitting soil and worms as actants, which have direct effects on the incorporation of manure into the soil and release of nutrients, opens the way for different approaches to farming the land. A biodiverse grassland may not be as productive as intensively managed pastures with perhaps just two species of grass, but it allows the livestock agency to select the species grass or forbs that meet its immediate nutritional requirement. As an additional reward for the farmer, such fields will echo to the sound of curlews calling in the summer. If the aim of ANT is to bring nonhuman actants into the foreground, regenerative farming extends consideration to the organisms that decompose manure and detritus in the soil. Coming full circle, this way of farming breaks down the barrier between domesticated and wild species, when they are interacting one with another in a dynamic and shifting series of events. ANT requires us to follow these relationships beyond the entities that are on the financial balance sheet.

The farm has much in common with the way the land was farmed before the invention of artificial fertilisers, antibiotics and wormers. One change is that Rebanks has sought out advice from an ecologist to get the best out of his land. For example, by allowing grass to remain longer it would maximise the area exposed to the sun for photosynthesis. Where streams had been straightened during the 'modernising' phase, he dug meanders and planted trees. The reward from this regenerative agriculture is a richer biodiversity of the farm. This way of farming converges on the rewilding by reintroducing wild herbivores such as beavers.

Stop and think

Beavers, sheep and cows are all herbivores. From the viewpoint of these animals, how do the management systems of beaver reintroduction and regenerative farming with sheep and cows differ? Can beavers really be described as wild if they are closely monitored, relocated from time to time and lethally controlled if they threaten human interests? What effects do these animals as actants have on the human entities that engage with them? Sentience is seen as a an important factor in the animal turn in the humanities, but both rewilding and regenerative agriculture are based on the understanding that worms, insects and other invertebrates are actants in the network and their presence is critical if the system is to be sustainable. How does the admission of animals with lesser claims to sentience change an animal studies reading of a literary text?

Is ANT just ecology by another name?

The texts discussed above were interwoven with ecological narratives. With its origins in the sociology of science, ANT confronts terms like 'society' and 'nature'. Over the three-generation span in Rebanks' book, ecology has changed markedly. The original idea that each location had a climax community of species, which it would progress to if human interference was removed, is now contested. For most of England it was expected that succession stages would progress towards a climax community of broad-leaved forest and for the Highlands of Scotland to Caledonian pine. This myth of the wildwood has since been discredited. An important development was the idea that ancient forests would have been grazed by large herbivores, including red deer, aurochs and wild boar. Attempts to replicate such a system by breeding approximations of cows and horses to their wild forebears have been plagued by trouble. Without predators, such as grey wolves, the population of these herbivores will grow to the point where they die in large numbers from starvation. Even if humans are excluded from the system, they soon become aware that animals are being left to die. Further, some of these breeds are very difficult to handle. In England, rewilding is mostly done by bringing back traditional breeds of domestic animals, such as the Old English Longhorn cattle used at the Knepp Estate in Sussex.

Ecology has had to come to terms with the dynamic nature of the ecosystem. There is no single climax system towards which the community of species will proceed through a known succession path. It therefore shares with ANT the idea that relationships are constantly changing. Ecology has, in the past, focused on 'natural ecosystems' with anthropogenic effects coming from outside the system. ANT can help to refocus this viewpoint to bring humans into the system and to show that they are dependent on the functioning of an ecology where often ignored organisms play an essential role. It should be stressed that ecology is a developing science and that there are many different ways of studying the relationships between species. For example, population ecology considers a single species in terms of variables such as survival rates within species biodiversity or dispersal. By narrowing the focus, investigators can quantify their findings. In community ecology the approach is more descriptive. The relationships between species may then be expressed in terms of energy and nutrient flows up the trophic levels and through the decomposing pathway. In the process, the individual animal gets lost. ANT, with the emphasis on the sometimes fleeting interactions between actants, is also descriptive. It reinforces current thinking in ecology about the dynamic nature of relationships, and encourages us to consider entities that we might otherwise ignore. Its principal contribution to an animal studies reading of literary texts is to open our minds to all the possible actants in the system. It widens the view of an animal studies reading that is preoccupied with sentient or social animals that are like us. Further, unlike ecology as science, it admits the affect that humans have for nonhuman others as an effect of relating to another actant. Ecologically informed conservation management has, however, already recognised affect as important. That is what saved the beavers on the River Otter, and most projects will include interpretation and ranger services to present the animals to people.

Further reading

Dawkins, Marian Stamp and Bonney, Roland (eds) (2011) *The Future of Animal Farming: Renewing the Animal Contract*. Hoboken, NJ: Wiley-Blackwell.

Harman, Graham (2016) 'Demodernizing the humanities with Latour', *New Literary History* 47:2–4, pp. 249–74.

Tree, Isabella (2018) *Wilding*. London: Pan Macmillan.

References

Austin, Mary (2001 [1906]) *The Flock*. Reissued edition. Reno, Nevada: University of Nevada Press.

Beer, Amy-Jane (2022) *The Flow: Rivers, Water and Wildness*. London: Bloomsbury.

Bewick, Thomas (1804) *A General History of Quadrupeds, with Some American Animals*. New York: G. and R. Waite.

Bewick, Thomas (1834) *A General History of Quadrupeds, with Some American Animals*. Second American, eighth London edition. New York: J. Booth & Son.

Gow, Derek (2020) *Bringing Back the Beaver*. White River Junction, VT: Chelsea Green.

Kerson, Arnold L. (2000) 'The Republic of Beavers: an American utopia', *Utopian Studies* 11:2, pp. 14–32.

Latour, B.(1996) 'On Actor-Network Theory: a few clarifications', *Soziale Welt* 47, pp. 369–81.

Latour, Bruno (2005) *Reassembling the Social: An Introduction to Actor-Network Theory*. Oxford: Oxford University Press.

Latour, Bruno (2017) *Facing Gaia: Eight Lectures on the New Climatic Regime*. Cambridge: Polity.
Muir, John (1894) *The Mountains of California*. New York: Century Co.
Nelson, Barney (2000) *The Wild and the Domestic: Animal Representation, Ecocriticism and Western American Literature*. Reno, Nevada: University of Nevada Press.
Rebanks, James (2020) *English Pastoral: An Inheritance*. London: Allen Lane.

6

Attentiveness and the poetic imagination

In the previous chapters, we have been challenged to think differently about animals in their environment. Haraway asked us to move beyond a model for animals, including ourselves, as bounded individuals. Latour introduced us to the actor–network theory in which animals were actants alongside other living and non-living entities. The ephemeral nature of these relationships was stressed, as only when an actant was producing an effect, could it be seen to be relevant. The examples used to illustrate these ideas were drawn from creative non-fiction in which facts were to be respected within a literary format. If we are to make progress in this way of thinking, we need to be more attentive to what we see around us and to be more flexible in how it is represented in literature. This chapter looks further into the idea of attentiveness and asks what role poetry might have in disrupting norms, finding new meanings, and seeing facts in ways not constrained by what Plumwood called the master model.

Attentiveness in a multispecies world

In their contribution to a special edition of the journal *Environmental Humanities* on multispecies studies, van Dooren, Kirkby and Münster suggested that 'passionate immersion in the lives of fungi, microorganisms, animals, plants is opening up new understandings, relationships and accountabilities' (van Dooren, Kirkby and Münster, 2016: 1). Thinking more deeply about what we are seeing can unsettle the given notion of species. For example, elsewhere in the same issue, Lorimer makes the case for the human individual to be an assemblage of all the other organisms that live closely with it, including the gut biota and all the other microorganisms that find a place to live, both internally and externally, on the human body (Lorimer, 2016: 57–76). Some of these organisms are commensal in that we get a direct benefit from them, for example, in digesting our food, and others are less benign. Before we can construct new meanings, we must cultivate the art of attentiveness that includes the concept of ourselves as a community of organisms.

All beings exist in multispecies assemblages and the authors cite Bateson in suggesting the 'the fundamental unit of survival is the "organism in its environment"' (van Dooren, Kirkby and Münster, 2016: 2). The entanglements between species that have a shared heritage through coevolution is what they describe as 'the rich processes of cobecoming'. 'This cobecoming involves the exchange and emergence of meanings, immersion in webs of signification that might be linguistic, gestural, biochemical, and more' (van Dooren, Kirkby and Münster, 2016: 2). To make sense of this complex world we have to search across the disciplines, including the natural sciences, and perhaps take them in new directions. We should not restrict ourselves to sources from within the colonising master model, but admit also the different ways of thinking of Indigenous people, which is explored in greater depth in chapter 8.

This complex multispecies world requires practices of attentiveness to the relationships we have with others. It requires a broader taxonomic scope of enquiry to that privileging sentient animals that has traditionally been taken in animal studies. Is this the point at which we abandon 'animal studies' as a discipline? Although multispecies studies demands more of us than examining the dualism between *Homo sapiens* and one or more nonhuman animal species, I propose to treat it as a development of animal studies rather than a complete paradigm shift to a totally new way of thinking. In common with Latour's ANT, multispecies studies 'focuses on the multitude of lively agents that bring one another into being through entangled relations that include, but always exceed, dynamics of predator and prey, parasite and host, researcher and researched, symbiotic partner, or indifferent neighbour' (van Dooren, Kirkby and Münster, 2016: 3). All of these relationships are dynamic. As with Latour, these authors admit non-living agents, including stones and weather systems.

Taking their cue from Haraway, the authors stress that the term 'species' is used in its generic sense, rather than being tied to the strictures of western taxonomy.

The art of attentiveness has a broad range, which acknowledges the diversity of interlocking ways of living. It aims to produce 'thick accounts' that pay attention to what matters to the life form we are attending to. This requirement has echoes in the development of farm welfare based on what the animals want that was discussed in chapter 2. This way of thinking has to consider the part played by less attractive animals, which humans may not feel to be charismatic, or that overshadowed by the headline species named in conservation plans. Some such species have so few followers, that reading widely may be a challenge. Taxa at the margins may be unknown except to taxonomists wanting to make their name by describing a species 'new to science'. The passionate immersion advocated by the authors asks us to become curious and entangled so that we learn to care a little differently (van Dooren, Kirkby and Münster, 2016: 6). Haraway on primates and Despret on baboons, sheep and Arabian babblers have shown how critical and creative readings of contemporary natural scientific literature can 'deconstruct and reconstruct truth claims towards a better understanding of others' (van Dooren, Kirkby and Münster, 2016: 7). These scholars have spent time in the field with scientists, observing how they go about studying animal behaviour. Attentiveness is as much about careful reading and watching scientists at work, as it is about watching the animals themselves. Part of this approach is to challenge how knowledge is constructed: 'aiming to decolonize and more broadly challenge dominant assumptions about knowledge, expertise, and who is authorized to speak for Nature' (van Dooren, Kirkby and Münster, 2016: 8). In particular, to pay close attention to Indigenous communities, which may have alternative ways of seeing the natural world. Above all, this type of attentiveness makes space for the animals themselves to be inventive, particularly when they live with us as companion species, but also as we use modern technology such as 'critter cams' to watch their intimate lives.

The authors of this paper refuse to make a choice between 'unreconstructed realism and easy relativism' (van Dooren, Kirkby and Münster, 2016: 12). There is a real world out there, but it is not our task to describe it. Rather, they advocate the notion of 'worlding', which is an interplay between the material world and its semiotic expression. This approach breaks down the 'absolute division between epistemology and ontology' (van Dooren, Kirkby and Münster, 2016: 12). This chapter considers how the practices of the poetic imagination and the critical reading of poems can contribute to this process.

On the poetic imagination

Poets craft their work by employing a wide variety of forms and literary devices. Also they are not so bound by factual accuracy as those writing literary non-fiction. Much may be unsaid between the lines of a poem, and it is sometimes here that we must look for the animals and other actants that make up their multispecies worlds. How all this works has been a concern of poets since Aristotle. The concept of 'mimesis' is one of Aristotle's contributions to debate in literary circles. It seems that not everyone is sure what he meant by mimesis, and are divided on whether it is a good thing or to be avoided. For Halliwell, 'the idea of mimesis has become symbolic of the uncertain position of the *Poetics* in the factionalised world of modern literary theory' (Halliwell, 2012: 2). Is it an abstract theoretical principle or 'an acknowledgement of poetry's (and, more generally, literature's) open-ended possibilities of practice' (Halliwell, 2012: 3). If it is the latter, can it be useful in casting light on the demanding world of multispecies relationships? While Aristotle didn't equate mimesis with 'imitation of nature', that is one meaning that others have taken from it (Halliwell, 2012: 3). Halliwell interprets his idea as having several levels that build on the inborn human trait to engage in mimesis, which has 'cognitive, emotional and ethical ramifications' (Halliwell, 2012: 4). This trait is expressed through the practice of the mimetic arts in media, such as language, visual forms and musical patterns, aspects of human experience, in actions, emotions and ethical qualities, and in modes such as different narratives and points of view (Halliwell, 2012: 4). I return to this discussion below in considering how poets have echoed nature and have rendered their work as 'true to nature'.

The Romantic poets spent a good deal of their time thinking about their craft. In his preface to the third edition of the *Lyrical*

Ballads, Wordsworth had revolution in mind 'in what manner language and the human mind act and re-act on each other, and without retracing the revolutions, not of literature alone, but likewise of society itself' (Wordsworth, 1802: iv). He felt that poetry should have a worthy purpose, which emerges when his description of objects and his habits of meditation excite his feelings to the point where they carry a purpose (Wordsworth, 1802: x). The necessity of producing pleasure is not a degradation of the poet's art:

> It is an acknowledgement of the beauty of the universe, an acknowledgement the more sincere because it is not formal, but indirect: it is a task light and easy to him who looks at the world in the spirit of love: further, it is homage paid to the native and naked dignity of man, to the grand elementary dignity of pleasure, by which he knows, and feels, and lives, and moves. (Wordsworth, 1802: xxxiii–xxxiv)

For Wordsworth, the poet 'considers man and the objects that surround him as acting and re-acting upon one another, so as to produce an infinite complexity of pain and pleasure' (Wordsworth, 1802: xxxiv–xxxv). How far are these ideas in tune with a multispecies world in a dynamic relationship between actants, each sometimes producing an effect on another object or sometimes through silence ceasing to be an actant? Wordsworth talks here about men, but includes the 'entire world of nature, from which I am at liberty to supply myself with endless combinations of forms and imagery' (Wordsworth, 1802: xliv). For Coleridge it is evident that the first task of the poet who works in this way is to pay close attention to nature itself: 'there is no profession on earth, which requires an attention so early, so long, or so unintermitting as that of poetry' (Coleridge, 1847: 46). For a contemporary poet that will mean attuning themselves to the possibilities of a multispecies world.

For Shelley, 'poetry in a general sense, may be defined as the "expression of the imagination"' (Shelley, 1840: n.p.). He saw that there was a principle in all human beings and perhaps all sentient beings, to produce harmony as well as melody. This inclusion of all sentient beings is perhaps an early indicator of the way the animal turn would gradually enlarge the range of species that are thought to have moral standing. Shelley saw poetry as the image of life expressed as its eternal truth, which differs from a collection of facts. This expression is 'universal, and contains within itself the germ of a relation to whatever motives or actions have place in the possible varieties of human nature' (Shelley, 1840: n.p.). But in the context of considering how the poetic imagination might offer an insight into multispecies relations, his suggestion, in contrast to ethical science, is that

> Poetry acts in another and diviner manner. It awakens and enlarges the mind itself by rendering the receptacle of a thousand unapprehended combinations of thought. Poetry lifts the veil from the hidden beauty of the world, and makes familiar objects be as if they are not familiar; it reproduces all that it represents, and the impersonations clothed in its Elysian light stand thenceforward in the minds of those who have once contemplated them as memorials of that gentle and exalted content which extends itself over all thoughts and actions with which it coexists. (Shelley, 1840: n.p.)

Thinking in a multispecies world is a challenge and I would suggest that it is to poetry that we must look to confront the persistent ideas that stand in our way. Attentiveness is a practice that is necessary for a poet to have the material that will set their imagination to work. The radical use of language, form and rhythm further challenges us to look deeper into the complex relationships on which our very survival as a species may depend.

Some contemporary poets look to the form of their poems as a means to explore radical themes. In her anthology of radical landscape poetry, Harriet Tarlo has selected 'poets whose formal techniques are exploratory and experimental enough to be called radical, poets whose ideological pushing of the boundaries is to be found integrated into the forms their poems inhabit' (Tarlo, 2011: 8). She has argued that such poetry can be particularly powerful in 'the necessary mental and emotional adjustments to environment that we need urgently to make' (Tarlo, 2011: 10). As an example, she cites Carol Watts, whose work shows lyric poetry under stress, through the use of internal mathematical logic. Each poem is named after a prime number and has nineteen lines (Tarlo, 2011: 11). By resisting narrative and realist conventions, such poetry can create a truer reflection of reality itself. Although this anthology is of landscape poetry, many of the poems included can be read from an animal studies perspective;

examples are Mark Godwin's 'Dark bird with corner' and Helen Macdonald's 'Skipper/copper' (Tarlo, 2011:16, 149–50, 162). The landscape here is another actant in the network that makes it possible to apply the level of attentiveness required in a multispecies reading of these poems.

Apart from works that are mimetic, poetry rarely clings closely to the referent. There are real objects out there and some of them are living or inanimate species that play a part in a multispecies world, but there is not the same obligation to dwell on their description as there might be in creative non-fiction. 'Words refer to things in the world, but it can be argued that they do not do so in a one-for-one kind of way' (Eagleton, 2008: 51). For poetry a word denotes through the complex interrelations it has with other words. Further, 'it is a characteristic of poetic language that it gives us not simply the denotation of a word (what it refers to), but also a whole cluster of connotations or associated meanings' (Eagleton, 2008: 110). The use of imagination does not stop with the writer, but continues as the reader makes new associations and arrives at new meanings. In this chapter we look to the meanings that perhaps were not foreseen by the poet, that can emerge when we read a poem from a multispecies perspective. We rely here on there being sufficient life in the poem to allow our imagination to work. Not all the connotations and new meanings we find will yield a multispecies reading, while they may have value in their own right, they are not what we are looking for here. In following the referent, even when it is between the lines or otherwise absent, we can admit some narratives of science, but must guard against making the poem conform to what Plumwood called the 'master model' that was discussed in chapter 4.

Case study: should we adhere strictly to western taxonomy?

In the anthology *The Poetry of Birds*, edited by Simon Armitage and Tim Dee, most of the poems are grouped under the species name of their subject. Two well-known poems caught my eye, both placed by the editors to the species of Whooper Swan: Yeats's 'The wild swans at Coole' and Heaney's 'Postscript'. For those who search the internet there are plenty of analyses of these poems, but not much mention of the birds themselves. An attentive multispecies reading would start with the birds and spread out to the other species that are in the poem or hidden between the lines. It was Heaney's poem that unsettled me with the line 'In September or October, when the wind' (Heaney in Armitage and Dee, 2009: 33, line 3). One of the joys of living on a Hebridean island is that day in mid-October when the whooper swans announce their arrival with their loud bugling call, some to stay with us for the winter, others to fly over on their way to winter in Ireland. Heaney knew his birds, so something is wrong here, whooper swans would be unlikely in Ireland before mid-October. Heaney does not name the species of his swans in what he saw as a drive by impression on an autumn day; are we then right in assuming that he must have meant the same wild swans that Yeats was seeing at Coole? We can identify the lake from his description as Lough Muree, which is blocked at the seaward end by a shingle bank. The road runs along this bank. Can we verify Armitage and Dee's placing this poem under the heading of whooper swan?

The first thing to do is to check whether whooper swan is likely at this location. Lough Muree is a hotspot on the eBird website with 52 species being seen by observers since 2010 – whooper swan is not among them. On the other hand there were 36 mute swans present on 24 September 2023, and a high count of 71 on 23 November 2021 (ebird.org, accessed 23 July 2024). The line 'Their fully grown headstrong-looking heads' would make sense if these were mute swans, which have a prominent knob where the bill meets the head. It seems that the editors of this anthology have taken the known admiration that Heaney had for Yeats and the nearness of this lough to Coole, to pair the two poems. Further the phrase 'among stones' in line 5 also resonates with 'among the stones' in Yeats's line 5. We will return to stones.

Now that we are suspicious, we can turn to the wild swans at Coole. Were they whoopers? Until 1830 'wild swan' was a species name to differentiate these migratory swans from the mute swan. Unusually for birds living in the wild, mute swans are owned, some by the Crown and others by university colleges. In 1830 William Yarrell described the smaller race of wild swans as a separate species, which he named after the famous engraver Thomas Bewick. In taxonomic terms, it is a 'splitter' that would name two species where there was one. Coole Lake was once a wintering site for both Bewick's and whooper swans. In 1998–99 the mean peak for whooper swans was 324 and for Bewick's 79 (Coole Park Nature Reserve, n.d.). Yeats might have deliberately reverted to the older name to avoid counting the species separately, an activity that he had kept up for 19 years. The lines 'Among what rushes will they build / By what lake's edge or pool' make sense if some were whoopers which come to Ireland from Iceland and others were Bewick's, which breed in the European taiga. Since Yarrell split the race into two species, the 'lumpers' have made an additional revision to assign both Bewick's and the North American whistling swan as separate subspecies of a new species – the taiga swan.

Does this discussion help us in an attentive reading of these two poems? It places these birds in their place where each species has its own reasons for being on one or both of these loughs. Taking the multispecies reading further, consider the stones. In 'Postscript' the location is mentioned as by Flaggy Shore. The karst landscape of this area of County Clare is dominated on the surface by limestone pavements broken into blocks, with underground sinkholes and streams. Between the blocks wild flowers and miniature trees are able to flourish away from the grazing pressure of livestock. Coole Lake, which is in the nearby karst landscape of County Galway, is seasonally fed by underground streams. It is the largest of these lakes in this area, where they are known as 'turloughs'. Some dry out completely in the summer, others to just a pool. Yeats's line 'Upon the brimming water among the stones' (line 5) makes sense here. These turloughs have a distinctive vegetation, which may be one reason why they are attractive to the swans. Lough Muree is fed by fresh water in the same way, but also by percolation of the sea through the shingle bank. It is brackish with a salinity between that of sea and fresh water. The Gregory family planted both native and exotic trees at Coole, and this feature also gets a mention in the first two lines of the poem. This wonderful landscape is now designated as a Special Area of Conservation under the EU Habitats Directive.

I have another copy of this poem in a facsimile edition with an introductory note by George Bornstein (Yeats, 1919). The cover of this version was designed by T. Sturge Moore, an English writer and artist. Bornstein describes this cover as follows:

> Stamped in gold on a blue background, the new cover featured a swan in a circle looking down and the top half of a swan at the bottom, both in flight. They thus reinforced the prominence of the title poem of the book, and at the same time enacted one of Yeats's favourite dichotomies of up/down, as above, so below. (Bornstein 'Introduction' in Yeats, 1919: xx)

Again I am troubled by these images. The lower swan has a knob on its beak, which would make it a mute swan. Yeats's lines 'Unwearied still, lover by lover, / They paddle in the cold / Companionable streams or climb the air' (lines 19–21) reflect his understanding that swans migrate as family units, with male, female and that year's offspring flying together. Further, the upper bird in heraldic pose lacks the knob and seems to have a hooked beak. As the next poem in this collection, 'In memory of Major Robert Gregory' laments his death, while serving in the Royal Flying Corps during the First World War, we can perhaps explore what the upper bird might mean. A search of the web for an image of Gregory's war grave has at the head of the gravestone the emblem of the Royal Flying Corps, later adopted as the emblem of the Royal Air Force. This is of a generalised hawk in a near identical pose to that used for the upper bird on the cover of this facsimile edition. It is hard to know if this is accident or design. It does not invalidate Bornstein's reading of the image, because that is where his imagination took him, but for me the unnatural nature of the image was unsettling and leads to a different set of meanings and associations.

Does this discussion help or hinder a reading of these fine poems for their literary merit? Does it provide yet more opportunities to find metaphor in the works? Does it help to know that the brimming lake is the seasonal evidence of a complex hydrology in this special landscape? Without this seasonal filling there would be no swans here.

Perhaps the lines in the third stanza have alternative meanings: 'I have looked upon these brilliant creatures, / And now my heart is sore. / All's changed since I, hearing at twilight, / The first time on this shore, / The bell-beat of their wings above my head, / Trod with a lighter tread'. Do they refer to changes in his personal life, the loss of Major Robert Gregory, or the changing makeup of the flock of wild swans? Or does one thought flow from another? Whooper swans fly directly to Britain and Ireland from Iceland. Bewick's swans have the option of stopping off en route in continental Europe, and with global warming, few now reach Ireland. Even the huge flocks at Slimbridge on the River Severn in England and the Ouse Washes in East Anglia are getting smaller, as more birds opt to spend the winter on continental Europe. Of course all of these associations could be valid as perceived change in the multispecies sphere, could lead onto connotations in the personal sphere, if only to miss the company of someone who would have shared an interest in the swans at Coole.

We see in this example, that the taxonomists have been busy with the swans. Bewick's swan was first split from whooper swan and then lumped with the whistling swan as the taiga swan. Poems can still work with ambiguity; I would not have questioned Heaney's 'Postscript' without it being misfiled under whooper swan by Armitage and Dee. The resident mute swans and the migratory wild swans (both species) are closely related in the same genus; the imagery works just as well with any combination, but a multispecies reading does open up new facts and associations for the poet's imagination and for the reader to search out new connotations that can add to the enjoyment of the poem.

Stop and think

Attentiveness, as advocated by van Dooren and others, requires us to see the organism in its environment. Further, we need to abandon the idea of a bounded individual, for ourselves and for the other animals that we pay attention to. Not all of these aspects will be evident just by looking. When we look at one another we have no sense that another's gut biota is there, and even less of what it might be up to. Poetry can cope with this uncertainty, because it is economical in its use of words and we will be accustomed to the idea that some animals are present between the lines, for example, the sheep in a pastoral poem might not be referred to directly, but the poem will make sense if we understand that they are there. I have taken the liberty to question the poet laureate in his assignation of the two poems discussed above to the species of whooper swan. That was not a huge error, but for me the possible connotations from both poems make more sense if the species is uncertain, for Heaney's because I then do not need to puzzle about why whooper swans might be on the lough in September and for Yeats's because the uncertainty over which wild swans are present opens up new possibilities for metaphor. A close reading of these poems will take, for example, the word 'brimming' in relation to Coole and see where that takes us. Discovering that the lough dries out in summer makes more sense here. It also introduces the dynamic nature of these relationships. In the same way the 19 years over which Yeats has counted swans has been a period of great change, personally, in relationships, and as the natural world changes from year to year. Assuming that what we see on the lake today was the same as it would have been 100 years ago, makes no allowance for the constantly changing assemblage of natural actants.

Attentiveness, true to nature and mimesis

It takes a particular type of attentiveness to write a poem, and another to read one, but when real, as opposed to mythical, animals appear in poetry, attentiveness to living animals also has a part to play. Ted Hughes's essay 'Capturing animals' gives an insight into how he brought these two kinds of attentiveness into the creative process. His early experience was with his brother, where they shot all manner of animals. The excitement of the hunt is, for Hughes, comparable to that when making a poem:

> The slightly mesmerised and quite involuntary concentration with which you make out the stirrings of a new poem in your mind, then the outline, the mass and colour and clean final form of it, the unique living reality of it in the midst of general lifelessness, all this is too familiar to mistake. This is hunting and the poem is a new species of creature, a new specimen of life outside your own. (Hughes, 1994: 11–12)

A multispecies reading of this poem must see this new species in its environment, literary and material. Recognising the link between the text and the material species that informed it is very much part of our responsibility as attentive readers of such work.

Discussing his own poem 'The Fox', Hughes stresses the need to see the real fox: 'If I have not caught the real fox there in the words, I would never have saved the poem' (Hughes, 1994: 14–15). Alice Oswald, in the introduction to *A Ted Hughes Bestiary*, asks the question: 'What is it that turns language into an animal?' She concludes that it is the percussion: 'there is something irresistible about a Ted Hughes poem, which makes every word of it connected and essential' (Oswald, 2014: xiv). Hughes shows how to escape from factual prose by combining the imaginative leap needed to create a poem, with the attentiveness that still captures the real animal. Poetry is not the only medium that can make this leap, but as Hughes shows, it has the intensity and focus of the imagination that is needed to cross species lines.

For attentiveness, few poets have the intensity of John Clare. In his poem 'The nightingale's nest', we are breathless with him as he practises the field craft of finding her nest. This 93-line poem takes us into the wood, so that by the time he finds the nest, we know just what that wood looks like and all the species that populated the place that the nightingale chooses for its summer home. Clare listens to the song, not just to appreciate its beauty, but to connect with the bird as it sings:

> Her wings would tremble in her ecstasy
> And feathers stand on end as 'twere with joy
> And mouth wide open to release her heart
> Of its out-sobbing songs – the happiest part
> Of summer's fame she shared – for so to me
> Did happy fancies shapen her employ
> But if I touched a bush or scarcely stirred
> All in moment stopt – I watched in vain
> (Clare, 1990: 109)

In this extract we see Clare being faithful to the myth that it is the female bird that sings. Attributing joy to the bird is anthropomorphic, but the description of the bird's behaviour while it sings is based on close observation in the wild. Further, he understands that the bird's singing is conditional on him keeping quite still. There is kinship established across the species divide and respect in retreating once the nest has been found, so as not to risk its desertion or to expose it to predators. There is plenty in this poem for an attentive reading that recognises the structural integrity of the place where the bird has made its nest. As practices such as rotational coppicing in woodland – for this seems to be the habitat Clare is describing – die out, so the nightingale has fewer places to nest.

Another nightingale poem that draws on the same habits of attentiveness is Samuel Taylor Coleridge's 'The nightingale', written in 1798 and included in Volume 1 of Wordsworth's *Lyrical Ballads* (1802). He turns his back on the association of the nightingale with melancholy:

> And hark! The Nightingale begins its song
> 'Most musical, most melancholy' Bird!
> A melancholy bird? O idea thought!
> In nature there is nothing melancholy
> – but some night-wandering Man, whose heart was pierc'd
> With remembrance of a grievous wrong,
> Or slow distemper, or neglected love
> (Coleridge in Wordsworth, 1802: 91)

A footnote is rather apologetic for alluding to a line in Milton's 'Il pensero', in scare quotes above, with the excuse that 'it is spoken in the character of the melancholy man'. However, the nightingale is such a popular subject for poets, and carries such a burden of mythology, that the poet has to make a conscious choice to escape convention, if they are to find kinship with this species. In the lines 'When he had better far have stretched his limbs / Beside a brook in mossy forest-dell / By sun or moonlight, to the influences / Of shapes and sounds and shifting elements', Coleridge takes the poet out into the field to practise the kind of attentiveness that is necessary for his imagination to create something that is true to the nature of this 'venerable thing'. 'By sun or moonlight' shows that he knows the nightingale also sings by day, but for many people that his song would be hidden among a cacophony of noise from all the other songbirds.

In this poem, it is the expression in words of the song that take us to this wood: ‘That crowds, and hurries, and precipitates / With fast thick warble his delicious notes / As he were fearful, that an April night / Would be too short for him to utter forth / His love chant, and disburthen his full soul / Of all its music’ (Coleridge 93). The song ends with ‘musical and swift jug, jug / and one low piping sound’. The footnote below this poem was rather defensive about the possible accusation of ‘mere description’, however the ‘jug, jug’ from the lines above is onomatopoeic. What part can mimesis (imitation) play in a poem?

Many poets have tended to avoid mimesis, perhaps with a concern that it is too descriptive. One artist and performer has instead deliberately embraced this type of imitation as a way to get closer to the natural world. For Hanna Tuulikki:

> mimesis opens one’s sensory awareness to ‘other’
> mimesis is a process of attunement to the more-than-human
> mimesis is a meeting point, a space in between
> mimesis is a way of directing attention to earth-others
> mimesis is a method of thinking-with and feeling-with
> mimesis is an embodied practice of becoming-with
> (Hanna Tuulikki tumblr hannatuulikkidiary, 5 November 2020)

Searching traditional verse and song in English, she found very few examples of mimesis. She has recorded on video two of those she did: ‘Blackbird’ and ‘Song Thrush’ were performed in the open air (Tuulikki 2020a). When the words are sung, the effect is to imitate the way each bird expresses itself in song through melody, repetition and pauses. Tuulikki found more scope to develop her concept in traditional Gaelic song and verse. In an ambitious composition for a choir of ten, Tuulikki ‘weaves together fragments from the Gaelic songs and poems that are imitative of birds’ (Tuulikki, 2020b). *Air falbh leis na h-eòin* (Away with the birds) was performed live on the Hebridean Island of Canna. There were five movements: on the shoreline, on the cliffs, ebb tide – lament, flock and skein, and night-flight to the burrow. The sounds include those of wading shore birds, and sea birds both in flocks and wheeling around the cliffs. For the live performance on Canna, the singers were dressed in black with red pleats showing from behind and red legs. Costume design is an important part of Tuulikki's creative process. The nighttime return of the shearwaters to their nesting burrow imitates the eerie call these birds make to let their mate know that they are coming. Shearwaters are clumsy on land and if they returned in daylight they would make easy prey for a great black-backed gull or other predator.

Far from limiting her creative imagination, Tuulikki has found mimesis to be an effective way to get closer to other species. In 'Blackbird' and 'Song Thrush' she imitated a single species, but took her performance to a place where they would feel at home. 'Away with the birds' is also site specific, but the use of the many voices of a choir places these birds very much in their environment. We know that the shearwaters are calling to their mates and timing their return to avoid predators that would either kill them or force them to regurgitate the food that they have carried home. These works deploy mimesis to bring together the attentiveness of the multispecies world, with the creative imagination to bring the listener onto the shore, cliff and hillside of this remote island.

Stop and think

We see from the footnote to Coleridge's poem in the *Lyrical Ballads* that the authors were sensitive that their departure from the conventions and myths that attended the nightingale, might be interpreted as criticism of Milton and that it might seem to be mere description. Paying close attention to detail does not mean that all detail has to be recorded. Latour makes the point that if an actant is not having an effect, then it is not an actant. The same is true of some of the detail we gather from paying close attention to an animal in its environment. In evolutionary terms it is assumed that all structures must have a function if they are to persist over evolutionary time, but we are not necessarily looking over evolutionary time. It will often strain our attentiveness when there are relationships or structures that are important to the animals within our gaze, which we are not equipped to perceive. Telling one individual animal from another may be a particular challenge, but the animals recognise their young, and can read the nuances in what might look to be stylised behaviour. As with Coleridge, we have to clear our mind of prior assumptions and ways of looking imposed by the master model. Representing an animal that is true to life as Hughes would require is a work of the imagination; it is not mere description. Does our reading of a poem take us closer to the animal?

Seeing things differently: embodiment, neurodivergence and the animal other

Poets and philosophers have been theorising about the creative process for millennia. The much younger field of neuroscience has also started to show an interest in how the mind works, both during the creation of literary works and in their reading. For her doctoral research, poet Helen Mort brought these two disciplines into dialogue with one another. The two disciplines offer different ways of 'thinking about the notion of qualia' (Mort, 2015: 238). Qualia is a term used in phenomenology to mean introspectively accessible, phenomenal aspects of our mental lives, that is, a subjective conscious experience. The focus here is on what it feels like to experience a poetic text through the introspective, phenomenal aspects of our mental lives that are accessible to us. Such work is in its infancy, but for this book it is worth extracting two aspects that have a direct interest for beginners in animal studies. Firstly, by making common cause with neuroscience, we are grounding the creative process and reading in the material processes of the brain and hence the body. This offers us the opportunity to close the mind–body gap and to avoid reliance on metaphysics to explain creative activity. It happens that French philosopher Maurice Merleau-Ponty (1908–61), in his theory of phenomenology, had brought together gestalt psychology and early neuroscience to examine the concept of embodiment. His ideas are discussed further below.

The second aspect that flows from the new interest in neuroscience is that not all humans are the same. It seems that some people react very differently to the world in front of them to those that are classed as neurotypical. It is claimed that some neurodivergent individuals have a closer affective relationship with animals than their neurotypical counterparts, that their ways of expressing themselves in creative works differ, as do the meanings they take away from reading the work of others. These issues are all important in approaching an animal studies reading of a text, both to respect the diversity that might have contributed to its form and expression, and to be open to the idea that different people will read the same text in different ways. This idea is also explored in greater depth below.

In the 1940s Maurice Merleau-Ponty developed a philosophy that 'focused on the body as it was enmeshed within the dynamic matrix of the biosphere' (Westling, 2014: 5). By taking the body seriously he was able to collapse the dualism between realism centred on an objective material world and idealism that depends on an eternal reality outside experience. For Westling:

> No metaphysics of presence is suggested in this long and painstaking examination of embodiment. Merleau-Ponty relied consistently on Gestalt psychology and the neuroscience of his day in making his case, always emphasising the mediating neural structures of the brain in perception, the destruction of cognitive abilities caused by brain damage, the body's functioning as a limiting situation that determines what we can perceive, and the ways our tools become extensions of our bodies in our interactions with the world. He also took into account individual predispositions and the way ethnicity and personal experience shaped perception. (Westling, 2014: 5–6)

Later he drew on Uexküll's theory of a distinctive *umwelt* for each organism and individual. The 'human *Umwelt* is a sort of bubble created by our perceptive abilities and cultural formation in dynamic interchange with our surroundings' (Westling, 2014: 6).

Of particular significance in the context of this chapter is the respect that Merleau-Ponty had for the attentiveness of the scientists. He valued 'the careful attention to nature that science alone provides, while at the same time his critical distance enabled his style of phenomenology to complement scientific findings by identifying their limitations and placing them within a larger, more complex frame of interpretation' (Westling, 2014: 18). This attentiveness makes the way for an embodied experience of the natural world. Westling illustrates the concept of embodiment with two phenomenological readings of literary works: a short story by Eudora Welty that includes 'a description of a meditative baptismal swim' and W.

H. Auden's poem 'A New Year's Greeting' (Westling, 2014: 39–42). For the short story it is the perception of the water on the swimmer's naked body that emphasises the important part that the body plays in experiencing nature. Auden is more concerned with the other creatures that share his body.

> For creatures your size I offer
> a free voice of habitat,
> so settle yourselves in the zone
> that suits you best, in the pools
> of my pores or the tropical
> forests of arm-pit and crotch,
> in the deserts of my fore-arms'
> or the cool woods of my scalp.
> (W. H. Auden, cited by Westling, 2014: 41)

This recognition that we share our bodies with numerous other small organisms is similar to the point made by Lorimer about our gut biota discussed above. For Westling this poem nibbles away at human exceptionalism 'as the conscious individual disappears back into the mass of pullulating life forms that Merleau-Ponty describes as the "perpetual pregnancy, perpetual parturition, generativity and generality, brute essence, which are the nodes and antinodes of the same ontological vibration"' (Westling, 2014: 42). A new frontier in neuroscience is the possibility that the organisms in our gut can activate neurotransmitters that make their presence felt in the brain.

The engagement with neuroscience raises the issue of neurodiversity. Not all people perceive the world or express themselves in the same way. Of particular interest is the markedly different view of the world and especially of animals, between those who are classed as neurotypical and those on the autism spectrum. In her memoir, *Animals in Translation*, Temple Grandin relates how animals saved her (Grandin and Johnson, 2005). She found particular empathy in riding horses that had in the past been abused; although they were difficult, she found she loved them and took care of them. Riding horses requires a particular kind of attentiveness:

> I remember looking down to make sure my horse was on the right lead. When a horse is cantering around the ring one of his front hooves has to thrust out further than the other one and the rider has

> to help him do that. If I leaned my body just the right way, it helped my horse get on the right lead. My sense of balance was so bad I could never learn to parallel ski no matter how hard I tried, though I did reach the advanced snowplough stage. Yet there I was, moving my body in sync with the horse's body to help him run right. (Grandin and Johnson, 2005: 5–6).

This particular skill is not the sole preserve of those with autism, but Grandin is suggesting that it comes more easily to those who can think like the animal. By using her whole body to communicate with another animal, she combines the embodied processes within her brain, the focus of neuroscience, with those of the rest of her body.

Although many subjects in the traditional school curriculum defeated Grandin, she had good visual skills, which she was able to combine with her understanding of how animals felt, to design equipment for use in reducing stress in cattle bound for slaughter. She suggests that animals are like 'autistic savants'. They 'have special talents normal people don't; the same way autistic people have special talents normal people don't; and at least some animals have special forms of genius that normal people don't; the same way autistic people have special forms of genius' (Grandin and Johnson, 2005: 8). That someone on the autism spectrum could feel empathy for nonhumans, which they might not for their fellow humans, is a further advancement of the idea of affect in animal studies, but Paton suggests that the therapy that animals offered to Grandin might not be transferable to others. While her experience may have been serendipity, 'using animals as replicable therapy funded by organisations requires consistent evidence of efficacy' (Paton, 2013: 354). Despite Paton's reservations, Riding for the Disabled has an established presence in the UK. Also the Paws for Progress programme between the Dogs' Trust, Stirling University and HM Prison Service reports success from taking difficult dogs into Youth Offender Institutions. Grandin's assumption was that autistic brains and animal brains worked in the same way, but for Paton that does not imply that cross-species empathy is automatic (Paton, 2013: 356).

Knowing that she was herself a visual thinker led Grandin to study visual thinking in animals. Her approach was at odds with conventional behaviourist approaches to studying animals in the laboratory with rewards based on securing food and electric shocks as punishment. She studied animals in their environment, which for cows is the feed yard. When she saw 'cattle baulking or acting scared', she looked at it from the animal's point of view to see that shadows or chains hanging down could make them baulk (Grandin and Johnson, 2005: 19). Animals share with those on the autism spectrum a way of seeing the real world as detail rather than as an 'idea of the world' (Grandin and Johnson, 2005: 31). The general theme of attentiveness in this chapter calls on those who would get closer to other species to pay more attention to the small details that they would otherwise miss. Grandin admits that she was being just as anthropomorphic as other researchers by assuming that animals shared her way of thinking visually. The autism spectrum is very complex, not everyone on it will be as strong in visual thinking as Grandin. It should be noted that the reception to Grandin has been mixed. For example, for Muller and McNeill, her 'complicity in the animal-industrial complex renders her status as an animal advocate questionable' (Muller and McNeil, 2021). Lamey, while praising her success in designing humane slaughterhouses, criticises her 'for not engaging with the moral status of animals with the depth and rigour it deserves' (Lamey, 2019).

Perhaps this is a moment to pause. For many people who are drawn to human–animal studies, in particular those who take the activist/academic route of critical animal studies, the idea of the humane slaughter of nonhuman animals as a resource will be taboo. Grandin, whose autism has brought her close to animals, has worked for much of her life designing equipment to make the process of slaughter as humane as possible. The moral imperative here is not to avoid slaughter, but to reduce the stress of the process. She criticised the closing of US facilities for the slaughter of horses because there was no alternative programme for mitigating severe horse welfare problems, and suffering was therefore prolonged (Paton, 2013: 360). This line of thinking is close to that of Marian Dawkins discussed in chapter 1.

If Grandin has shown that being on the autism spectrum has helped her think like an animal, what would that kind of attentiveness do for a poet? Although she has not had a formal diagnosis for autism, poet Jen Hadfield 'definitely recognise[s] an interesting array of neurodiverse traits within [herself] that are often associated with Aspergers' (Chong and Hadfield, 2020: n.p.). Some of these traits have been difficult to live with, 'others have felt like genuine boons'. Hadfield has recognised these traits within herself. It would be a step too far to make a diagnosis of neurodiversity based on a reading of her poetry. While some of these traits make some types of attentiveness come naturally, other poets might have trained themselves to be attentive to the detail in an image or animal encounter. In traditional schools of art, visual artists spent many hours drawing to help them develop both the attentiveness to detail and the eye–mind–hand coordination to represent an image on paper or other medium. 'Again there are all these other manifestations of diversity too, so why do we insist on calling ANYONE normal?' (Chong and Hadfield, 2020: n.p., original emphasis) For Hadfield there has been the added difficulty that 'women present differently and the clinical approach hasn't quite caught up yet'.

Sometimes it is difficult to talk, but at other times, where she is genuinely interested in a subject and she is relaxed, she can be quite articulate. 'Sensitivity to sounds, smells and colours and textures can be a really delicious thing under the right conditions'.

> A friend said she wondered how people could take on what I was saying about struggling to speak when I was talking about it so fluently in poetry! The point is that writing a poem very practically helps you rehearse what you need to say. And to say it as powerfully as possible. To score in breath when you know you will need a breath. To take out clusters of sounds that are difficult to say. And to self-hypnotise into a calm state where speaking is more possible. Also, I think if you can hypnotise yourself with the poem's rhythm, you probably also hypnotise a willing audience. (Chong and Hadfield, 2020: n.p.)

Hadfield is also a visual artist and many of her poems draw on visual imagery or deploy it through the arrangement of words on the page. In her poem 'Ladies and gentlemen This is a horse as Magritte might paint him' from her 2008 collection *Nigh-No Place*, even without the reference to the surrealist artist, it is her surreal use of metaphors that challenges us as she paints the visual picture: 'Consider this percheron in the climate – / controlled hold, gimped up for the flight / in blinkers and bridle and drugged of course' (Hadfield, 2008: 28). The percheron is an imposing heavy draught horse, which at between 16 and 17 hands couldn't be further away from the diminutive Shetland ponies of her island home. The 'climate-controlled hold' seems to suggest that the animal is pulled into a collected posture favoured in the show ring. A bearing rein will pull the head forward and at a trot the legs will be lifted high. It is the 'climate-controlled' metaphor that startles us. How do these very different types of control play off each other? Describing the wearing of blinkers and bridle as being 'gimped up' is a reversal of the usual use of that term when the wearing by humans of bridles, blinkers and other forms of restraint is seen as a fetish. If it is a fetish for humans, could it also be a fetish for a horse, controlled for display and the pleasure of the human gaze? The poem ends with an invitation to a toast or a prayer: 'May the horse never wake / that stands in mid-air'. It is echoed twice in repeat on lines in italic, justified to the right. It is here that she moves from an impression of weightlessness to a more surreal imagery. Does the high-stepping gait suggest that the horse is standing in mid-air? Or is this just a surreal play on the imagery that is so deftly deployed in this poem? Hadfield's poem is not an ekphrastic homage to a particular Magritte image, but it does echo the way he played with the images of horse, for example, of a woman riding a collected horse through a woodland, where some parts of the horse and rider are in front of trees, others behind trees that seem further in front and parts of the horse and rider disappearing where they should be visible through a gap in the trees.

This poem challenges us to think about the animal behind the imagery. The use of metaphors is very original and requires our attention when we read the words as they draw us into a re-evaluation of the control that humans have exerted, for example, through bearing reins. Are we giving it subtle signs that bring out a natural gait, or is this constraint making the horse do something unnatural? Hadfield is a very creative poet and provides us with work that merits close reading from a human–animal perspective. We cannot say what part her Asperger's traits have played in the creation of this work and what part was played by her hard-earned literary skill.

In another poem in the same volume, 'Dead-trae' [slack tide] the first couplet, which repeats through the poem, reads: 'I go to the rockpool at the slack of the tide / to mind me what my poetry's for' (Hadfield, 2008: 35). In this world, that is closed at low tide, but open to the sea when the tide is in, she finds all manner of drama, from 'its Little Shop of Horrors' to 'its cross-eyed beetling Lear'. In another stanza she draws on the imagery of cloistered monks: 'For monks, it has barnacles / to sweep the broth as it flows, with fans / grooming every cubic millimetre', which is much more expressive that the marine biologist's designation of this crustacean as a filter feeder, albeit one confined in adult life to the cell of its shell. This imagery comes from a poet who has paid attention and has embodied the experience of peering into the rockpool. She returns to the rockpool in her 2021 collection *The Stone Age.* Again written in couplets, the poem starts 'Above the rockpool / everything is tilt or // rough, glazed in / weed like afterbirth' (Hadfield, 2021: 2). The blurb on this collection states that it 'is a timely reminder that neurodiversity is a gift: we do not all see the world in the same way' and suggests that her work provides 'a portal into a different kind of being'. It is not specific about whether that portal is into the mind of the poet or into the world of nature that she brings to us.

Grandin claims to think like a cow, which has practical implications for the welfare of farm animals. Hadfield regards her neurodiversity as a gift and the unspecified traits that she detects in herself may play some part in her creative process. What remains for us to consider is the role that neurodiversity can play in the reading of a poem. This is a question that Bruhn takes up in relation to the poetry of Wallace Stevens. For Bruhn:

> Many individuals with ASD [autism spectrum disorder] are prone to process *any* linguistic sequence as if it were poetry, dedicating heightened attention to an utterance's perceptible features and thereby delaying and sometimes compromising their ability to decode its semantic content and pragmatic function. (Bruhn, 2015: 182, original emphasis.)

This way of reading seems to align with Wallace Stevens's way of writing: that delays 'automatic semantic processing by foregrounding language's perceptible dimensions – its visual-spatial arrangement of letters, words, lines, and stanzas on the page; its audible rhymes, alliterations, and assonances; its kinesthetic rhythms; and so forth' (Bruhn, 2015: 182). Bruhn gives particular prominence to Stevens's use of the literary device of 'chiasmus', in which the words in one clause are inverted in another, which seems to reflect in 'the precise terms of cognitive science, an embodied schema that derives from the bilateral symmetry of our bodies, especially as expressed in the hemispheric and mirror-symmetrical organisation of our brains' (Bruhn, 2015: 187). Citing Mark Turner, Bruhn suggests that 'we produce or recognise bi-lateral symmetry in discourse' (Bruhn, 2015: 185). As we embody our subjective experience of other species we subject them to the way our brain works. It is outside the scope of this book to pursue these intriguing ideas further, but we should acknowledge the part that neurological processes play in attentiveness, embodied experience and individual difference in perception, in creative writing and in reflexive reading, that allows connotation to follow new paths. All can help to disrupt a rigid schema placed on us by western taxonomy and established ways of doing academic science.

At this point it is perhaps best if we fall back on Hadfield's suggestion that we should regard diversity as the norm and learn to live with differences, in our ability to close the subject/object gap between ourselves and other animals, in the poet's ability to bring a range of perceptual talents into their close attention to the natural world, and their ability to express what they perceive in literary form that can be read by people who have diverse ways of relating to text and shapes on the page. Added to this is the reader's contribution in following new pathways of connotation to embody the experience of reading the poem and that of relating to the animal and inanimate actants that inhabit our shared world.

Further reading

Blok, Anders, Farías, Ignacio and Roberts, Celia (eds) (2023) *The Routledge Companion to Actor-Network Theory*. New York and Abingdon: Routledge.

References

Armitage, Simon and Dee, Tim (eds) (2009) *The Poetry of Birds*. London: Viking.

Bruhn, Mark J. (2015) 'A mirror on the mind: Stevens, chasms and autism spectrum disorder', *The Wallace Stevens Journal* 39:2. Special Issue: Stevens and the cognitive turn in literary studies, pp. 182–206.

Chong, Cat and Hadfield, Jen (2020) 'Inhabiting a space of love'. *Discussion*, 10 July. Guillemot Press. guillemotpress.org, accessed 26 June 2024.

Clare, John (1990) *Selected Poems*. London: Penguin.

Coleridge, Samuel Taylor (1847) *Biographia Literaria or Biographical Sketches of my Literary Life and Opinions*, vol. 1, edited by Henry Nelson Coleridge and Sara Coleridge. London: William Pickering.

Coleridge, Samuel (1802), 'The Nightingale', in William Wordsworth, *Lyrical Ballads: With Pastoral and Other Poems*, vol. 1. London: Longman, pp. 90–6.

Coole Park Nature Reserve (n.d.) *Nature & Wildlife*. https://www.coolepark.ie/nature-wildlife/ (accessed 24 July 2024).

Eagleton, Terry (2007) *How to Read a Poem*. Oxford: Blackwell.

Grandin, Temple and Johnson, Catherine (2005) *Animals in Translation: The Woman Who Thinks Like a Cow*. London: Bloomsbury.

Hadfield, Jen (2008) *Nigh-No Place*. Hexham: Bloodaxe.

Hadfield, Jen (2021) *The Stone Age*. London: Picador.

Halliwell, Stephen (2012) 'Aristotelian mimesis between theory and practice' in S. Isomer (ed.) *Rethinking Mimesis: Concepts and Practice of Literary Representation*. Cambridge: Cambridge Scholars Publishing, pp. 1–22.

Hughes, Ted (1994) *Winter Pollen: Occasional Prose*. London: Faber & Faber.

Lamey, Andy (2019) 'The animal ethics of Temple Grandin: a protectionist analysis', *Journal of Agricultural and Environmental Ethics* 32, pp. 143–64.

Lorimer, Jamie (2016) 'Gut buddies: multispecies studies and the microbiome', *Environmental Humanities* 8:1, pp. 57–76.

Mort, Helen (2015) '"Something else, then something else again": neuroscience and connection-making in contemporary poetry', unpublished PhD thesis. University of Sheffield.

Muller, S. Marek and McNeill, Z. Zane (2021) 'Toppling the Temple of Grandin: autistic-animal analogies and ableist-species nexus', *Rhetoric, Politics and Culture* 1:2, pp. 195–225.

Oswald, Alice (ed.) (2014) *A Ted Hughes Bestiary: Selected Poems*. London: Faber and Faber.

Paton, Priscilla (2013) 'Temple Grandin and the neuroscience of empathy', *JAC*, 33:1–2, pp. 352–63.

Shelley, Percy Bysshe (1840) 'A defence of poetry' in *A Defence of Poetry and Other Essays*. Project Gutenberg eBook.

Tarlo, Harriet (ed.) (2011) *The Ground Aslant: An Anthology of Radical Landscape Poetry*. Exeter: Shearsman.

Tuulikki, Hanna (2020a) 'Song Thrush' (Song of the day) *Folk Radio UK*, 1 July.

Tuulikki, Hanna (2020b) *Away with the Birds*. Bandcamp: Digital Album.

van Dooren, Thom, Kirksey, Eben and Münster, Ursula (2016) 'Cultivating the arts of attentiveness', *Environmental Humanities* 8:1, pp.1–23.

Westling, Louise (2014) *The Logos of the Living World: Merleau-Ponty, Animals and Literature*. New York: Fordham University Press.

Wordsworth, William (1802) *Lyrical Ballads: With Pastoral and Other Poems*, vol. 1. London: Longman.

Yeats W. B. (2017 [1919]) *The Wild Swans at Coole*. Facsimile edition with introduction and notes by George Bornstein. New York: Scribner.

7 Affect, empathy and altruism in animal fiction

Throughout this book, I have made frequent references to the affect that humans feel for animals, as put forward by writers including Ritvo, Midgley, Haraway and Latour. This chapter brings together two strands in this discussion. The first is the finding by ethologists that at least some animals are capable of feeling empathy for others of their species, and perhaps are also able to extend that feeling across the species boundary. The second is the role of fiction in expressing empathy and engendering feeling in readers. The chapter then looks at some of the difficulties in reconciling the differing views of empathy in ethology and in literary studies, and how these are further complicated when we extend the field of interest to include animals.

Defining the terms

This chapter draws on a cross disciplinary approach that uses terms which some disciplines regard as their own. Before we start mixing them up together it would be prudent to understand the genealogy of each concept. *Affect* is a term in behavioural psychology that divides behaviour into three domains: cognitive, conative and affective (thinking, doing and feeling). Behaviourists will argue that, of these, we can only see the behaviour that is externally expressed, we cannot know exactly what another person, let alone an individual of another species, is thinking or how their brain is processing information. The same is true of affective behavior: we might interpret a smile or an expression of interest as friendly, but we do not have direct access to how another feels. Although behaviourism is falling out of use, the term 'affect' for feeling or emotion has been retained where the user cannot be assumed to be operating within the constraints of the behaviourist model.

Uncertainty about another individual's feelings is directly challenged by the next two concepts. *Empathy* between individuals is where one can share a feeling with another. For Suzanne Keen that would be expressed as 'I feel what you feel' or 'I feel your pain'. While these examples emphasise negative feelings, empathy can also occur for positive feelings of happiness or elation. Keen associates such pleasure engendered in readers with what 'French literary theorists have described with the felicitous term *jouissance*'. She contrasts that with *sympathy* as 'I feel a supportive emotion about your feelings' or 'I feel pity for your pain' (Keen, 2007: 5). Wispé, cited by de Waal, has the following definition of sympathy: 'The definition of sympathy has two parts: first a heightened awareness of the feelings of another person, and second, an urge to take whatever actions necessary to alleviate the other person's plight' (de Waal, 2019 [2009]: 88). For either of these two concepts to have any validity, it is necessary that we have a reasonable ability to read the affective state of another individual. To apply it to literary animal studies we have to have grounds for claiming to be able to read the affective state across the species divide.

Altruism has a general meaning when one individual does something that benefits another with no gain and even at a possible cost to themselves. The term has been particularly troublesome for evolutionary biologists. If a trait, such as altruism, had no benefit to the individual expressing such behaviour, it cannot contribute to fitness, and therefore cannot be an evolutionary stable strategy. This trait should therefore die out over evolutionary time. Various models have been developed to explain how such behaviour might contribute to fitness including kin selection. This line of thought is not followed here, but it would be wise to bear in mind that altruism can be a contested topic.

For Frans de Waal behaviourism, as the school of psychology that dominated for a century, 'has wreaked more havoc than any others' (de Waal, 2019 [2009]: 12). We cannot see directly how people are feeling nor the cognitive processes that are informing their actions.

For behaviourists it is only the behaviour that we can see that we should care about. For ethologists this led to a taboo about considering the inner life of animals. Further, as animals were considered to be machines, terms that had human connotations had to be avoided. In *The Age of Empathy* de Waal makes the case for breaking free from the constraints of both behaviourism and the Cartesian model of the animal as machine. Much of his work has been on primates, but there is evidence that it is also relevant to other species. For example, he cites Canadian work on empathy in mice that were influenced by the sight of another individual in pain (de Waal, 2019 [2009]: 70).

If we are to feel empathy for another, we need to be able to read their emotional state in their face or in the way they hold their body (de Waal, 2019 [2009]: 82–3). The ability to read another's body language is important both for empathy and for sympathy. For de Waal 'empathy is [his] bread and butter, and [he] has made many a discovery by closely following the lives of animals and trying to understand why they act the way they do' (de Waal, 2019 [2009]: 89). From his observations on baboons, he has concluded that they go further than just reacting to external signs of distress, such as calls or facial expression. It matters to them that the situation is recovered, for example, that a fallen infant gets up again and is reunited with its mother (de Waal, 2019 [2009]: 145).

For de Waal, empathy is a skill that is essential if he is to gain insight into the social life of the animals that he observes. This skill or competence may draw on a complex interaction between cognitive and affective behaviours, and the resulting empathy will influence both how he feels and what he then knows about the emotional state of another. While admitting feeling into the record, he will offend some scientists for whom this threatens his objectivity, but will also help to restore the subject status of these same animals. Having regard for the feeling of other species is a key part of the animal turn.

There are several parts to empathy as a competence. There is the competence for an individual to express how they are feeling though external signs, such as facial expression or body posture; there is the competence for another individual to be able to read these signs, and finally there is the competence to process these signs cognitively, as knowledge, and affectively as feeling. The term 'emotional intelligence' has been introduced to capture the ability to be self-aware, to have empathy and the social skills to conduct relationships with feeling and sensitivity. More recent research in neuroscience challenges the idea that emotions and rationality are separate features of our experience. Keen introduces work on cognitive neuroscience by Joseph LeDoux and Ronald DeSousa who recognise the rationality of emotions (Keen, 2007: 27). This young hybrid 'discipline of Social Cognition is more likely to reflect the understandings of affect and cognition as intertwined' (Keen, 2007: 27). 'Human empathy clearly involves thinking and feeling. Memory, experience, and the capacity to take another's perspective (all matters traditionally considered cognitive) have roles in empathy' (Keen, 2007: 27). It is significant that de Waal chose the example of empathy to challenge the behaviourists' emphasis on observable behaviour, as so many other aspects of behaviour are required to feel what another feels.

The end result of feeling empathy can be very different. Individuals will vary about how closely they are able to feel with another. Altruism does not always flow from sympathy, nor is sympathy always predicated on empathy. Keen notes that the cognitive domain may also have a role in influencing what Eisenberg and Strayer called pro-social behaviour (Keen, 2007: 22). Keen does not explicitly refer to the reservations that sociobiologists have for altruism that confers no advantage to the giver. This argument is, however, hovering in the background in the evidence she cites of examples, such as those people who rescued Holocaust survivors at considerable risk to themselves. She also cites examples where people have been criticised for helping others in order to feel good about themselves.

As a further complication, not all altruistic 'helping' contributes to just social solutions. Keen cites an example from Batson 'where feeling empathy for another member of the group in a social dilemma created an altruistic desire to allocate resources to that person as an individual, thus reducing the common good' (Keen, 2007: 22). In practice Keen suggests that two motives are interacting, one for empathy-induced altruism and the other to uphold the moral principles of justice. Sometimes these motives are in accord and at other times they conflict.

Stop and think

If ethologists such as de Waal and Goodall have found insights about other species by learning to read their emotional state and feel empathy with them, who else could have this competence? Is it possible that huntsmen, shepherds, horse-riders and dog-handlers experience and draw on empathy gained through their close association with individual animals? Is it possible that the insights can be expressed in writing? Affect can be negative as well as positive; pain or pleasure; we can show coldness as well as warmth. To what extent is the attentiveness discussed in chapter 6 necessary to bring all the senses to bear on both cognitive and affective domains of mental activity? If affect, empathy and altruism are such contested terms, can they have any relevance in the critical reading of fictional works? These issues are considered in the next section.

Empathy in fiction

Over time, ideas about the benefits or otherwise of reading fiction have changed. Keen notes that in the eighteenth century there was a fear that 'an appetite for frivolity would drive out the useful and serious (non-fictional) works and that "obscene" works pouring in from France, would corrupt the young' (Keen, 2007: 37). Samuel Richardson's *Pamela* (1740), though, sought explicitly 'to show virtue in the strongest light', which might have led to unrealistic views about marriage (Keen, 2007: 27). Empathy entered the discussion as a factor in the social impact of fiction in the early twentieth century. In the middle of that century the identification of 'a Great Tradition in English fiction (by F. R. Leavis in 1948), enforced the separation of the novel from its origins as a consumer product sustained by buyers' (Keen, 2007: 39). The raised status of fiction in the academy and the cultural status of emotional intelligence paved the way for discussion about empathy as a worthy feature of fictional works.

The emotions had been a topic for discussion in previous literary movements. Introducing empathy to a critical reading of works created before terms such as empathy and emotional intelligence had entered the discourse, must recognise that a contemporary reading may find things in the text that would not have been recognised by the original author or their contemporary readers. For the Romantics, it was in poetry that 'the emotionally involved reader and the sympathetically imagining writer joined in mutually reinforcing processes of cultivating feeling selves' (Keen, 2007: 51). For modernists 'appeals to sentiment and feeling fell out of favour as merely conventional', just as ideas about empathy and the cultural value of fiction were taking hold (Keen, 2007: 56). Keen ends her review of changing ideas about the place of empathy in fiction, citing Hardwick, with a caution:

> By advertising novels as so relevant, personally beneficial, and immediately useful to self and society, do we not render unpalatable the very product we want to place in the hands of the young? Even if empathy for fictional characters were to be demonstrated a short cut to altruism and compassion, should novel reading be asked to bear such a heavy freight? (Keen, 2007: 64).

So far we have considered the idea of empathy as a behaviour that is not limited to our own species, and the potential role of fiction to engage readers empathetically with the characters in a novel. For animal studies we must now look at the issue of whether it is possible for readers to feel empathy with the animal characters in a fictional account. Bringing animals into a discussion of empathy in fiction adds another layer of complexity. Does our feeling of empathy across the species divide help us to deal with other challenges associated with animal studies, such as closing the subject/object gap? Can we feel sympathy for an animal whose feelings bear no direct relationships to those that a human might have?

Empathy in literary animal studies

There is a risk in highlighting any one facet of animal studies that it overwrites insights from another perspective. As discussed above, empathy for an individual can lead us to prioritise their need at the expense of the collective good and may therefore violate moral principles of justice. Literary animal studies grew out of the animal rights movement that followed the broadening of civil rights to support the equality for women, all races, social class and gender identity. Danielle Sands suggests that by raising the importance of empathy we are trading these rights for relations (Sands, 2021: 8). 'Rights presuppose an individual human subject who is discrete, autonomous and rational' (Sands, 2021: 9). Extending such rights to animals might include the great apes, but exclude those animals not thought to be sufficiently rational. Writers such as Haraway have stressed the need for us to form kin relationships in a multispecies world. This approach works best with companion animals, which are dependent on support from a human companion, who is attentive to their shifting behaviour and moods. It works less well for animals where contact is fleeting and where we may not know one individual from another. We may be able to detect that an animal is in distress, but it will be a challenge to identify any nuance in their emotional response to another of their species and we would not expect any signs of affection.

Sands suggests that progress in admitting affect to literary studies came from 'an unexpected alliance between "continental" thought, aligned with the body and affect, and an ethological discourse, epitomised by Marc Bekoff and Frans de Waal, increasingly keen to affirm the value of emotional and anthropomorphic approaches to nonhuman life' (Sands, 2021: 9). For Sands there is a further potential problem, in that the turn towards affect in animal studies is predicated on the denial that literary studies is the inheritor of deconstruction. Literary animal studies is an interdisciplinary enterprise. As we bring ideas from ethology and psychology into the discussion, and then add in the idea that other animals may be subjects, these disciplines will rub up against one another. In the process, there is a risk that we do not build on the strengths of each of the contributory disciplines. This denial both of deconstruction and the problems that it set out to confront allows for such taxing problems to be set aside (Sands, 2021: 6). Citing Lori Gruen, as an approach to the distinction between ontology and ethics, Sands introduces the concept of 'entangled empathy' (Sands, 2021: 12). Following Gruen, she introduces entangled empathy as 'a type of caring perception focused on attending to another's experience of wellbeing' that blends emotion and cognition with the understanding that we are in relationships that are built around attending to each other's needs (Sands, 2021: 12).

Empathy in Hardy's Wessex novels

In common with de Waal, sheepherders, over thousands of years, have had to pay close attention to the lives of their sheep and those of the dogs that assist in guarding and herding them. There are many ways of herding sheep and some require closer involvement in their lives than others. Some sheep need assistance in giving birth, some shed their wool each season and do not need to be sheared, others need to be brought into shelter each night to guard them from wolves and other carnivores, and for others the sheep follow their nomadic shepherd across the wider landscape. What these different ways of tending sheep have in common is that the shepherd must pay close attention to the individuals in a flock. Is a ewe bleating for a lost lamb, is another finding a place to give birth, circling around and lying down, perhaps picking up dead leaves in her fleece, has she licked her lamb after birth to get to know its distinctive smell, and has it started to suckle?

Many shepherds pride themselves on knowing each individual sheep, its history and its individual differences in behaviour. Since biblical times this care for the individual has been a model of care of God for each of His followers. In common with the discussion in chapter 6, this care is predicated on an attentiveness across the species divide. It also requires feeling for each individual in the flock expressed at least as sympathy and arguably as empathy. While such care might have an economic impact, the shepherd will also act in ways that can only be seen as altruistic. Paying a veterinary surgeon to perform a cesarean on a pregnant ewe will cost more than the market value of the ewe. In the same way rearing a lamb on formula milk will cost more than its eventual market value. That such care can be expended on animals that will end their days in the abattoir is one of the immediate challenges for an animal studies reading of rural texts. The rest of this section considers how Thomas Hardy treated these conflicting demands on the shepherd's cognitive and affective sensibility.

In her study of animals in Hardy's novels, Anna West draws attention to the conclusion he drew from Darwin's theory of natural selection: 'which revealed that all organic creatures are of one family, [that] shifted the centre of altruism from humanity to the whole conscious world collectively' (Hardy cited by West, 2017: 1). With this understanding in mind, West shows that the naming of individuals in *Far from the Madding Crowd* is relevant.

> Like the human characters in the novel, the sheep and dogs exist within the shared environment of the farm. As domestic creatures they occupy a liminal ground somewhere between human and nonhuman animal, participating in acts that place them in unusual roles, they learn to use human tools, grieve, adopt orphans, and receive life-saving operations, they alert others to danger, scheme for rewards, and perceive lingual cues. (West, 2017: 47)

Through the narratives of sheep and dogs, Hardy argues for the moral sense in nonhuman animals and the consequent need to extend a 'moral obligation to all creatures' (West, 2017: 83). While sharing with humans the same 'wants and fears' the nonhuman animals retained their individual identity (West, 2017: 84). Hardy called the mutual feeling between individuals 'altruism', which as discussed below, other authors have called empathy (West, 2017: 83).

In creating characters that Hardy's readers could understand, and 'on some level feel with', Eve Sorum emphasises the 'role played by geographic perspective taking in the creation of empathy for these characters' (Sorum, 2011: 180). For Sorum, Hardy brings together geography and empathy as an 'alternative narrative practice in which subject-making – the imagining of interior life and emotions – is no longer the primary method of engaging empathy'. By doing so Hardy 'anticipates the intersection of cognitive and affective theories of perspective-taking that are central to studies of empathy today' and in so doing overcomes the challenge by the division of emotion and cognition that was raised by Keen (Sorum, 2011: 180). While such empathy makes it easier for the reader to experience, cognitively and affectively, the perspective of another, it does not necessarily, but might, lead to feelings of compassion for the character (Sorum, 2011: 183). Hardy developed his approach after responses from the 'too genteel reader', so that in the preface to the fifth edition of *Tess of the d'Urbervilles*, he introduces the phrase 'imaginative intuition' to bring together 'the cognitive act of adopting another's perspective, and intuition, which is a pre-reflective and often emotionally informed process of apprehension' (Sorum, 2011 :190). If Hardy is capable of inducing empathy for the human characters in his novels by placing them within a geographical perspective; can he do the same for the animal characters? Can he also raise the status of animals to be characters in their own right? In portraying characters whose stock in trade is their ability to feel for the animals in their charge, is it in fact the presence of animals in the landscape that is essential for the narrative practice that raises the status of affect?

In Sorum's geographical perspective, the sheep are relegated to a feature in a bucolic scene (Sorum, 2011: 197). One of the challenges in animal studies readings of pastoral literature is to bring sheep into focus, to allow them to have agency and feelings, but above all to recognise the interplay between shepherds, individual sheep and the dogs that herd or guard them. Kreilkamp takes a different approach that brings sheep into the foreground as an object of pity (Kreilkamp, 2009: 474–81). In his analysis of *Far from the Madding Crowd*, he suggests that the 'novel can be read not as a narrative rooted around singular human subjects, possessing automatic priority, but as a representation of multiple life forms in interaction and interrelation – even a kind of "archive of creaturely life"' (Kreilkamp, 2009: 474). Because the sheep and sheepdogs have coevolved with humans, he cites Haraway's claim that these species are 'in obligatory, constitutive, historical, protean relationship with human beings' (Kreilkamp, 2009: 474). Here Haraway is accepting that relations with other species will be complicated by their shared history. In *Where Species Meet* (2008), Haraway only makes two references to empathy, both in footnotes. In one it is to contrast the huge exercise to genetically modify mice for research, with a paper in the same issue of the scientific journal as one on empathy in mice (Haraway, 2008: 338–9 n34). In the other, empathy is mentioned in the title of a paper she cites, but she directs her attention at terms such as 'animal joy' and 'friendship' that have not found favour with journal editors (Haraway, 2008: 375, n55). These terms have looser meanings than empathy, but seem to align better with Haraway's embracing of the complexity of relationships between species.

For Foucault 'pastoral' power as a mode of care that is a basic element of western modernity had its origins in the practices of sheepherders (Kreilkamp, 2009: 475). In particular it is 'the sheepherder and his ability to turn cross-species pity or empathy into the action of protective care and governance' (cited by Kreilkamp: 475). For Kreilkamp, *Far from the Madding Crowd* can teach the readers to pity sheep, that even though they may be slightly disgusting and prone to injury, they deserve the care that the shepherd, Gabriel Oak, extends to them. Particularly significant for an animal studies reading, is that 'Hardy ascribes self-recognition to the lambs themselves; such recognition is not Gabriel's gift to bestow, but only to assist them in achieving for themselves' (Kreilkamp: 476). In this novel Hardy is able to extend his empathy to Fanny Robin, as he holds her wrist that 'was beating with a throb of tragic intensity' similar to the 'quick hard beat in the femoral artery of his lambs when overdriven' (Kreilkamp: 477). It is worth considering whether this propensity for empathy towards fellow humans has coevolved with the care of sheep, as suggested by Foucault and here by Kreilkamp, or is it that only shepherds who can show empathy to those of their own species will be successful in attending to the behavioural clues that tell them how a sheep is feeling.

The emergence of modern veterinary science came at about the same time as *Far from the Madding Crowd* was published in 1874. Informed by this science, Gabriel was able to treat Bathsheba's sheep for bloat after they had broken into a field of clover. Through the tragedy where Gabriel's sheep are driven over a cliff by his overexcited dog, Hardy addresses the conflict between caring for the living and facing up to their destiny to end as a meat. 'A shadow on his life had always been that the flock ended as mutton – that a day came and found every shepherd an errant traitor to his defenceless sheep. His first feeling now was one of pity for the untimely fate of these gentle ewes and their unborn lambs'. (Hardy cited by Kreilkamp: 478)

In her reading of three of Hardy's rural novels (*Far from the Madding Crowd* (1874), *Tess of the D'Urbervilles* (1891) *and Jude the Obscure* (1895)), Richter explores 'the entangled relationship between human and nonhuman companion animals in his work' (Richter, 2020: 104). In including sheep, with dogs, under the heading of 'companion animals', she suggests a closer relationship than if they are merely regarded as domesticated. It is the regard Hardy shows for individual animals that suggests a kinship across species boundaries. Richter suggests that

> vulnerability as a condition of living and empathy with individuated creatures are compatible, and figure across Hardy's works. Instances of empathy between individuated humans and animals indeed appear in later works, but they can also be found in *Far from the Madding Crowd*, notably in the support a stray dog gives to an exhausted Fanny … On the other hand, both *Tess* and *Jude* show characters' encounters with non-individuated animals that precisely establish a sense of ontological continuity. (Richter, 2020: 109)

To achieve such empathy between individuated humans and animals requires work. 'The use of animals in agriculture is hence work with, not on animals; it demands collaboration' (Richter, 2020: 110). Hardy allows the cows at Talbothays Dairy to 'have a degree of agency, the ability to express by bodily cooperation or resistance, their preference for particular milkers, or rather their hands … it is the cows that invite a relationship or reciprocity and collaboration with their milkers rather than the other way around' (Richter, 2020: 110). Richter suggests that the question of animal agency deserves greater attention in literary animal studies; in particular by taking note of McHugh's three imperatives for animal studies, discussed in chapter 2 (Richter, 2020: 111). To be successful in this approach requires us to see animals in their own right and not just as metaphors for human subjects. We cannot approach the interior life of animals by anthropomorphic projection of our own thoughts and feelings onto animals. The necessity to avoid making assumptions about what that life might be is a problem for empathy that crosses species boundaries. We have to be open to the possibility that our ability to read an animal's feelings may be limited. Both Richter and McHugh draw on Haraway by directing the focus on 'embodiment, surfaces, and exteriority' (Richter, 2020: 111).

Stop and think

In focusing on empathy and sympathy we are also placing the emphasis on the relationship between an individual human and an individual animal. What is right for that animal might not be right for others of its species or for the wider ecosystem in which different species must coexist. It shifts the emphasis away from animal rights to relationships and therefore narrows the perspective of an animal studies reading of a novel. Consider why fiction has been credited with such power in engendering in its readers empathy for others including those of another species. Does this risk the cooption of fiction for a social purpose? Would that matter, or would writers of fiction prefer to avoid any accusation of a didactic purpose?

Loving and fearing wolves

Affective behaviour can involve both positive and negative feelings. Marvin's essay on wolfish behaviour brings this contrast in feeling into sharp focus. Wolf behaviour, and in particular their role as apex predators, is both natural and necessary in a functioning ecology. The complexity comes from the way we they have been 'constructed by humans, as a moral ecology, and the human judgements of the morality of that ecology construct the nature of wolves' (Marvin, 2020: 34). Wolves are rarely seen, even where they are present. I have seen them once in captivity, with a brief glimpse in their large enclosure at the Highland Wildlife Park. Some years ago, walking in the Picos de Europa in northern Spain, we were surprised to see a farmer with a gun standing at every gap in the hedge, until they explained that a wolf had been reported. Their unseen presence was marked by the obvious anxiety of the waiting men. Driven nearly to extinction in both Europe and North America, wolves are making a comeback.

Wolves can cover 20 km in a day without stopping (Kassabova, 2024: 51). This constant roaming increases their propensity to move into new territories. With the laws on wildlife protection passed in the twentieth century, wolves have started to return to their former range from the remoter parts of Europe and North America. Traditional sheepherding practices in eastern Europe are in decline, but it is there that we must look to understand the origins of the myths that we have constructed, and their portrayal in literature. We face a new future, where it is the nomads and transhumant pastoralists whose culture is at risk of extinction, and the wolf that is becoming more common.

Kapka Kassabova embedded herself with one of the few remaining transhumant sheepherders in the Pirin Mountains of Bulgaria. The ancient breed of Karakachan mountain sheep she met are in a remarkably unadulterated state. 'This in itself was a sign of the long-standing nomadic existence of these people and animals'. (Kassabova, 2024: 46) These are sheep that would have been familiar to Virgil. Maintaining the breed characteristics, by carefully selecting breeding stock, relies on the cultural memory of what the sheep should look like, and on maintaining traditional transitions between lowland and mountain pastures. They needed guard dogs to keep them safe from wolves and bears. The same dedication was needed to maintain the Karakachan mountain dog. Kassabova and the shepherd set off on their trek to the mountain with 600 sheep, the guard dogs and a horse with her foal at foot.

Once on the mountain, they are constantly alert to the presence of wolves:

> Sásho [the shepherd] didn't like wolves. It's hard to like them when you're a shepherd. They take more animals than they need, like avaricious people, Sásho said, and they kill for fun. With the bear it's different – it takes one and makes it last. (Kassabova, 2024: 101)

At night the flock must be counted and gathered into pens. In the morning they must be looked over for signs of blood (Kassabova, 2024:242). When the horse, Mimi, lost her foal, wolves were suspected because they had set up camp nearby (Kassabova, 2024:241). Although there are only a small number along the route, and they are seldom seen, they are a constant presence in the imagination. Sásho wants this story to be told. 'Nine years I have roamed these mountains. I see things but there's nobody to tell. You must write it all just as it is' (Kassabova, 2024:277). These special sheep, and the shepherds that tend them, are close to extinction. Kassabova's first-hand account of the ancient culture of nomadism and transhumance should be read against literature that relies on folklore and myth. Marvin agrees that we must look to the shepherds in pastoral society, who have experience of wolves, to make sense of what wolf predations mean to them (Marvin, 2020: 41). He does, however, ask that we separate fact from feeling in their reports.

Marvin warns against taking such accounts at face value. In particular where it is expressed in affective terms (Marvin, 2020: 36). That Sásho hates wolves, constructs their behaviour in terms of morality. Of all the large predators capable of taking livestock, it is the wolf that is most feared. Marvin attributes this fear to them being pack animals (Marvin, 2020: 38). He also repeats Sásho's point that they kill more than they need. The owners of livestock attribute evil to such behaviour (Marvin, 2020: 38). Not everyone hates wolves.

Before trekking up the mountain, Kassabova followed Marina, a wolf biologist who, twice a year, tracked the wolf population of Pirin (Kassabova, 2024: 53). She estimates there are 800 individual wolves in Bulgaria. But hunters had a tendency to exaggerate their numbers, to justify indiscriminate hunting (Kassabova, 2024: 54). Marina stopped several times to call the wolves; on this occasion they didn't answer (Kassabova, 2024: 36). 'Marina had nature's mind. She saw how fragile the web had become and it made her frantic. She was running out of time' (Kassabova, 2024: 54). She is a dying breed, as modern biologists prefer the laboratory to the extremely harsh life of a wolf biologist trekking the wilderness. She is also misunderstood:

> Because the impersonal nature of her mission was still incomprehensible to the masses, there was a conspiracy about people like Marina: that they 'released' wild animals into nature. Wolves, bears, snakes and dangerous creatures in general, just to be perverse, just to be witches. What else was a lone woman doing in the forest? (Kassabova, 2024: 58)

Being known to call to the wolves would perhaps reinforce this prejudice. Public relations is an important part of the wolf biologist's role. As wolf ethology, and its role in flourishing ecosystems, becomes better understood, so does the need to publicise its importance as a keystone species. The success of the wolf reintroduction programme in Yellowstone is widely cited in support of this role (Boyce, 2018). While the wolf can make its own way across continental masses of Europe and North America, in Britain, it would need to be reintroduced. For many years, reintroduction has been discussed as a means of controlling the deer that prevent the regeneration of Scotland's Caledonian pine forest, which in turn supports scarce animals including the pine marten and the capercaillie. Sarah Hall's novel is set in such a background, at a time when Scottish independence, which seemed a possibility, would have made it easier to bring such plans to fruition.

The narrative in Hall's *The Wolf Border* begins with Rachel Caine, an English biologist attached to a wolf monitoring project in Idaho. She is considering an offer of a similar post in her native Cumbria, to study the ethology of a captive breeding pair, which are to be enclosed on a large estate. Having devoted ten years of her life to monitoring wolves on an Indian reservation, her sympathy is with the wolves. When a radio tracking collar from a missing wolf is returned, she is very worried about how it died. 'She hopes he has been shot, rather than trapped or run over or anything worse' (Hall, 2015: 61). Later aerial footage arrives of a known pack that had cornered a grizzly and cub in a lake. Named individuals, Tungsten and Moll, are clearly recognisable threatening the cub, which flails around. We do not see the end, but as Marvin notes, a wolf kill of a large animal is a protracted affair (Marvin, 2020: 36). Rachel anticipates what it would be like. 'They are matchless predators; they exist supremely, she is irrelevant to them' (Hall, 2015: 74–5). Any love that wolf specialists have for their study species, while it may be deep, is not reciprocated. This understanding makes it easier for her to take the post in England.

In Cumbria, an English aristocrat with a large estate and deep pockets has erected a wolf-proof enclosure with high fences, buried deep into the ground at their foot. The initial pair are to be brought from a rescue centre in Romania. When they arrive by freight at the airport, Rachel's worries begin, that they will escape and vanish into an English countryside quite unprepared for such an addition to its fauna. This fear, for the wolves, for the idea of captive breeding, for her credibility, continues to give her nightmares, which are amplified by vocal opposition from some in the community. 'It will be up to her to convert suspicion and fear into something positive' (Hall, 2015: 83) Marvin echoes the fear and suspicion felt for wolves (Marvin, 2020: 43). He also suggests that the ethological studies of new champions for the species can, in time, create new cultural configurations (Marvin, 2020: 44). It is worth considering here whether novels such as *The Wolf Border* can play a part in constructing new ways of seeing this iconic species.

When they arrive, the male and female, who she has named Ra and Merle, settle into their enclosure after being checked by the local vet, who will feature in Rachel's personal life. As is usual in captive breeding for release, the wolves are not to be allowed to become habituated to their human carers (Hall, 2015: 195). Even enclosed, they are to be treated as wild. Briefing a new volunteer, she explains that: 'They will be rarely seen – defined as much by their absence as their iconography' (Hall, 2015: 93). It is likely that the unseen wolves will, however, see the humans, which leads the volunteer to conclude that being seen by a wolf is nearly as good as seeing one (Hall, 2015: 270). It would be worth checking this statement against Derrida's essay, 'The animal that therefore I am (more to come)', discussed in chapter 1.

The novel concludes with Ra, Merle and their four cubs escaping through a hole cut in the fence. The first sighting is from a Cumbrian farmer, who came across the pack attacking one of his ewes. He shoots one of the cubs, but not fatally. Again Rachel's sympathy is for the injured cub as she tracks it into a wood. Lacking the means to euthanise the animal, she uses anaesthetic darts to ensure that it dies without suffering pain. There is no mention of sympathy for the ewe. A helicopter is sent up to track the pack as it makes its way to the Scottish border. At the end, it emerges that it was the plan all along to engage in a form of aristocratic guerrilla rewilding, predicated on the supposed empathy for the species across the border that would accommodate rather than eliminate the incursion.

Marvin discusses the way that science and sentiment over wolves are in opposition (Marvin, 2020: 44). In Hall's novel, this opposition is part of the narrative structure. Their long history in folklore and myth makes wolves a rich subject for literature. Marvin's essay is in support of the other contributions to George and Hughes's edited book. The ability of this species to be both absent and present contributes to its mystery and to its imaginative presence in the Gothic novels discussed in that volume. This section has stayed close to the actual animals, but it demonstrates how stories begin with shepherds deep in the mountains, living with this unseen presence, that is mythologised by those who let their imagination run wild. Hunters experience a similar dissonance when they kill a species that they are fond of.

Killing those we love

Some years ago, before the passing of the Hunting Act 2004, I came across the master of the local fox hunt walking in the woods with his son. He told me with enthusiasm how they had just been watching a litter of fox cubs playing outside their earth (den). It struck me as strange how someone could be so engaged with the play of the young foxes, when in a few months they would be out cub hunting, where inexperienced hounds, newly entered to the pack, would be attempting to kill these same cubs. Watching young animals play is always a joy. Watching my own lambs racing around in gangs, as they seemed to play games that I recognised as playing when I was a child, was a delight in early summer. One game had particular resonance for me, as a group of half a dozen lambs raced across the field to see who could be the first to take possession of a rock projecting above the ground. As the winning lamb jumped about in triumph, I could imagine it chanting the lines of the nursery rhyme: 'I'm the king of the castle and you're the dirty rascal'. Yet as Hardy noted above, I was to betray them by autumn when two thirds of them would go to slaughter. Is it possible to reconcile the positive feelings of the one, with the act of killing a short time later?

The art of hunting with dogs has a long history and its own language and narrative form. This narrative starts as soon as the hunt sets out. The huntsman, there is only one, who is in charge of the pack of hounds, blows his horn as the hunt moves off. Each action has a different call on the horn, through which he maintains a constant dialogue with the hounds. Many of the followers, known as the field, will only have a limited view of what the hounds are doing and it is through the narrative on the horn that they are involved in the hunt. The huntsman will watch his hounds closely as they start 'feathering' with their nose to the ground and their tail wagging, which is sign that the hounds suspect they are detecting the scent of a fox or hare, but are not yet certain. Once they have a clear scent they will start barking. Hounds are valued for the quality of the 'music' that tells the rest of the pack, the huntsman and the followers that they are off on a scent. It is at this stage that the hunted animal becomes an individual, whose sole aim is to avoid being captured, and becomes a character in the narrative.

An interview by Cook (2015) stressed the respect that hunters have for animals that succeed in escaping. This narrative progresses with the hunt and will be retold after it is over. A friend who attended a hunt in France reported that at the end the hunt, the huntsman, hounds and field assembled in the courtyard of the big house where they had met and the huntsman then told the story of the hunt on his horn for the benefit of the 'ladies' who had not been among the followers. Telling the story of the hunt has an ancient pedigree, for example, in *Sir Gawain and the Green Knight* in the late fourteenth century, three hunts are narrated in detail to support the overall tale of a quest in which the successful outcome of the hunts plays an important role.

Cook reported a small scale programme of interviews to identify variations in the structure of discourse from a variety of those with an interest in the natural world. Of particular interest were two interviews with people with opposing views of hunting and killing animals for meat: a representative of the Vegan Society and one from the Countryside Alliance. The latter group supports hunting with dogs, and its representative stressed the importance of following the tradition where, for example, foxes are called Charlie and are always assigned male gender and hares are called Puss and are assigned female gender. This interviewee claimed this fox-hunting language reflects the 'admiration' and 'love' for the quarry species. Cook reports that '"respect" for the quarry occurs 17 times in the interview' (Cook, 2015: 600). In contrast to the hunter's desire to preserve old terms and style of discourse, the representative of the Vegan Society was keen to introduce new terms such as 'dead bodies' for meat, 'companion animal' for 'pets' and 'free-living animal' for 'wild animal'. Cook drew attention to the small number of species that were mentioned in these single issue groups. In another series of interviews, not reported in detail in his paper, conservation-minded broadcasters, including David Attenborough, Chris Packham and Alice Roberts, made 'a strong case for conservation to focus on saving those ecosystems as wholes' (Cook, 2015: 602). In this respect they are more aligned with the actor–network theory discussed in chapter 5, than with empathy that inevitably favours interaction between individuals.

In his discussion of these interviews Cook notes that although hunting is entangled with political and class divisions, 'this need not preclude recognition that certain kinds of skilled hunting do nevertheless involve both close encounters with "quarry" and knowledge and understanding of their behaviour: a kind of intimate interaction which industrialised procedures preclude in contemporary urban contexts' (Cook, 2015: 601). As these skills are lost, it may be difficult for a contemporary reader to understand the way that quarry animals are characterised in fiction written when both the skills and the rationale of the hunt were well understood. In D. H. Lawrence's novella *The Fox* (1923), the titular animal is given character, agency and the ability to affect the three human characters: the two women, March and Banford, and the returning soldier Henry Grenfel. The fox disrupts the economy and peace of the farm by regularly taking hens, which had also been remarkably reluctant to lay eggs. In part, the story is about the battle with the fox, which March is unable to shoot, but Henry understands what is needed to bring a hunt to a successful conclusion.

> It is not so much what you do when you go out hunting, as how you feel. You have to be subtle and cunning and absolutely fatally ready. It becomes like a fate. Your own fate overtakes and determines the fate of the deer you are hunting. First of all, even before you come in sight of your quarry, there is a strange battle, like mesmerism. Your own soul, as a hunter has got to fasten on the soul of the deer, even before you see any deer. And the soul of the deer fights to escape. Even before the deer has any wind of you, it is so. It is a subtle, profound battle of wills, which takes place in the invisible. And it is a battle never finished until your bullet goes home. (Lawrence, 2023 [1923]: 24)

It is significant that Lawrence has Henry choose a deer as the prey species, as the metaphor for his pursuit of March, rather than the male gendered fox. Although the fox is a fully rounded character in this novella, it also has a metaphorical role. March is affected by the fox and Henry, the hunter, sets out to hunt March with the same dedication he would apply to hunting another species.

When March first comes face to face with the fox, it is she who is mesmerised. 'He was looking up at her. His chin was pressed down, and his eyes were looking up. They met eyes. And he knew her. She was spell-bound. She knew he knew her. So he looked into her eyes, and her soul failed her. He knew her, he was not daunted' (Lawrence 2023 [1923]: 10). It is March who identifies Henry with the fox (Lawrence 2023 [1923]: 18). Henry identifies as 'a huntsman and not a farmer, and not a soldier stuck in a regiment. And it was as a young hunter, that he wanted to bring down March as his quarry, to make her his wife' (Lawrence 2023 [1923]: 24). The fox is assumed male until his sex is confirmed when he has been killed. It is 'a lovely dog-fox in its prime', described in the text in admiring detail that would have deserved sympathy 'if it wasn't such a thieving wretch' (Lawrence 2023 [1923]: 41). Later, the convention of regarding all foxes as male is put aside as they go in search of the vixen.

This novella builds on what would have been common knowledge about the relationship between hunter and hunted in the more rural parts of the country. Although Cook's interviewee was speaking of the discourse of organised hunting, the same intimate relationship would exist between poachers and their prey. Foxes that take poultry and young lambs are regarded as vermin, yet they are admired for their beauty and cunning. A new generation is relating to the foxes that have thoroughly colonised urban spaces. They will fix their gaze on this new audience, just as they did on March. Here, too, they need to make sure that pets and chickens are securely protected from them and that lids on rubbish bins are fastened each night, but the foxes will be tolerated for their charm.

As a symbol of female virtue and companionate marriage, Henry Fielding, in *Joseph Andrews* (1742) and *Tom Jones* (1749), takes the hare, which as discussed above is assigned female in hunting narratives. In her analysis of these novels, Ramos suggests that: 'Amatory hare-hunting metaphors place the male suitor in the dominant position of a joyous huntsman, animalize women by representing them as the timorous yet wily hare, and connect the consummation of male desire to killing and eating game' (Ramos, 2020: 179). The hare has a cultural value from centuries of hunting narratives, that for Ramos illustrates the ambivalent status of Fielding's heroines, where 'innocence and vulnerability afford them moral worth and agency' but just 'as the hare's value in the in the hierarchy of the hunt does not negate her status as prey, the moral worth that humanises Fielding's heroines does not preclude their subordination to men' (Ramos, 2020: 181). For feminist readings, the association between women and animals, through the assignation of some prey species as female, is deeply problematic. By giving status to the animal, these narratives take it away from women. 'The woman-hare parallel is not, by any means symmetrical and its implications are best understood when set against Fanny sympathizing with game' (Ramos, 2020: 184). She is shown to have a 'tender heart' and 'maternal instincts' but this is offset against the rules of the hunt in which the hare that is torn to pieces in front of her, though Joseph makes the case that it has been killed fairly (Ramos, 2020: 185).

For Ramos, 'Fielding's short but significant articulation of animal sympathy shed light on the hierarchy of moral concern that informs the novels. In particular, criticising the Europeans for their cruelty to horses, that deserve our special regard. Based on his belief in the 'horse's Wisdom and Sagacity and ability to feel pain', Fielding looks to the possibility that a law could be enacted that would protect the horse from barbarities (Ramos, 2020: 185). The part played by allowing sympathy for horses a special place in the move to animal protection is considered in the next section.

Can reading fiction make the reader more likely to have concern for animal welfare?

There is a widespread belief that some novels have played an important part in changing attitudes and in the promotion of pro-social behaviour. For animal welfare, the most frequently cited example is Anna Sewell's *Black Beauty, His Grooms and Companions: The Autobiography of a Horse* (1877). Hansen has addressed 'how moral discourses are narrated through sentimental fiction and melodrama' (Hansen, 2010: 727). This work employs anthropomorphism in which Black Beauty is the narrator of his own story and in the conversations he has with the mare Ginger and the 'schoolmaster' pony Merrylegs. In the process it imagines what Black Beauty is feeling about the kindness and understanding, and its absence, that he is shown by different human owners and grooms. For Hansen, there is a tension between Sewell's call for change in the behaviour of master towards servant, both human and animal, and the grounding of the novel in 'liberal humanist values' (Hansen, 2010: 727). It is not a posthuman work even though it foregrounds the animal as worthy of consideration. '*Black Beauty* upholds existing class hierarchies, justifying social and economic inequalities among humans and enforcing human domination over nonhuman animals' (Hansen, 2010: 730). It works to improve the welfare of animals, not to radically alter the relationship people have with them.

In the process, as Black Beauty is 'broken in', he has to suffer being separated from his family, being physically confined and constrained by a harness, and becoming used to all manner of frights such as locomotives. In the case of the use of a bearing rein to force the horse to hold its head unnaturally high, Hansen suggests that, the mare Ginger 'links the psychological constraints on horses' and women's body' (Hansen, 2010: 734). Ginger complains that her human tormentors 'fail to consider her as a sensitive, responsive and communicative individual' (Hansen, 2010: 736). While the anthropomorphic use of 'translated' horse language can engender sympathy in the reader, it is questionable whether that is based on empathy in terms of feeling what the horse feels. Sewell places the reader in the position of moral judge, 'this narrative strategy at the same time forces identification with the equine narrator, drawing readers into sympathising with Beauty's suffering and the suffering of other horses whose stories he tells' (Hansen, 2010: 744). Melodrama works to concentrate on the point of view of the victim (Hansen, 2010: 745). This approach has limitations.

'The empathy that links the reader to the victim implies an active empathiser, but a passive object' (Hansen, 2010: 746). Drawing on Despret, Hansen argues that while accepting that this empathy transforms the one feeling empathy, that is, the human reader, it does not allow for the horse to become a subject (Hansen, 2010: 746). The novel reflects the rights model of human–animal relations that emerged in the nineteenth century, and reinforces the desire to 'rescue' suffering animals (Hansen, 2010: 748). Urban dwellers in the nineteenth century would be able to witness animal suffering at first hand. That the novel continues to appeal to readers in the twenty-first century, leads Hansen to question what this has to say about the 'moral health' of our nations and suggests that 'this moral health remains constrained within the humanist legacy of categorical exclusions' (Hansen, 2010: 749).

If *Black Beauty* moved opinion as dramatically as claimed, what would happen if the next book a reader picked up was R. L. Stevenson's *Travels in the Cévennes with a Donkey* (1879)? Stevenson had enjoyed a reputation as humane and kind to animals, but when he met Modestine, the truculent and unwilling donkey that was to be his companion on this journey, that kindness became progressively eroded. Taking advice from the locals, he first acquired a switch with which to beat the unfortunate animal, but he became concerned that he was being watched beating it with increasing exasperation and little effect. Later, another native introduced him to the goad, a length of wood with a nail on the end that he could use to prick the unfortunate Modestine each time she refused to move. If fiction can increase our empathy and sympathy for other species, would Stevenson's travel writing desensitise us to the feelings of the donkey? Conversely would our prior ideas about humane behaviour towards companion animals make us recoil from his account?

The answer to these questions is crowded out by other considerations in travel writing. In his criticism of the book, Holmes finds '*Travels with a Donkey* to be a record of some of the powerful ideological elements – in particular nationality – that informed the contradictory realm of Victorian interspecies morality' (Holmes, 2009: 109–10). Modestine was with Stevenson for almost two weeks, and is very much a central figure in the narrative (Holmes, 2009: 110). That the animal is allowed subjectivity, but not shown sympathy, is one of the disturbing features of the account. Holmes includes a rich analysis of this book in his chapter, in which he examines the representative functions played by Modestine, for example, the projection of Stevenson's body on her own abject body (Holmes, 2009: 111). On nationality he suggests:

> A theory of historical 'displacement' does not, however, sufficiently explain Modestine's plight. Instead, an awareness of the general human propensity towards violence against individuals and groups considered beyond the pale – for example of religion, of nationality, of species – brings us closer to Stevenson's behaviour and his subsequent literary record of those actions. (Holmes, 2009: 111)

Stevenson helps us to see the part that 'nationally-inflected custom and prejudice play in shaping humans' attitudes and relationships towards other animals over which they have authority' (Holmes, 2009: 111). In the genre of travel writing it is the attitudes of the people that he meets that write over the status of Modestine as a valued companion.

The local inhabitants show Stevenson the way that Modestine would expect to be treated. Rather than abandon his trek, he seems to have gone along with this regime:

> How was Stevenson able to present his transformation from a young man unable to 'brutalise' an 'innocent creature' into someone, who, just three days later, possessed a heart so flinty that his companion's gory suffering elicited no sympathy? The answer lies in a shedding of the Scottish traveller's guise of humane 'Englishman' in favour of the role of the callous Continental European. (Holmes, 2009: 114)

The suggestion here is that by adopting the customs of the country that he is visiting, Stevenson is able to shift the blame for this treatment onto the callous natives.

Returning to the issue of the power of writing to instil empathy in the reader raises the question of whether the lack of empathy shown by Stevenson would transfer to his readers, with the same rationale that they were 'away from home'. From the response of critics it would seem not:

> Since one cannot wholly divorce oneself from the ethical feeling of one's age, I must confess that I would have liked Mr. Stevenson better if he had beaten his donkey less unmercifully, and above all if he had not used that wooden goad with its eighth of an inch of pin. (Novelist Grant Allen in his review of the book, cited by Holmes, 2009: 115)

The suggestion here is that the 'ethical feeling of one's age' limits the susceptibility to internalising a less humane attitude. If readers were resistant to influences against the current ethics, could we be sure that *Black Beauty* was the prime force in this change of empathy? Was the influence of this book to impart knowledge about bearing reins? Having a horse as narrator avoids having to identify with those who ill-treated their equine companions. Perhaps the sympathy generated in the reader was mainly as a reinforcement of the changes that were in hand in society towards the more humane treatment of horses. Can we be sure that literature has any power to shift attitudes, through empathy and sympathy? This issue is addressed in the next section.

What does science have to say about literature and empathy?

The answer to that question is relatively little. A psychological research study in Poland attempted to interrogate the considerable power credited to literary fiction 'to improve attitudes towards out-groups' (Małecki, Pawłowski and Sorokowski, 2016: 1). The author recruited respondents to an attitude survey with an offer of the opportunity to read a short passage from a soon to be published novel by Marek Krajewski. The respondents were divided into two groups: one of which read a section depicting animal cruelty to a monkey, the other a 'neutral' piece. The topic selected was considered relevant to 'existing research on the so-called empathy-altruism hypothesis' (Małecki, Pawłowski and Sorokowski, 2016: 2). A questionnaire, which was administered before and immediately after these volunteers had read the excerpt, was modified from the Animal Attitude Scale. The animal welfare questions, scored on a seven-point Likert scale from 'completely agree' with a statement, to 'completely disagree', were included, with more general attitude questions so that it was not immediately obvious that it was about animal attitudes. A market research agency was hired to create and manage the on-line questionnaire.

What this survey showed was that those who had read the piece that included the text about cruelty to a monkey changed their attitudes from before to after, compared with those who read the control group excerpt. The changes were of a magnitude to be statistically significant, although when shown on a bar chart they do not seem to be massive, allowing the authors to conclude that literary fiction can change attitudes to animals to make readers more in favour of increasing animal welfare (Małecki, Pawłowski and Sorokowski, 2016: 4). Literary fiction seems to be more powerful in this respect than approaches based on moral argument (Małecki, Pawłowski and Sorokowski, 2016: 6). The authors do, however, accept that it is morally questionable to use literary fiction for that explicit purpose. In this respect they echo Keen and Hardwick, discussed above, in being hesitant to ask novel reading to bear such a heavy freight.

There are a number of limitations to the research, which stem from the need to control the experiment. We do not know how readers will feel when they have read the whole novel. We do not know if this attitude change is permanent, or will be changed back by social pressure and further reading of fiction and non-fiction. The authors cite existing 'research in philosophy and experimental psychology which argues that moral attitudes (including attitudes towards the welfare of others) are based on basic, implicit, intuitions that are highly resistant to being changed through moral argument' (Małecki, Pawłowski and Sorokowski, 2016: 6). As discussed above, feeling empathy is a complex activity that draws on cognitive as well as affective domains of behaviour. It is perhaps best if we embrace this complexity and use more general terms favoured by Haraway, Richter and. Gruen's concept of entangled empathy is also useful as a way of placing empathy in its context. It is likely that when we use terms such as empathy and sympathy in the discussion of literary texts, we do not rely on a definition that can be tested statistically for significance. It is comforting to know that literary fiction can make us more sensitive to the plight of others, including animals. It also seems that we also need support from the ethics of our age for this to take root.

Further reading

George, Sam and Hughes, Bill (eds) (2020) *In the Company of Wolves: Werewolves, Wolves and Wild Children*. Manchester: Manchester University Press.

Małecki, Wojciech, Sorokowski, Piotr, Pawłowski, Boguslaw and Cieński, Marcin (2019) *Human Minds and Animal Stories: How Narratives Make Us Care About Other Species*. New York and London: Routledge.

References

Boyce, Mark S. (2018) 'Wolves for Yellowstone: dynamics in time and space', *Journal of Mammalogy* 99:5, pp. 1021–31.

Cook, Guy (2015) '"A pig is a person" or "You can love a fox and hunt it": innovation and tradition in the discursive representation of animals', *Discourse & Society* 26:5, pp. 587–607.

de Waal, Frans (2019 [2009]) *The Age of Empathy: nature's lessons for a kinder society*. London: Souvenir Press.

Hall, Sarah (2015) *The Wolf Border*. London: Faber & Faber.

Hansen, Natalie Corinne (2010) 'Horse stories: perverse victimisation', *JAC* 30:3–4, pp. 727–54.

Haraway, Donna J. (2008) *When Species Meet*. Minneapolis: University of Minnesota Press.

Hardy, Thomas (1993 [1874]) *Far from the Madding Crowd*. Ware, Hertfordshire: Wordsworth Editions.

Holmes, Morgan (2009) 'Donkeys, Englishmen, and other animals: the precarious distinctions of Victorian interspecies morality' in Richard Ambrosini and Richard Dury (eds) *European Stevenson*. Cambridge: Cambridge Scholars Publishing, pp. 109–24.

Kassabova, Kapka (2024) *Anima: A Wild Pastoral*. London: Jonathan Cape.

Keen, Suzanne (2007) *Empathy and the Novel*. Oxford: Oxford University Press.

Kreilkamp, Ivan (2009) 'Pitying the sheep in *Far from the Madding Crowd*', *NOVEL: A Forum on Fiction*, 42:3, Fall, pp. 474–81.

Lawrence, D. H. (2023 [1923]) *The Fox/The Captain's Doll/The Ladybird*. London: Penguin.

Małecki, Wojciech, Pawłowski, Boguslaw and Sorokowski, Piotr (2016) 'Literary fiction influences attitudes toward animal welfare', *PLOS One*, 22 December.

Marvin, Garry (2020) '"Man is a wolf to man": wolf behaviour becoming wolfish nature' in Sam George and Bill Hughes (eds) *In the Company of Wolves: Werewolves, Wolves and Wild Children*. Manchester: Manchester University Press, pp. 34–47.

Ramos, Adela (2020) 'Female virtues and companionate marriage in Henry Fielding's *Joseph Andrews* and *Tom Jones*' in Karen L. Edwards, Derek Ryan and Jane Spencer (eds) *Reading Literary Animals: Medieval to Modern*. New York and London: Routledge, pp. 179–93.

Richter, Virginia (2020) 'Collaborative agency: animals in Hardy's rural novels' in Karen L. Edwards, Derek Ryan and Jane Spencer (eds) *Reading*

Literary Animals: Medieval to Modern. New York and London: Routledge, pp. 123–39.

Sands, Danielle (2021 [2019]) *Animal Writing: Storytelling, Selfhood and the Limits of Empathy*. Edinburgh: Edinburgh University Press.

Sorum, Eve (2011) 'Hardy's geography as narrative empathy', *Studies in the Novel*, 43:2, pp. 179–99.

West, Anna (2017) *Thomas Hardy and Animals*. Cambridge: Cambridge University Press.

8
Reading animals in postcolonial literature

In this chapter priority is given to listening closely to Indigenous voices, particularly where they might have insights into the wider objectives of animal studies, and are able to recognise the animal subject in its environment, with sentience and agency. Listening to Indigenous voices is particularly problematic for a non-native reader or researcher. The original text may be in an unfamiliar language, it may be an oral story rather than a written text, and have an internal logic or form that has no equivalent in the western tradition. If the Indigenous author has chosen to write in a western language to take their story to an audience outside their own community, they have already embraced a cultural form that may be alien to that community. Anthropologist Darren J. Ranco, 'a member/citizen of the Penobscot Indian Nation', finds that even when studying stories from his own people, he cannot wholly escape the theoretical and ethical concerns that face the non-native researcher (Ranco, 2006: 61). Anthropology is a western construct that the Penobscot have become familiar with, as objects of study. In his first attempt to study the stories of his people, they agreed that his observations were accurate, but 'ultimately uninteresting to them' (Ranco, 2006: 66). A further problem is that meanings are inserted by the critic or reader that westernise the narrative.

To ensure that he was as true as possible to the object of his study, Ranco adopted a hermeneutic theory approach that 'postulates a subject (the analyst) who aims to understand an object (a text, a social practice, the Indian himself) as it is in itself. This means that the subject must be as open-minded and unprejudiced as possible, approaching the object without preconceptions'. (Ranco, 2006: 62). This means setting aside a reading practice that allows the reader to explore the connotations they find, as they play with the text in the light of their own sentiments and interests. For Ranco, even staying closely to the denotations in the text, there is no unbiased research. Preconceptions and prejudices are what makes understanding possible (Ranco, 2006: 63). There is, however, a difference if those preconceptions and prejudices are those familiar to an Indigenous audience, rather than those of the western academy. He cites Maori scholar Linda Tuhiwai Smith, who 'asks us to differentiate between the "community action projects" within our Native communities and the research we formulate within academic institutions' (Ranco, 2006: 76). In practice he finds the lines being blurred. He also wants community action projects to count in his academic profile. Here it is likely that western academic readers will apply their own rules for academic rigour to the resulting discussion, which might be alien to a Native audience. All of these issues are made more difficult when the objects of study are stories from the oral tradition.

Jo-ann Archibald, whose Indigenous name is Q'um Q'um Xiiem, is from Stó:lõ/Soowalie First Nation in British Columbia, has a problem memorising the stories she hears the elders tell (Archibald, 2018: 233). Her training as first a school teacher and then a university professor was to rely on written prompts to remind her of the story. In academic texts, accurate reproduction is prized, while in the oral tradition a degree of variation is possible as the narrator reads the response from her audience. An elder suggested that the way to remember a story was to write it on her heart, to make a seamless connection to her memory (Archibald, 2018: 236).

Telling the stories through structured repetition, aided by the family, was one way to develop a storied memory (Archibald, 2018: 237). Archibald notes that these practices have been under long-term assault from colonisation under a variety of practices, including community separation in residential schools. The task of the Native researcher is to resist these pressures, to recover language and to appreciate Indigenous peoples' resilience. New stories of 'oppression, genocide and various forms of abuse were remembered and told through residential school survivor stories' (Archibald, 2018: 238). These are their stories seen through their own cultural framework.

This chapter looks at the intersections between postcolonial narratives and literary animal studies. It asks whether it is helpful to consider the two forms of othering as being related, or does it introduce new ways to avoid allowing animals to become the subject in a narrative. If the previous chapter traded rights for relations, an intersectional approach would highlight the rights of both Indigenous peoples and nonhuman animals. Extending postcolonial literary studies to include animals, and including Indigenous voices in literary animal studies, both increases the power of these separate lines of enquiry and offers opportunities for cross-fertilisation between the disciplines.

Animals in the colonial project

Animals have played a central role in empire building and colonisation from the so called Columbian exchange in 1492. They continue to be actors in the still unfinished colonial project. Philip Armstrong claims that postcolonial studies have largely ignored this role. 'One reason might be the suspicion that pursuing an interest in animals risks trivializing the suffering of human beings under colonisation' (Armstrong, 2002: 413). He suggests that while in western society comparison to animals was insulting, it would have been considered an honour in Native American cultures. The superiority of humans over other animals 'owes a great deal to the colonial legacy of European modernity and … that the Indigenous cultural knowledges that imperialism has tried to efface continue to pose radical challenges to the dominance of Western value systems' (Armstrong, 2002: 414). For Armstrong the most promising area for collaboration between postcolonial and animal studies will be 'in the production of sharp, politicized, culturally sensitive, and up-to-the-minute local histories of the part that animals and their representations have played – or been made to play – in colonial and postcolonial transactions' (Armstrong, 2002: 416). Citing Ingold, Armstrong suggests that the two areas of study share concerns over 'the human', 'the natural' and 'the cultural' (Armstrong, 2002: 414). More recent work that addresses this deficit illustrates the value of looking beyond western ways of thinking about animals.

Columbus and other explorers made a point of introducing useful European food animals to the countries they reached. Haviing found no domesticated animals on his first voyage, 'On his second voyage in autumn 1493, the Admiral of the Ocean Sea brought a veritable ark, the passengers on the seventeen ships included horses, dogs, cows, sheep, pigs, and chickens, as well as approximately 1,200 humans' (Norton, 2024: 76). As we shall see below, they saw the conversion to agriculture of Indigenous hunter gatherers as part of their civilising mission. The spread of European diseases among Indigenous populations that had no immunity to them was to prove fatal for many Native Americans, but it is the movement of animal species in both directions than concerns us here.

Trying to replace native species with those that were familiar back home continued well into the twentieth century, as part of an acclimatisation strategy in Australia and New Zealand (Armstrong, 2002: 416). The introduction of the European starling to North America offers a cautionary tale. It was, for many years, widely accepted that all these birds can be traced back to the release of 100 birds on 6 March 1890 by Eugene Schieffelin as part of an eccentric plan to introduce to America all the birds mentioned by Shakespeare. Fugate and Miller demonstrate that this story is mostly untrue. Starlings had been released in the decades prior to this as part of an acclimatisation strategy, and others had escaped from those kept as pets. Fugate and Miller trace the elements of this story by reviewing literary works that show where false claims enter the discourse. In particular they show how one writer amended his account over time to 'track closely with those of American attitudes towards introduced species, demonstrating how these stories about the starling's release were subject to larger political and cultural forces' (Fugate and Miller, 2021: 309). The supposed threat to American agriculture was also shown to be false, with the starling's control of agricultural pests being a net benefit. Most introductions fail, and only a tiny percentage of species introductions cause serious problems. It will pay to give close attention in any animal studies review to terms such as 'alien', 'exotic', 'invasive' or 'native'. These terms are never neutral, often changing and should always be interrogated.

This transfer of species worked both ways, as animals were brought back to stock menageries, zoological gardens and parkland collections. Some species escaped into the wild, among them several species of deer from parks, including that of the Duke of Bedford at Woburn. Sika deer and muntjac deer are among the 'exotic' species added to the British fauna by becoming naturalised after escapes from parkland. Parks such as Woburn have found themselves to be the custodians of species that are at risk of becoming extinct in their native land. One such is the Père David's deer, originally native to the subtropical river valleys of China. A successful breeding programme has allowed them to be reintroduced in that country. Poet Melanie Bowman shares her fears:

> … the men speak of leading
> Père David's deer home. It's just one more doing or undoing,
> and why am I afraid for the story's end? You say
> they may thrive. And I say may. Up there, behind panes
> that break the December sun, there is talk of teaching animals
> what men remember for them
> a cold plain with no fences
> the white China wind, a perfect design of one long,
> wandering season when no bell chimes over the short,
> dark syllables of a rumor not to shoot. (Bowman, 1986: 28)

This species of deer, the only one in its genus, bears the marks of the colonial project. Named after the French missionary priest and zoologist Armand David (1826–1900), the deer was one of many species that he sent home to France, from where the 11th Duke of Bedford acquired a breeding herd. It highlights the role played by priest naturalists in documenting the natural world. Now it is Bowman's 'the men' who one assumes are western zoologists, that hold the memory for what life would be like for the deer back in the wild. Indigenous voices are absent, with even the Chinese name for this species being obscured by western 'discovery' and naming of species, discussed in chapter 1. Would 'the men' also have to teach Chinese rural peoples how to conduct themselves around the reintroduced deer? Engaging culture and science to hold off the extinction of species is discussed in the next chapter.

This section has argued that the movement of animals to and from the colonies played an important role in westernising other nations and in extracting wealth from them. With the development of the Atlantic trade in enslaved people in the sixteenth and seventeenth centuries, humans became yet another category of livestock to be transported to the new colonies in the West Indies and the Americas. The complexity of this trade and its importance for human–animal studies is explored in the next section.

Animals, Africans and the Americas

The people taken to the Americas brought with them the cultural meanings that they associated with animals from their homeland, and those meanings that evolved through the way they were treated before, during and after the Atlantic passage. Not only were human cargoes treated as livestock in the triangular Atlantic trade in enslaved people, nonhuman animals were used in their purchase from the native traders in enslaved people. Blakley has shown how the Royal African Company adapted to the trading conditions in West Africa to exchange animals, such as sheep for ritual sacrifice and cowrie sea snails from the Indian Ocean as part payment for the human slaves. 'These exchanges gradually produced and constituted an ecocultural network of human and animal social relationships and cross-cultural negotiations that enabled the expansion of England's involvement in the slave trade from the Gambia River to the Bight of Benin' (Blakley, 2019: 85). The European traders 'adopted West African cultural values and rites involving sheep as sacrificial offerings to forge bonds of trust, commerce and mutual alliance' (Blakley, 2019: 91). This adaptation illustrates how all those involved in the slave trade were altered culturally, not least the humans traded in exchange for animals.

Since antiquity, the shells of the marine gastropod cowrie, *Moneteria moneta,* had been used as money in trading in the Indian Ocean. European merchants purchased the shells directly in the Maldives and elsewhere on the Indian subcontinent. Blakley shows how the cultural significance of the animals became loaded with new symbolic meaning, as stories were woven around the association between these animals and the slave trade. Oral tradition held that cowries fed on the blood from the bodies of enslaved people thrown overboard, and that the best place to harvest them was on the routes for trading enslaved people (Blakley, 2019: 105). Vermin animals, particularly rats and worms, threatened this trade by 'infesting supplies of food and goods, by evading plans for their elimination and by endangering the health of the enslaved' (Blakley, 2019: 105–6). The export of ivory from Africa, and whale oil and furs from North America, added complexity to the exploitation of both humans and animals, which had the overall purpose of enriching commercial interests in England. It commodified animal products as international goods of exchange and altered the relationships between Indigenous hunter-gatherers and their animal prey.

Blakley notes that few historians have studied the role of animals in the slave trade, but gives as an exception Marcus Redeker who suggests that the presence of sharks trailing the slave ships helped to contribute to the 'system of terror' (Blakley, 2019: 87). Further, once they reached the New World, the enslaved people might have come in contact with new plants and animals, citing as an example the mangrove swamps of Brazil, 'in a terraqueous ecology for shelter, food and refuge from slavery' (Blakley, 2019: 87). In another paper, Blakley surveys the ways in which the historiography of slavery has intersected with human–animal studies. Before the 'animal turn' in the 1980s, historians wrote about chattel slavery in terms of labour involving animals, and about the dehumanising function of slavery as an economic system (Blakley, 2025: 33). Enslaved people were required to look after the animals brought to the Americas in the Columbian exchange; in turn they were treated very much like animals, whose reproduction was controlled, any surplus was sent to auction and individuals were branded with their owners' marks. Blakley cites Stuckey's analysis of how the enslaved people used animal folklore to covertly challenge the enslavers' ideas. 'Tales such as Brer Rabbit and other trickster figures derived from West African literary traditions further provided a shared repository of narrative through which a Diasporic African identity could be forged from storytelling' (Blakley, 2025: 36).

Just as humans that were enslaved were treated as animals, other writers have suggested that domestication of nonhuman animals could be regarded as chattel slavery. In the preface to the first edition of Marjorie Spiegel's *The Dreaded Comparison* (1988), 'Alice Walker discussed the violence inflicted on animals in American society, specifically the "enslavement of animals" for cosmetics and pharmaceutical research, zoological captivity, and meat production' (Blakley, 2025: 38). Spiegel identifies the 'auction house as a crucial site for commodification and power'. The threat of sale and separation had a destabilising effect on family bonds and kinship of both people and animals (Blakley, 2025: 39). As discussed in chapter 1, the development of ideas on animal rights drew strongly on the other liberation and rights movements. Here the rights of animals are compared to those of emancipated slaves, whereas we also have to consider how humans came to be treated as animals.

The written sources for studies of the human–animal interactions in slavery largely rely on legal documents and the reports of factors for the owners of enslaved people. A promising line of research has been opened up by Jodi Skipper at the University of Mississippi, which combines archaeological techniques with anthropology, to investigate living quarters for enslaved people in the 'Behind the Big House Project' (Skipper, 2022). Excavations have found numerous animal bones. A student participating in the dig gave her preliminary observations: 'I can tell they wreak havoc eating sheep. We can tell how they were butchering cows and maybe they were using the bones for soup. I can see they had ribs and a number of domestic animals, and a lot of birds' (Newsom, 2015: n.p.). There is a suggestion that different nationalities of owners of enslaved people varied in their preference for cuts of meat, sending those cuts they rejected to the slave quarters. This enigmatic information gives us a glimpse of a human–animal interaction that would have shaped the culture of the enslaved people. The oral tradition inherited by their descendants will therefore have passed through a number of cultural shifts as they moved through capture, to transportation, to slavery, which may or may not have involved the care of animals, to emancipation. Much of this culture is now concealed from view.

What has changed little is that most history and literature has been written by white people. Against the odds, the African diaspora and allied people of colour are now starting to write back against the one-sided view that erases non-white culture. A group of Black interdisciplinary scientists explore the way that identities explicitly influence how they interact with the natural world (Yitbarek et al. 2021: 742). In particular, they use Hardin's concept of the 'Tragedy of the Commons' to show how 'the complex sociological processes that drive the use of common-pool resources' highlight how inclusive engagement of all social groups can avoid environmental tragedies. Such interdisciplinary research is a necessary precursor to literary animal studies, which sets both oral and written narratives within the sociocultural world of black story-tellers, whose contact with, and ideas about, animals might differ from those of dominant white discourse.

Alice Walker is an African American writer who has accepted this challenge. Finding that her own introduction to literature was almost entirely from reading white authors, she set out to explore works by Black writers who drew from their own unique lived experience, and from the stories told by their mothers and grandmothers. In her collection of prose writing between 1966 and 1982, she develops a 'womanist' approach that is different to white dominated feminism. For Walker, womanist is 'a black feminist or feminist of color. From the expression of black mothers to female children, "You acting womanish." i.e., like a woman' (Walker 2005 [1984]: xi). In *Ecowomanism* Melanie Harris adds to Walker's intersection of race and gender to add spirituality and concern for the environment: 'Walker's commitment to a gender-inclusive justice movement underscores the focus of the womanist community to be the goal of liberation for all humans and the earth' (Harris, 2017: 90). For Walker 'humans and nature are related to one another' (Harris, 2017: 92). A reading based on gender alone misses the point that race, class and gender acting together determine how African American women are treated (Harris, 2017: 95). The 'eco-' prefix is treated rather generally in Harris's book and the relationship between humans and animals is not developed. We can, however, look to Walker's own writing to see this intersectional approach at work.

Perhaps the best known example is Walker's short story 'Am I Blue?' (Walker, 1989: 3–8). In this story a horse named Blue occupiers a field next to the home of the story-teller. Sometimes he is ridden for short periods, but mostly he is alone. The narrator relates to this horse and forms a loose bond by feeding him apples from the tree. Later he is joined by a mare, which in the story is given the name Brown. His joy in having a companion is evident but it doesn't last, as once she becomes pregnant Brown is taken away, leaving Blue seeming dejected. 'I had forgotten the depth of feeling one could see in horses' eyes. I was therefore unprepared for the expression in Blue's. Blue was lonely. Blue was horribly lonely and bored' (Walker, 1989: 4–5). Walker finds similarities between the horse's situation and that of enslaved people, who may be sold on at any time, disrupting friendships that have sustained them. For Walker, 'if I had been born into slavery, and my partner had been sold or killed, my eyes would have looked like that' (Walker, 1989: 7). Walker allows Blue to have feelings as if he was human: is that anthropogenic or is it making way for the richness of the social and emotional life that is the right of all horses? What would Blue's life be like as a stallion in the wild?

Górecka-Bruzda et al. have surveyed the literature to answer that question. The wild ancestors of domestic horses have been extinct for millennia, but feral horses take readily to life in the wild. Horses are naturally sociable, but that comes at a cost for stallions. Some will rise to dominance through fighting, either to control a harem of mares or to defend a territory within which they may mate with any mare that passes through (Górecka-Bruzda et al., 2023: 6). Colts and stallions that have not been successful in holding a harem may associate in bachelor groups (Górecka-Bruzda et al., 2023: 5). Horses in most parts of the world are not under constant pressure from predators, but are still ever watchful. In a herd one can keep watch while the others sleep. The main threat to stallions is injury through fighting, and the distress of being sent away from the herd when dislodged from their position by a new stallion (Górecka-Bruzda et al., 2023: 8). Although free-living can be stressful, it represents the best option for stallions. Those in captivity are separated from their mothers while they still need them, have no contact with females when they are young, and are socially isolated for most of their lives. Those that are not required for breeding are usually castrated so that they can live in the herd with mares, which satisfies their need for social interaction, while removing the biological urge to reproduce (Górecka-Bruzda et al., 2023: 15). Walker's empathy for Blue is therefore supported by the sociology of equine relations. This short story has been the subject of much critical interest.

In a statistical study with Polish students, Małecki et al. tested the hypothesis that Walker's empathy across the species divide would transfer to her readers. What they found was that after reading the story, compared with those who had read a 'neutral' story, there was not a positive change in attitude to other species in general. In another study a positive change of attitude towards horses was found (Małecki, 2020: 369–70). They suggest that it is the parallel that Walker draws 'between the oppression of human outgroups in general and the oppression of nonhuman animals in general' that 'stops the progress of emotive associations' (Małecki, 2020: 370). The conclusions from this study differ from the positive attitudes towards animals from reading Sewell's *Black Beauty*. While the oppression of African Americans is an urgent topic for decolonising literature, so too is the need to raise the subject status of nonhuman animals. It is a core objective in human–animal studies that is being addressed in critical readings of African literature considered below.

African American women, including Walker, make sense of the stories handed down by their mothers, and claim a space for a distinctive literature based on their own experience of being Black in a society where the canon is dominated by white authors. So, too, does a specifically African literary criticism that is becoming established to consider writers from that great continent. Iheka widens literary enquiry from the postcolonial concern in which 'an account of human agency gives way to a distributed network of agency between human beings and other components of the ecosystem. Agency here is based not exclusively on intentionality but on actions or effects produced by both humans and nonhumans' (Iheka, 2018: 3). The complexity of these ecosystems must be taken into account (Iheka, 2018: 5). In African literature the closeness between humans and ordinary nonhuman and supernatural entities demands 'recognition of their interconnectedness in our reading practices' (Iheka, 2018: 22). In effect, these practices demand that the place of nonhumans in African literature should be taken seriously (Iheka, 2018: 23). Iheka gives the example of a dog, in a novel by Naganang, which shows signs of resistance. He makes the case for 'offering an alternative to the usual treatment of animals as allegories for humans in African literary criticism' (Iheka, 2018: 25). It is perhaps a weakness of intersectional approaches that one component dominates the narrative, and the other components are used in support of that dominant narrative. Iheka is making the case for the unique experience of Africans, and

Walker for those of African Americans, to enrich animal studies. Seeing the human–animal relationship from another perspective helps to challenge entrenched positions to improve the quality and relevance of literary animal studies.

Paying close attention to Indigenous narratives about animals

Spivak's influential 1988 essay 'Can the subaltern speak?' explores the concept of the subaltern, which, taking her example from India, is separate from the dominant groups, both foreign and operating at the all-India level. She acknowledges that this concept is complicated by the violence of the imperialist project and by the practice of the Indian elite, who have acted as informants for first world intellectuals interested in the voice of the other (Spivak, 2013 [1988]: 78–9). For this chapter it is incumbent on us to take note of what the subaltern has to say about animals. In postcolonial literary studies we have to listen very carefully to Indigenous voices.

The lack of interest in animals in postcolonial literary studies, reported by Armstrong above, is now being addressed. Woodward and McHugh have considered 'how the "animal turn" in scholarship informs revaluations of Indigenous knowledge, in ways that launch new possibilities for shared human-animal futures' (Woodward and McHugh, 2017: 2). For these authors it is important not to dismiss narratives, for example, those that are seen as prime symbols of, inter alia, animist gods, familiars, or 'co-creators of multispecies cosmologies', that seem to conflict with Eurocentric intellectual traditions:

> With the rise of animal studies, the conventionally dismissive stance towards such associations as primitive symbols for more vital human relations gives way, revealing an ongoing struggle to engage with indigenous epistemologies at face value, on their own terms, and as vital players in the lives of cultures. (Woodward and McHugh, 2017: 2)

In addition to making room for all these narratives that might offend western sensibilities, their book, *Indigenous Creatures*, assumes that human–animal studies provide the opportunity for a different model to that taken by postcolonial ecocriticism. In particular, they make the case for intersectionality that embraces the complexities, rather than trying to prioritise from a feminist or animal studies viewpoint (Woodward and McHugh, 2017: 4–5). To this end they 'foreground and celebrate indigenous imagination rather than being deflected by postcolonial perceptions' (Woodward and McHugh, 2017: 5).

While it is imperative to listen closely to Indigenous voices, particularly to gain from their close association with nonhuman animals and the meanings they assign to them, we must not make the error of romanticising these viewpoints. One particular error is to assume that Indigenous people can always be relied upon to use natural resources sustainably. Krech (2000), taking his examples from North America, sets out to debunk the myth of the 'ecological Indian' as a construct devised by 'myth makers', which on close inspection is unsubstantiated. Fleisher's 1999 review of Krech's book is a useful summary of his analysis. This cautionary tale does not mean that we must always give priority to western rationality over Indigenous narratives. Also it should be remembered that the myth which sustains the idea of the ecological Indian is a western construct. As we will see below, there is always a risk that we take unfounded western prejudices and assumptions with us when engaging with Indigenous narratives. To understand how American Indians used natural resources, we must take account of their cultural premises, especially that religion and economy are not separate. The buffalo on the plains were assumed 'to be sentient beings capable of seeing, hearing and responding to us in different ways' (Fleisher, 1999: n.p.).

In her tribute to Australian philosopher/activist Val Plumwood, Deborah Bird Rose stressed how she challenged the arrogance of western narratives where the assumption is that these are the only ones to have an active voice (Rose, 2013: 100). For Plumwood the 'hyperseparation' in western thinking produced binaries that make it harder to access both the natural world and the Indigenous Australian way of connecting to it. These binaries include: 'nature/culture, matter/mind, savage/civilised' (Rose, 2013: 94). Setting these binaries aside and rethinking our most basic cultural narratives is essential if we are connect to aboriginal Australians thinking about 'a world that is buzzing with multitudes of sentient beings, only a few of which are human' (Rose, 2013: 95).

Plumwood's interest in Indigenous animism was a way to encounter the lived experience of ideas she was thinking about theoretically. She did not seek to appropriate this way of thinking, but rather to build on these insights to develop western philosophy (Rose, 2013: 93):

> In sum, Plumwood's philosophical animism 'opens a door to a world in which we can begin to negotiate life membership of a community of ecological beings.' Her use of the term 'kindred' means beings with whom we are kin; she was claiming an earth kindred or kinship among those she called earth others. We tend to think of kinfolk as organic beings, but Val was open even to thinking about kinship with stones and other inorganic 'beings'. (Rose, 2013: 98)

In effect, Plumwood is widening the cast of actors, rather as Latour did in his actor–network theory discussed in chapter 5. In common with Latour, Plumwood recognised the complexity of relationships between organisms. 'Country exists because of the living beings who participate in the life of country, and country exists through looped and tangled relationships' (Rose, 2013: 100). The concept of kin is also taken up by Haraway (2016). It is evident that Indigenous voices have much to contribute to mainstream literary animal studies. In particular to navigate past the legacy of human exceptionalism that denies the sentience of nonhuman animals and its emphasis on the individual, and that overlooks the interdependence between all individuals and the other actors in their environment. Plumwood, cited by Rose, also calls upon the practices of listening and paying active attention that were discussed in chapter 6 (Rose, 2013: 102).

Stop and think

Bringing two lines of enquiry together in the hope that each can inform the other has to contend with the contradictions and complexities in each discipline. As we have seen, literary animal studies is not a unified critical method. Ways of engaging with animals have changed and multiplied since Aristotle, or arguably since some species were domesticated more than 10,000 years ago. Postcolonial literary studies as a way to access Indigenous cultures, including those around animals, is also complicated after generations have grown up under the influence of western attempts to 'civilise' them. Most of the examples in this chapter are written in English or translated into English. Some are the work of a diaspora fully integrated into western epistemologies, whose recollection of Indigenous narratives is coloured by foundation myths and hybrid forms. Reading postcolonial and animal studies together means embracing this complexity and taking time to sort through the muddle to find new meanings. Despite the challenges we face, as we enter this entangled multispecies world, the effort is still worthwhile, not least because avoiding this challenge means denying the interconnectedness of nature and culture. Important questions to consider include:

- The rationale for using an intersectional approach is that both animals and Indigenous people have been treated as 'other' in western narratives. How do these two types of othering intersect?
- What if we add other forms of discrimination, such as sexism, ableism or ageism, into the mix? Will that add value to our analysis?
- As discussed in chapter 2, an intersectional approach underpins critical animal studies, where academic study is closely associated with activism. Is that the direction in which investigating the intersection between postcolonial and animal studies will inevitably lead, even if there is no hint of didacticism in the literary text being considered?

Interrogating the assimilation of colonising animals into Indigenous practices

The colonisation of North America brought waves of European settlers, each with their own cultural traditions and ideas about animals. Spanish, Dutch and French immigrants had already left their mark on the continent, before English, and later Scottish and Irish, immigrants came to dominate. The form of colonisation covered plantations worked by enslaved people, yeoman farmers, pioneers opening up forests for livestock, and the grazing of vast rangelands. Resource extraction schemes, particularly for fur, were overseen by expatriates who would return to their homeland rather than settle. For Canada it was this commerce based on furs, particularly from the beaver, that would be the foundation for the nation (Backhouse, 2015; Nadeau, 2001). This section takes the example of dogs, sheep and horses to interrogate this complex set of relationships and the myths and misunderstandings that have accumulated as modernity tries to make sense of the contact between the settlers and the Native Americans, and between both them and their animals.

The Australian shepherd bitch, Ms Cayenne Pepper, is a central character in Haraway's *The Companion Species Manifesto,* where the shared intimacy of competing in the sport of agility has inspired her to look closer into both the human–nonhuman animal relationship and the myths of origin for this particular breed. 'My point is simple: Knowing and living with these dogs means inheriting all the conditions of their possibility, all of which makes relating with these beings actual, all of the prehensions that constitute companion species' (Haraway, 2003: 81). Dogs of various kinds came to North America as it was settled. Haraway interrogates the popular story that the Australian shepherd dog came to America from Australia with Basque shepherds. This story, which Haraway demonstrates to be false, is still included in the breed description of the British Kennel Club (The Kennel Club, n.d.). The history of these dogs and how they got their name is far from clear. It is likely that Cayenne's ancestors were dogs of the collie type that emigrated from the British Isles from early colonial times.

As for the Basques, they were not herders in Australia, but came to America 'in the nineteenth century with the millions lusting for gold and ended up herding sheep to feed other disappointed miners' (Haraway, 2003: 83). This origin myth, which Haraway picks apart, is as much about the organising principles of the show dog fancy that requires dogs in registered breeds to be pure-bred, as it is about historical accuracy. It is the practice among shepherds to breed from dogs that seem to have the instincts needed for herding, some to gather sheep off a mountain, others to drive sheep along a drovers' path. Cayenne's pedigree suggests that this was her origin, with Redding farm dog being one of her ancestors. The sheep that these dogs herded were introduced by the Spanish missions who advocated sheep ranching to civilise the Indians. Sheep originally of merino type came to the west coast from Australia and from the east coast with dogs coming in both directions. 'Dogs that look like contemporary Aussies might have gotten their name from being associated with flocks arriving by boat from down under, whether or not they came on those ships' (Haraway, 2003: 85).

The sheep that the Spanish missions used to civilise the Indians were descendants of the Iberian churra, which were well established by the seventh century. Other Native American peoples acquired these sheep for themselves by trade and raid, and bred them for three centuries to adapt to the rugged native pastoral conditions (Haraway, 2008: 98). These sheep were the ancestors of the Pueblo and Navajo churro, whose wool was used to make the Indians' distinctive textiles. 'In Navajo communities sheep are primarily owned by women and weaving has always been women's labor' (Haraway, 2008: 99). Where once sheep keeping was considered to be a civilising influence, most of the Navajo flocks were slaughtered by the US Army 'in the 1860s in retribution for Indian resistance to conquest and relocation to Bosque Redondo' (Haraway, 2008: 99). The Diné sheepherders were not 'civilised' by their sheep, but assimilated them into their own ways of living with each other and with other species. In particular, they developed their own culture around nomadic sheepherding. Marsha Weisiger has explored this culture and its later conflict with government agriculturists who did not take the time to understand it.

That there was a problem with overgrazing and desertification is not in dispute, but in the 1930s, after a tour lasting less than a week, government scientists decided 'to show the Navajo the logic of scientific range management through a demonstration project at Mexican Springs' (Weisiger, 2009: 35). In this way, a conflict between competing narratives was set up as 'range technicians, soil specialists, engineers, agronomists, and biologists – many of them the best in the region – swarmed across Navajo country' (Weisiger, 2009: 36). The failure of these scientists was in making assumptions about the supposed Edenic conditions they assumed existed before the Diné started grazing their animals: 'as they constructed stories about Navajo country, the scientists relied on assumptions about the land's historical condition they barely acknowledged and never scrutinised' (Weisiger, 2009: 38). They also relied on the then influential orthodoxy of Frederick Clements's 'climax theory' of ecology, which predicted that this land once would have included stands of shrubs and rich grassland.

Where they did consult with the Diné, they made further assumptions about the ownership of the sheep, which overlooked the way the Navajo society was organised around matrilocal residence and 'gave women a strong voice in their communities' (Weisiger, 2009: 94). Diné poet, Hershman R. John, draws on this matrilineal culture in his collection *I Swallow Turquoise for Courage* (2007). John was born to the Deer Springs People and grew up on the Navajo Reservation at Sand Springs, Arizona. In 'My Feminist Grandmother' he writes that she did not have to march to resist, she did not have a bra to burn:

> Grandma owns all the land, cows, corn.
> Her words are final; we listen,
> Arguments end. And the word
> Feminism doesn't exist. (John, 2007: 32)

Despite this she is under pressure to conform: 'Grandma, did you know you have to / Take on Grandpa's name? *Quit telling / Jokes like Coyote*' (John, 2007: 33, original emphasis). This culture, with its rich fund of stories and myths, particularly about the natural world, is one in which sheepherding could be assimilated to become integral to the natureculture of the tribal group. In 'Spider Woman's Children', as his grandmother cards wool:

> She sings the song slowly for her sheep,
> For her rug, for her hands, for the sun above and
> For her mother who taught her the words so long ago.
> (John, 2007: 59)

This mixture of myth, ways of relating to the natural world and the distinctive agro-pastoral society, depends on oral transmission down the female line.

In her contribution to the special edition of *Humanalia* on decolonising animal studies, Kelsey Dayle John 'highlights the relationship between violence against nonhuman animals and Indigenous peoples [and reframes] the conversation about horses by positioning horses as teachers and knowers for decolonization' (John, 2019: 42). Unlike sheep, whose wild ancestors were Eurasian species, horses evolved in the Americas from a small herbivore; they crossed to the Old World via the Bering Land Bridge. They became extinct in the Americas during the last Ice Age, so the animals that came with the conquerors would have been the first that Native Americans had seen for 9,000 years (Lobell and Powell, 2015: 33). John, who describes herself 'as a Diné woman, horse trainer, and activist scholar' includes nonhumans in an Indigenous ontology in the hope that this can avoid the dualism of the western world. As was the case with sheep and rangeland management discussed above, she confronts the settler colonial regulations imposed both on horses and people (John, 2019: 43). It is these injustices that fuel her activism, but it is the special relationship she has with horses that offers a different way of looking at the meeting of species.

In her dissertation research she 'centers the Navajo horse as a central point of Diné decolonization'. This research was submitted to the Navajo Nation Research Review Board for approval, to ensure that the work represents stories that are common to the Diné and not only her own family (John, 2019: 44). Situated at the boundary between settler colonial studies and animal studies, she could not base her research on one theoretical discipline. This problem of possibly conflicting methodologies needs to be addressed in any interrogation of postcolonial texts for an animal studies reading. Finding that her connection to horses is a 'window into a set of beliefs and traditions that characterize our existence as Dine' she used her own experiences to tell stories (John, 2019: 45). Her article reserves traditional Navajo knowledge about sacred horse practices for a Diné audience, in order to concentrate her attention for a wider audience on the way that settler colonial ideologies destroy horse/Navajo/land relationalities and to show how the Diné resist these violences. It would be fascinating to see behind this curtain to be able to distinguish between distinctive Indigenous relationships with horses and western approaches to the same questions. She does, however, give us some hints.

'Horses are present in Diné creation stories alongside Nahooká Diyin Dinéé and are understood as an integral part of the Diné narrative from the beginning' (John, 2019: 56). Horses are linked to the Earth and the four sacred elements. 'At their introduction, the horses came to the Earth's surface and are made to be a tool for and a gift to Diné' (John, 2019: 56). There is an obvious conflict here between the narratives around the Columbian exchange that brought horses back to the continent where they had evolved and their role in Navajo origin stories. Do we have to set aside what we know about the acquisition of horses from the settlers, by trade and raid, in order to relate to this sacred narrative? Is this western scepticism the reason that John has kept these stories for a Navajo audience? While the Indigenous North Americans may have known horses before the last Ice Age, we will never know how that has informed the world view of their ancestors. It seems more likely that horses became integrated within an existing narrative about the connection between land, people and nonhuman animals. Further the education, primarily from maternal grandparents, that introduced children to horse training before formal schooling, would have helped this cross-species relationship become second nature. The importance of introducing children to horses, often before they can walk, is understood by western parents who had themselves grown up within a horse culture. How, then, does John differ in her practical engagement with horses from western horse handling?

In the examples she gives, the horses are 'wild' or 'feral', depending on one's point of view, taken from the land. These Navajo horses, through their association with Indigenous people, are judged as less valuable than Non-Navajo horses (John, 2019: 49). While western horses may have been bred on the farm and handled from birth, the experience of being captured is likely to be traumatic for these mustangs. It is this hurt that John sets out to alleviate as she works with a new horse.

> *So I stay in the round pin an extra 30 minutes with a little mustang horse picked up off the highway. I try to understand why she resists, work with her and not against her, hear my dad's instructions, and embody his patience. I go slow with ropes and work through her trauma from being rounded up. I postulate that my studies in settler colonialism resonates with her, too.* (John, 2019: 58, original emphasis)

By holding back the spiritual part of the narrative for a Navajo audience, it is not immediately evident how this way of working differs from that used by western trainers such as Monty Roberts. Based on a study of horse psychology, Roberts claims that what horses most fear is being excluded from the herd. Working in a round pen as John does, he drives the horse away until it drops its head, whereupon he turns away from it and waits for it to join up with him walking at his shoulder. Soon afterwards it will accept a saddle and a human mounted on its back. Roberts uses the term 'join up' rather than 'breaking' in traditional methods where a lunge rein and whip would be used to 'school a horse'. The cruelty in some of the more drastic practices for breaking a horse are undeniable, but it should be noted that by separating the horse from the herd and driving it away, Roberts's method is still exploiting the horse's fear, even though the term 'join up' seems less aggressive. In her poem, 'Dancing with Ms. Bambi', John deploys 'patience, kindness and empathy':

> So I dance with Ms. Bambi
> Move with intention
> Raise my arm slowly
> Change my thought patterns
> Resist frustration and anger
> Change direction
> Dancing with Ms. Bambi (John, 2019: 64)

John has had to learn to move holistically and to be sensitive to context from moment to moment. She sees the relationship with her horse as a way of healing and resisting the violence in settler colonialism. The Diné epistemology 'foregrounds the agency and autonomy of nonhumans' and in this way is closely aligned with what animal studies is trying to achieve (John, 2019: 62).

Also tackling the problem of how to read Indigenous narratives in the absence of an agreed comprehensive methodology, Ziarkowska starts with Wolfe's discussion of how difficult it is to avoid humanist and anthropocentric perspectives when we study nonhuman animals. Further, the western paradigms, in which human-nonhuman animal relationships are hierarchical, are divorced from Indigenous cosmologies. Ziarkowska, as a non-Indigenous scholar, believes that 'it is ethically sound not to read [Indigenous texts] vis-a-vis Indigenous knowledge of which [she] is not a co-creator and co-owner' (Ziarkowska, 2024: 2). Instead she offers a theoretical framework derived from the work of Vinciane Despret to read Linda Hogan's collection of stories *The Radiant Lives of Animals* (2020). Hogan is a distinguished Chickasaw writer with a special interest in documenting the lives of animals around her. Hogan's description of her complicated relationship with horses is a useful second Indigenous view to add to that of John.

The horse, which is always present in many Native people's mythologies and has a central role in ceremonial practices, is fundamental not only to the Plains Indians.

> The Chickasaw, who before the Removal in 1837 occupied parts of today's southwestern Kentucky, western Tennessee, northern Mississippi and northwestern Alabama also kept horses … Theirs, however, were smaller than the Plains breeds and were descended from the horses brought to the colonized lands by the Spanish in the mid-nineteenth century. According to records these animals, swift and robust, were bred into a unique subspecies that were later referred to as 'Chickasaw ponies'. (Ziarkowska, 2024: 10)

Hogan, in *The Radiant Lives of Animals*, claims this beloved breed, now extinct, as lost kin. She obtains her new horse from horse rescue where the interaction is dominated by 'anthropomorphic attribution of human characteristics and intentionality to animals' (Ziarkowska, 2024: 10). While Hogan uses language that claims to know the horse's intentions, 'what begins to dominate in the interactions is the role of their bodies and how they affect Hogan's perception of their agency' (Ziarkowska, 2024: 11).

The tool of communication between human and horse is the body. With regard to the empathy that Hogan feels for her horse, Ziarkowska cites Despret: 'Empathy is not, in this case, experiencing with one's own body what the other experiences; it is creating the possibilities of an embodied communication' (Ziarkowska, 2024: 11). Ziarkowska suggests that a traditional horse trainer would interpret this response to Hogan as the horse having been trained to respond to specific cues through punishment. In contrast a 'horse whisperer', such as Monty Roberts would claim it, is this specific human's special gift of communicating with horses. It is likely that Hogan is aware of these techniques, but it is communication 'on the level of the body and affect that plays the main role in the event' (Ziarkowska, 2024: 11).

The conquistadors in the early colonial period in South America were also to remark on the Indigenous people's affinity with horses, in particular that they spoke to a horse as if it were a rational animal. 'Europeans viewed horses as exemplary vassal animals, but Cei's Indigenous interlocutors attributed far greater subjectivity to the animals' (Norton, 2024: 250). A Jesuit writing in the late eighteenth century reported how the Indian trains a riding horse by mounting it without a bit or a saddle and despite it bucking and galloping rides it across the savannah. After allowing it to 'laze' for several days, the process is repeated to new challenges until it 'converts, as they say, into a sheep'. The horses were not confined after this, but instead would choose to stay with their master and follow him anywhere (Norton, 2024: 251). This description has some similarities with the 'join up' terminology of Monty Roberts.

Stop and think

The authors considered in this section have all been reticent about drawing directly on the language and cosmologies of their Indigenous tradition, or in the case of Ziarkowska of trying to enter a culture in which she had not been a co-creator. Do we need to understand how these cosmologies construct the relationship between the human and the rest of the animal world, or is it enough to work with the end result as it challenges western narratives and assumptions? All agree that Indigenous people do not make the binary distinction between human and nonhuman life that is the bane of the humanist tradition. Meeting Indigenous narrators as they interpret their culture for a western audience, we do not have to overcome the ideas than humans are exceptional, and that animals are machines, with no culture or sentience. Can we learn from these exchanges to listen more closely to what nonhuman animals want? Can we pursue the shared goals of posthumanism and post colonialism in a single reading?

Settling animals and the poetry of resistance in Palestine-Israel

As I write this chapter war is raging in Palestine-Israel, which makes it difficult to look away from the suffering of humans to engage with other animals. Poets are being arrested and libraries destroyed, so that even literature, with its claims to be politically neutral, has a part to play in the conflict. However, the quiet and authoritative research by Irus Braverman, which uses a settler colonial framework to examine critically the practices of the conservation regime in the region, helps to ground an animal studies reading in reason and fact. Growing up in West Jerusalem, Braverman is an insider in the nature conservation community. 'During my military service, not only was I being indoctrinated, I was indoctrinating others to the value of nature and its powerful connection to the Jewish people' (Braverman, 2023: xi). She remains committed to the overall objectives of nature conservation. The research for her book, *Settling Nature*, was based on interviews with conservation colleagues in Palestine-Israel and on her exposure to conservation scientists around the world. This wider context informed her research methodology 'with which to tackle the ethnographic challenges of fieldwork in the region' (Braverman, 2023: x).

For Braverman the 'recent resurgence of settler colonial studies brings novel insights into [the framework of conservation in Palestine-Israel], which can arguably be further strengthened through engagement with more-than-human perspectives' (Braverman, 2023: xii). She proposes a new outlook for animal studies. 'Rather than decentering humans, which is referred to as the "non-human turn," [her] book brings attention to the ways in which colonial dynamics juxtapose between and therefore alienate (certain) humans from (certain) nonhumans' (Braverman, 2023: xiii). The book attempts to show 'the dangerous implications of such colonial alienation between humans and nonhumans'. She challenges much of the European-based conservation that is the model for Israeli protection of natural areas and species, as problematic 'for its imperial, colonial, racist, sexist, and capitalist foundations' (Braverman, 2023: xi).

In common with many cross-disciplinary approaches to animal studies, she has been under pressure from specialists to go into further detail in their own area of expertise. In particular, her 'colleagues in geography and critical theory felt that my story-telling style renders the underlying theory too elusive and the book needs more theory to pull it all together' (Braverman, 2023: xiv). Among her early influences was Amotz Zahavi, who in her high school years she often helped with his research into warblers and shrikes (Braverman, 2023: x). Despret has discussed how Zahavi developed a methodology that was at odds with the dominant theory-led research into avian behavioural ecology as championed by the Edward Grey Institute for Field Ornithology at Oxford University. Did this early exposure to observing behaviour without a-priori models, or a null-hypothesis to test, predispose her to a story-telling approach?

In his translator's introduction to Despret's account of the way Zahavi approaches his research into the behaviour of the Arabian babbler, Bussolini notes how 'Despret focuses on Zahazi's approach and on the telling of stories as a general, philosophical frame for the process of research and thinking – in the natural and social sciences as well as the humanities' (Bussolini in Despret, 2021: xiv). Despret was able to observe Zahavi working in the field on the highly social babblers alongside a colleague from Oxford whose research followed the dominant model. Zahavi adopts what he calls an 'anthropomorphic model'.

> The spatial structure of the meeting between Zahavi and the birds is drawn as a space without limits between the observer and the observed. In an analogical manner, a common mental space can be seen to as corresponding to this limitless space, that is, the common mental space of anthropomorphic identification. (Despret, 2021 [1996]: 109)

This method produces an interpretation in which every action the animal takes has a meaning in behavioural sequences, which Zahavi understands to be the best possible compromise the animal can make. The research output from this post-priori method avoids the statistics of the dominant method in favour of a series of text narratives or stories that describe the behaviour. I follow this deviation here for two reasons: firstly it suggests what may have been an early influence on Braverman, and secondly because it shows that even in Israel, which has followed the colonising practices of the European conservation model, an independent researcher in the Negev desert is able to deploy a methodology in his research into avian ethology, that writes back against the dominant method. This post-priori method takes us closer to an animal studies approach that gives the nonhuman partner space to influence the research outcome in the coproduction of the stories that allow for individual difference and agency.

The main part of *Settling Nature* is given over to story-telling, with only a light input of theory in the later chapters. This approach is particularly valuable in informing an animal studies reading of literary works. Particularly striking are her stories about reintroduction of lost species and the development of conservation priorities based on evidence taken from the Bible. 'Symbolising the Jewish return to the Holy Land, animals associated with the Bible have been granted biopolitical priority' (Braverman, 2023: 55). One such is the Persian fallow deer: this species, which some authors regard as a subspecies of the closely related European fallow deer, was close to extinction in 1956, when two dozen were discovered in Iran. In 1978 Israeli conservationists managed to capture four deer from this remaining population and ship them out under false papers. As these were all female, they borrowed two males from a German zoo to form a founder population for a captive breeding programme. This story with the 'heroic rescue' of the deer, the involvement of the army and the success of the subsequent breeding programme is seen as 'the crown of INPA's [Israel National Park Authority] reintroduction projects'. Jerusalem now has the largest zoo-kept herd of Persian fallow deer in the world (Braverman, 2023: 58). Releasing them to the wild has been problematic. They were at risk of being killed as they crossed the Jerusalem to Tel Aviv railway line, or by packs of feral dogs. The culling of the latter has been justified by their not-wild status. Braverman accompanied one release, initially to a nature reserve where they can be tracked by satellite, fed and monitored before they are released more widely. This was an emotional experience for both Braverman and the keepers responsible for the release.

While the release of species to their previous range serves the narrative of connecting Jewish people to their homeland, it also modifies the contemporary landscape (Braverman, 2023: 62). The Palestinian practices of hunting, grazing and gathering must be adapted to this new reality as a form of dispossession. 'Israel's reintroduced deer therefore serve as agents of normalisation – a technology for rendering banal, innocuous, and even natural Israel's conservation agenda as well as its colonial control over the land and its particular settler imaginaries' (Braverman, 2023: 63). Braverman does not contrast this reintroduction to the role of the closely related fallow, present in the wild and in deer parks across much of Europe. While restoring the deer to their rightful land, on evidence in the Bible, means so much in the context of building the nation of Israel, very different meanings are given to the presence of their congeneric cousins in Britain.

British conservationists have an ambiguous relationship with fallow deer. For a start they were introduced by the Normans into large areas of land taken into ownership as hunting forests. Further introductions were made into the deer parks of the great estates. Even after a millennium, some biologists regard the fallow deer as not native. Further the extinction of the grey wolf means that there is no top-down pressure to control the species, and deer populations have been rising. The practice of coppicing woodland prevents woodland from forming a closed canopy that would suppress the field layer of wild flowers and shrubs that in turn supported a wide invertebrate community and encouraged birds such as the nightingale. Conservationists who have tried to revive the now archaic practice have found that new growth from the coppiced stools did not survive browsing by deer if their populations got out of control. The settler colonial Normans used acclimatisation practices to establish deer. They exerted very strict control over who could hunt them, which was continued through to the anti-poaching laws that penalised the rural poor. Braverman cites E. P. Thomson's 1975 study of poaching, in which the taking of red or fallow deer in England was made a capital offence (Braverman, 2023: 65). Now they must be culled if other valued habitats are not to be destroyed, and the animal species that depend on these habitats are not to become extinct. The return of Persian fallow deer is seen as an essential part of 'ecosystem restoration' but it also has meaning in exercising colonial control over the land (Braverman, 2023: 62).

Another human–animal interaction explored by Braverman is the keeping of caged songbirds by Palestinian households. These include both captive-bred canaries, which have a long history of domestication, and goldfinches taken from the wild or smuggled in from those parts of Europe where breeding 'wild' species is not illegal. Male goldfinches are crossed with female canaries to produce infertile hybrids which are known as *banduk* in Palestine and Israel, and mules in Britain (Braverman, 2023: 64). These hybrids are prized for their singing. Since the passing of the Wild Animal Protection Act 1955 in Israel, taking goldfinches from the wild has been illegal, as it has in England since its Protection of Birds Act 1954. Illegal bird catchers are held to be the cause of goldfinches becoming scarce in Israel, but the lack of rough grassland with thistles may also have contributed to the decline.

This legal framework is seen as enlightened. 'From the INPA's perspective, then, Israel operates as an island of humanism and legality, protecting its natural heritage, which includes vulnerable wild species, from the destruction wrought by the "Arabs"'. For Braverman, that her interviewees insisted on calling them 'Arabs' is another common form of erasure of Palestinian identity (Braverman, 2023: 66–7). By prioritising wild over domestic, and policing the boundary, the opportunity to form a closer relationship with a wild species may be lost. Braverman interviewed 'Daniel', an Arab Jew who has kept a few canaries and a *banduk,* and grew up hearing his birds sing. This gave her a glimpse of an alternative way of looking at the birds which occur in the wild but have the potential to be companion species:

> the birds' charisma and the caretaker's compassion have paved the way for a human-animal affinity that could potentially defy the colonial order of things, hinting that even at the heart of the colony, a decolonized space in which human and animal kinships flourish might be possible. (Braverman, 2023: 74–5)

It is with this potential for kinship in mind that I turn to a poem by a Palestinian American who is trying to make sense of her inherited identity.

In the title poem of her collection, *A Theory of Birds,* Zaina Alsous imagines the *banduk* (Alsous, 2019: 4–5). The poem, with fifteen three-line stanzas, begins:

> In Gaza City canaries are raised
> for sale: goldfinch hybrids,
> ornaments singing

The next stanza suggests song and the third the high price, 'the equivalent / of one month's salary'. This opening to the poem provides the context that was discussed by Braverman. The very high price is both a measure of the value placed by residents of Gaza and an indication of why it is worth the risk of arrest or being shot to trap birds in the wild or to smuggle them into the country. The *banduk* is an infertile mule whose production requires a constant supply of wild or imported captive-bred male goldfinches to breed with the captive-bred female canaries. In the fourth stanza and beginning of the fifth there is a turn: 'Rare birds eat / dust in al-Tuffah'. Warplanes frequently bomb this area to the north of Gaza City, and the birds that are valued companions in the home of the people suffer alongside them. In the last line of the fifth stanza there is another turn:

> In North Carolina I saw
> a cardinal once
> that could have been
> my grandmother

Alsous could, with justification, have contrasted the Northern cardinal which, like the goldfinch, was kept as a caged bird in the United States until the passing of the Migratory Birds Act 1918 made it illegal. The brightly coloured male cardinal is a striking bird, which has been adopted as an emblem by states and sports teams across the country. It readily comes to garden feeders with a liking for sunflower seed, to replace captivity with another way to form a human–animal bond. Instead Alsous takes this freedom as a metaphor for her grandmother: 'Finally, / she gets a chance / to travel …'. The remaining stanzas turn to her identity and wanting love more than history. There is a detachment between the exiled Palestinian becoming accustomed to a world in which cardinals are loved but free, and trying to make sense of a much narrower existence in Gaza City, where the companionship of a singing bird could mean so much. While metaphor comes easily to her, is it possible that the human–animal bond in such straightened circumstances could provide the love to mitigate the problematic history of Palestine since 1948, and before that under the British Mandate and Ottoman rule?

The title poem of Mosab Abu Toha's *Things You May Find Hidden in My Ear* is dedicated to Alicia M. Quesnel MD, the Boston based ear and skull surgeon who operated on him after he was hit by shrapnel in an Israeli bombing raid on Gaza. The second stanza tells her what she may find as she repairs the damage from the wound.

> You may encounter songs in Arabic,
> poems in English I recite to myself,
> or a song I sing to the chirping birds in our backyard.
> (Abu Toha, 2022: 92)

Abu Toha, who writes in English as a way of reaching a wider audience outside his Gaza home, founded the Edward Said Library in North Gaza to make English language books available to a population otherwise cut off from the literary world. That he would sing to the birds in his backyard is no surprise, for those whose movements are constrained will often take closer notice of their nonhuman companions that are close at hand. In his long poem 'Wounds', subtitled '*Israeli aggression against Gaza (December 27, 2008 – January 18, 2009)* (Abu Toha, 2022: 73–83), he recounts the background to his receiving such a severe injury. Even here the bond that his family has with birds, in this case fancy pigeons, contrasts the terror and displacement of this aggression.

The poem starts calmly, as aged 16 he discusses his final Arabic exam with his father: 'Home by noon, we stood on the roof of our house, / watched the pigeons my father raised as a hobby'. As they watched a loud explosion rocked the city.

> Birds from nowhere flew aimlessly in the open sky.
> Some hid in trees.
> The pigeons in their big coop trembled.
> Rock pigeons, Egyptian pigeons, king pigeons,
> and Halabi pigeons.
> A tiny egg fell. (Abu Toha, 2022: 73)

This fragment in the poem reminds us that it is not only humans who are terrorised by war. I have seen my own pigeons tremble in this way when threatened by a peregrine or a goshawk. The impressive selection of fancy breeds includes the rock pigeon, whose plumage is close to that of the wild rock dove, which is the ancestor of all the very different fancy breeds. The Egyptian and Halabi pigeons are fancy breeds, while the king is noted for its size. Braverman, in her visit to the Allenby Crossing where the authorities try to detect and confiscate birds, finds that pigeons are among the species smuggled (Braverman, 2023: 70). Israel does have some relatively 'pure' wild type rock doves in the Negev desert, but elsewhere, as in most major cities around the world, the wild type has been diluted with feral escapes of domesticated pigeons. It is therefore biosecurity against importing disease, rather than genetic contamination of the wild population, that would be the priority in intercepting smuggled pigeons.

When they have to leave their house Abu Toha's father has to add to this risk of interbreeding. 'The pigeons were set free, too. / He was sure they'd return when we were back'. If Israel invokes the idea of Noah's ark as the model for the repopulation of the Holy Land with animals mentioned in the Bible, it is as well to remember the symbolism of the dove returning with the olive twig as proof the flood was retreating. The dove has been a symbol of peace ever since and the olive twig is reproduced in the Palestinian keffiyeh. Further, the belief that the humans and birds will once more be together in their own home, has resonance in the slogan 'exist, resist, return'. In their affection for these birds, it was more practical to give them autonomy rather than to try to settle them into a new home. If the Palestinians' love of caged birds is erased in the dominant settler discourse, these lines in Abu Toha's long poem can be read as an act of resistance.

For a bird watcher, Palestine-Israel is a dream destination, with interesting resident birds and a great concentration of birds that pass through on the migration flyway between Europe and Africa. Jasmine Donahaye, whose enthusiasm for birds was discussed in chapter 4, is the English-born daughter of kibbutzniks. Her first visit to Israel as a ten-year-old to visit family was dominated by bird watching. 'Everywhere we go, it is not family, or ruins, or human stories that make the strongest impression on me, but birds' (Donahaye, 2015: 26). She had already prepared herself by reading her father's precious first edition of Henry Baker Tristram's *Fauna and Flora of Palestine* (Donahaye, 2015: 26). Tristram was a notable clergyman ornithologist who was a joint founder of the British Ornithologists' Union and its journal *Ibis,* the foremost source of authoritative papers on ornithological science. Based in Durham Cathedral, Tristram 'was in the pursuit of a story of God, and science, and the aspirations of Empire' (Donahaye, 2015: 106).

At seventeen, Donahaye had embraced the ideology of the kibbutz movement as she learned Hebrew through the intensive programme used to integrate Jews settling in Israel from across the world. Over the years, she started to question her own family's part in the dispossession of the Palestinians during the formation of her mother's kibbutz in Mandate-era Palestine. She realised that her 'whole story, my whole sense of self has been premised on reducing the humanity of Arabs in general and any Arab as an individual' (Donahaye, 2015: 70). In this sense she is reinforcing the point made by Braverman above, which avoids mentioning Palestine and casts all Arabs as other. All of these tensions are evident in her poem 'The Palestine or orange tufted sunbird' (Donahaye, 2009: 28). In the first two of the four six-line stanzas she imagines a return to Israel, seeing the brewer's blackbird and his cousin flashing red. As always she is watching birds while the other passengers are 'singing *HaTikva* as we descend / weeping for the effect'. In the third stanza she looks to Adam to imagine naming the species, but this was not good enough for science. As the first to obtain type specimens by shooting, Tristram was able to add many 'new to science' species to the Linnaean taxonomy. Braverman shows how Israeli conservationists defer to Tristram as the authority for the identification of birds and other animals in the Bible, which are backed by museum type specimens. In this way the Zionist nature management project is linked to the Anglican missionary surveys (Braverman, 2023: 56). The bird in the poem's title is reached in the final stanza.

Tristram shot several specimens of this sunbird in Northern Palestine in the spring of 1864; he claimed that before then 'the sunbird was hardly known in Europe, or so Tristram claimed' (Donahaye, 2015: 182). Echoing the performative singing 'for the effect' that ended the second stanza, Donahaye imagines Tristram's performance with this newly found species:

> and, for the effect, pressing his thumbprint
> on the iridescent sunbird with its scimitar beak,
> turning it in his unmarked palm
> to catch the light, ruffling the tiny tufts
> of orange fluff for which he names
> and adds to our divine taxonomy of gifts. (Donahaye, 2009: 29)

It is, however, the title that conveys the seeds of resistance. The very mention of the word Palestine is suppressed as a means to erase the existence of this inconvenient people in the shared landscape. For Donahaye it is 'Better that the name Palestine remain bulbous and burgeoning and difficult; better that I hesitate between naming this tiny iridescent bird an orange-tufted sunbird, or a Palestine sunbird' (Donahaye, 2015: 187). That birdwatching can be a subversive act in speaking against the dominant settler colonial narrative, for a bird that is very much tied to place, complicates an animal studies reading. As with Donahaye it is better that we embrace this complexity and understand that our own feeling of dissonance is an essential precursor to change. Is it possible that the Palestinian interest in caged birds could develop in time to the attraction of watching birds in the wild? For a community unable to travel outside the confines of Gaza, the birds' freedom to travel the world is evocative (Vidal, 2023: n.p.)

Decolonising literary animal studies

The strand of animal studies that draws on the common struggle for rights between Indigenous people and nonhuman animals would seem to be an obvious point of departure to progress decolonising discourse. However, other strands of animal studies are close bedfellows with both animal welfare and nature conservation. In particular, UK nature conservation 'has inherited both a romantic tradition that decried the impact of "modernisation", and a scientific rational tradition that seeks to manage nature for human enjoyment and material benefit' (Adams and Mulligan, 2003: 8). As Braverman has shown, the international reach of nature conservation is closely aligned with the colonial project, in particular as it erases the presence of Indigenous people and their culture of human–animal relations. John, as discussed above, suggests that:

> Decolonizing animal studies means recognizing that animal genocide is a tool used to control and subdue Indigenous peoples for the purposes of resource extraction and land seizures. Furthermore, the settler colonial narrative is delivered in all educational and research arenas and should not be only a concern of Native American or Ethnic Studies. (John, 2019: 48)

Animal studies conference organisers might decide that all catering will be vegan to avoid offending those who have embraced ethical veganism. But what of the pastoralists who have close relationships with their animals that are erased by that decision? In the binaries of animal studies do we always have to take a side between wild/domestic or human/nonhuman? Should we always be looking back at some mythical Eden when harmony between all species was the norm?

Above all, an animal studies reading has to cope with the continuous change both in human societies and in the communities of nonhuman animals that live with us. It seems likely that climate change will add to the instability of the natural world. Coproduction of discourse between colonisers and the colonised is now seen as an efficient way to build on traditional ecological knowledge, with the shared aim of preserving the diversity of life. Literature that disrupts established ways of thinking has a part to play in promoting change. A literary animal study should feel unsettled, and literary criticism that rejects human exceptionalism will venture into spaces that are poorly understood. Rather than imposing a single theory or ideology on this space, we should take time to look and listen to the human and nonhuman animals that inhabit it, rather as Zahavi does when directing his gaze at the Arabian babblers as they dance before him.

Further reading

Geroux, Robert (2019) 'Introduction to the special issue: decolonizing animal studies', *Humanimalia* 10:2, pp. 1–9.

References

Abu Toha, Mosab (2022) *Things You May Find Hidden in My Ear*. San Francisco: City Lights Books.

Adams, William M. and Mulligan, Martin (2003) *Decolonizing Nature: Strategies for Conservation in a Post-Colonial Era*. London: Earthscan.

Alsous, Zaina (2019) *A Theory of Birds*. Fayetteville: University of Arkansas Press.

Archibald, Jo-ann (2018) 'Indigenous storytelling' in Philippe Tortell, Mark Turin and Margot Young (eds) *Memory*. Vancouver: Peter Wall Institute for Advanced Studies, pp. 233–42.

Armstrong, Philip (2002) 'The postcolonial animal', *Society and Animals* 10:4, pp. 413–19.

Backhouse, Frances (2015) *Once They Were Hats: In Search of the Mighty Beaver*. Toronto: ECW Press.

Blakley, Christopher M. (2019) '"To get a cargo of flesh, bone and blood": animals in the slave trade in West Africa', *International Review of Environmental History* 5:1, pp. 85–111.

Blakley, Christopher M. (2025) 'Historicising the "beast-man": on slavery and human-animal studies', *Animal History* March, pp. 33–51.

Bowman, Melanie (1986) 'Saving Père David's deer', *The American Poetry Review* 15:1, January/February, p. 28.

Braverman, Irus (2023) *Settling Nature: The Conservation Regime in Palestine-Israel*. Minneapolis: University of Minnesota Press.

Despret, Vinciane (2021 [1996]) *The Dance of the Arabian Babbler: Birth of an Ethological Theory*. Minneapolis: University of Minnesota Press.

Donahaye, Jasmine (2009) *Self-Portrait as Ruth*. London: Salt.

Donahaye, Jasmine (2015) *Losing Israel*. Bridgend: Seren.

Fleisher, Mark S. (1999) 'Natural man: examining our belief in American Indians' innate environmentalism', *New York Times* on the web, 17 October.

Fugate, Laurren and Miller, John MacNeill (2021) 'Shakespeare's Starlings: Literary History and the Fictions of Invasiveness', *Environmental Humanities* 13:2, pp. 301–22.

Górecka-Bruzda, Aleksandra, Jaworska, Joanna and Stanley, Christina R. (2023) 'The social and reproductive challenges faced by free-roaming horse (Equus cabals) stallions', *Animals* 13, n.p.

Haraway, Donna (2003) *The Companion Species Manifesto: Dogs, People, and Significant Otherness*. Chicago: Prickly Paradigm Press.

Haraway, Donna (2008) *When Species Meet*. Minneapolis: University of Minnesota Press.

Haraway, Donna (2016) *Staying with the Trouble: Making Kin in the Chthulucene*. Durham, NC: Duke University Press.

Harris, Melanie L. (2017) *Ecowomanism: African-American Women and Earth Honoring Faiths*. New York: Orbis.

Iheka, Cajetan (2018) *Naturalizing Africa: Ecological Violence, Agency and Postcolonial Resistance in African Literature*. Cambridge: Cambridge University Press.

John, Hershman R. (2007) *I Swallow Turquoise for Courage*. Tucson: University of Arizona Press.

John, Kelsey Dayle (2019) 'Illustrating the Intersections between Animal Studies and Settler Colonial Studies through Diné Horsemanship', *Humanimalia* 10:2, pp. 42–68.

Krech III, Shepard (2000) *The Ecological Indian: Myth and History*. New York: W. W. Norton.

Lobell, Jarrett A. and Powell, Eric A. (2015) 'The Story of the Horse', *Archaeology* 68:4.

Małecki, W. P., von Mossner, Alexa Weik and Dobrowolska, Małgorzata (2020) 'Narrating human and animal oppression: strategic empathy and intersectionalism in Alice Walker's "Am I Blue?"', *Interdisciplinary Studies in Literature and the Environment* 27:2, pp. 365–84.

Nadeau, Chantal (2001) *Fur Nation: From the Beaver to Brigitte Bardot*. Abingdon: Routledge.

Newsom, Michael (2015) 'U.M. students dig for clues about slaves' daily lives', *University of Mississippi News* 6304.

Norton, Macy (2024) *The Tame and the Wild: People and Animals after 1492*. Cambridge, MA: Harvard University Press.

Ranco Darren, J. (2006) 'Towards a native anthropology: hermeneutics: hunting stories, and theorising from within', *Wicazo Sa Review* 21:2, pp. 61–78.

Rose, Deborah Bird (2013) 'Val Plumwood's philosophical animism: attentive interactions in the sentient world', *Environmental Humanities* 3, pp. 93–109.

Skipper, Jodi (2022) *Behind the Big House: Reconciling Slavery, Race and Heritage in the U.S. South*. Iowa: University of Iowa Press.

Spivak, Gayatri Charavorty (2013 [1988]) 'Can the subaltern speak?' in Patrick Williams and Laura Christian (eds) *Colonial Discourse and Post-Colonial Theory: A Reader*. New York: Columbia University Press, pp. 66–111.

The Kennel Club (n.d.) Pastoral breeds. https://www.royalkennelclub.com/search/breeds-a-to-z/breeds/pastoral/australian-shepherd/ (accessed 11 April 2024).

Walker, Alice (1989) *Living by the Word: Selected Writings 1973–1987*. San Diego: Harcourt Brace Jovanovich.

Walker, Alice (2005 [1984]) *In Search of our Mothers' Gardens: Womanist Prose*. London: Orion.

Weisiger, Marsha (2009) *Dreaming of Sheep in Navajo Country*. Seattle: University of Washington Press.

Woodward, Wendy and McHugh, Susan (2017) *Indigenous Creatures, Native Knowledge and the Arts*. Cham, Switzerland: Palgrave Macmillan.

Vidal, Marta (2023) 'How trapped Palestinians fell in love with bird-watching', *Daily Beast* 7 April.

Yitbarek, Senay, Bailey, Karen, Tyler, Sahara, Strickland, Jeramie, McCary, Matthew and Harris, Nyeema C. (2021) 'Inclusive sustainability approaches in common-pool resources from the perspective of Blackologists', *BioScience* 717, pp. 741–9.

Ziarkowska, Joanna (2024) 'Native American studies meets animal studies: Linda Hogan's *The Radiant Lives of Animals* and the problem of anthropomorphism', *European Journal of American Studies* 19:1, n.p.

9

Individuals and species in the sixth extinction

In 2016, just across the bay from our island home, an orca was washed ashore, seemingly killed by entanglement with discarded fishing gear. This misfortune caused considerable distress among those who had been watching this Hebridean orca pod for many years. The watchers had an emotional attachment to this individual, a female that they had named Lulu, as the hope for the future of the Hebridean pod. Each year they had searched for a calf that would guarantee the future of the only orcas resident in British waters. The subsequent necropsy found that she was about twenty years old, had never had a calf and that there was a high level of PCB (polychlorinated biphenyls) forever chemicals in her tissue. At 100 times the level PCBs are known to affect marine mammals, while not thought to be the cause of her death, it may have been sufficient to prevent a successful pregnancy. Lulu had inspired affect among whale watchers that they had tried to share with others. There is no evidence that she was aware that she was the object of this affection. Since 2016, the two remaining bulls of this pod, named John Coe and Aquarius, have been seen around the Hebrides and sometimes further afield, even as far as the south coast of England. This pod will now be functionally extinct, unless a female from another pod joins it. Orcas are not threatened with extinction at the international level, but this pod has some unique features, including unusually feeding only on other cetaceans. It seems that we must now watch as this species becomes extinct at a local level and in the process its distinctive behaviour is lost to the biodiversity of the species. Lulu lives on in stories and her skeleton is preserved in the National

Museums of Scotland. For the environmental humanities, the increasing concentration of forever chemicals up the trophic levels in such top predators will be an issue, but it is the personal connection that people have had with this charismatic species that invites an animal studies reading of this unreciprocated stream of affection that humans have for this animal. The aim of this chapter is to explore what animal studies has to offer a reading of extinction narratives.

The sixth extinction and challenges for animal studies

Extinction of species, in terms of coming to the end of the line, is a natural process. It is also closely related to the emergence of new species. Over time, the genetic makeup of a species will change through the combined effects of genetic drift and natural selection, so that the accumulation of tiny changes is such that a new species is formed. We trace the development of *Homo sapiens* from early hominids through such developments. Geographically separated populations might take separate paths so that sister species emerge. In this process some species cease to exist without leaving a closely related chronospecies. For some time biologists have been concerned that we now face a sixth mass extinction, in which the imbalance between speciation and extinction events leads to an overall loss of biodiversity (Leakey and Lewin, 1996). Unlike the other five mass extinctions, this one seems to be largely the result of human activities.

After the Rio Earth Summit in 1992, extinction and the resulting loss of biodiversity entered the political consciousness. The signatories to the United Nations Convention on Biological Diversity (CBD) are obliged to implement programmes to mitigate these losses. Mitchell, citing Heise, shows how these imperatives led to 'an instantly-recognisable trope of mass extinction … that frame extinction as the "disappearance" of species and the destruction of biodiversity' (Mitchell, 2015: 23). There is now a political framework that defines terms such as 'biodiversity' and that drives organised nature conservation. This framework dominates public discourse, but 'the rapid adoption of political projects that seek universal solutions [excludes or ignores] pluralistic debate' (Mitchell, 2016: 25). Such hegemony is alien to an animal studies reading, which must be attentive to nuances of meaning, alternative standpoints and the experience of the animals as they face this process. Mitchell examines critically the terms 'species' and 'biodiversity'.

Noting that species is a term used as currency both in biology and finance, she shows how contemporary discourses on conservation are 'dominated by financial language and concepts' (Mitchell, 2015: 25). However, the concept of species is problematic in that it 'emerged from the fundamentally metaphysical practices of taxonomy'. Different ways of defining species all treat them 'as categories that transcend the organisms, cell or genes that compose them, and that maintain their integrity despite the perishing of these components' (Mitchell, 2015: 26). One definition goes as far as suggesting that species can be seen as individuals. 'Species are spatiotemporally restricted, dynamic and integrated systems, and in this sense are complex wholes, i.e., individuals' (Rieppel, 2007: n.p.). While some stories focus on the last individual in a species (for example, Lonesome George, the last known member of his subspecies of giant tortoise on one of the Galapagos islands, for the most part, extinction narratives focus on species rather than individuals. Animal studies, with its origins in individual rights and later relations, will find it difficult to get purchase on narratives that operate at the species level.

Actor–network theory is one approach that has the potential to accommodate human–other animal relations that operate at both the individual and species level. Julia Bennett has explored the contribution that ANT could make in an ethnographic study of conflict between two different conservation standpoints, both with the aim of preserving hreatened habitats and the suites of animals that depend on each type. She based her study on a small National Trust area near her home in North West England. One conservation standpoint, backed by government agencies and the force of law, sought to preserve the site as an area of lowland heath, the other driven by local enthusiasts favoured allowing the self-seeded birch woodland that was invading the site, to progress from this pioneer species to mature oak woodland. For Bennett this 'story sits on the cusp of nature/culture debates' (Bennett, 2017: 159).

Much of her analysis concerns the actants in the form of official agencies, strategy documents flowing from the UK's obligation under the CBD, and the social construction of heathland as a heritage site with a 3,000 year history, which also has ecological importance in preserving biodiversity. Relevant to an animal studies reading is her use of ANT to explore the complexity of lowland heath. Once common, this heath is characterised by dwarf shrubs, including heather (ling), Erica and bilberry, which thrive on poor soils. This habitat is maintained by grazing animals and requires a cast of characters, familiar from Thomas Hardy's Wessex novels, to stop it tumbling back to woodland as birch and Scots pine seedlings take root. For Bennett:

> Time interacts with place and biological species to create a 'hybrid collectif' that as Sarah Whatmore (2002) points out, implodes the inside/out binary which defines social action as an individual property of discrete, unitary individuals or collectives. The vegetation on the hill has *agency* in shaping this site as do the grazing animals and the Iron Age hill population, whose presence is still felt in the rhetoric of an authentic landscape; although increasingly the intangible heritage of local knowledge around the traditional grazing rights and use of the land for collecting sand for household use and twigs for making brooms is disappearing. (Bennett, 2017: 165, original emphasis)

With the removal of the actants that have maintained the character of this lowland heath, the National Trust has to resort to management to maintain this 'natural' 'wild' area and to the threatened animals that depend on it. At a national level this loss and fragmentation of heathland accounts for the decline towards local extinction of species such as the marsh fritillary and silver-studded blue butterflies, the nightjar and the Dartford warbler, and the adder.

By using ANT, Bennett was 'able to pull apart some of the strands of this story and examine them from a number of different perspectives' (Bennett, 2017: 167). This approach has to account for the sandstone rock that disintegrates to form the sandy soil, the way this soil is converted to podzol as the nutrients are leached out in response to the acidifying rain and decaying shrubs, the human use of the heath and in particular the presence, and species, of grazing animals. Stories about animal extinction will inevitably lead us back into this complex interplay between conflicting conservation goals, ideas about what the landscape should look like and for some rare species, the specialist knowledge to know that they are there and, if so, whether they are threatened with extinction.

While not making any specific reference to ANT, Ladle and Jepson advance a biocultural theory for the avoidance of extinction, which looks beyond ecology to take account of the behaviour of human actors including 'conservationists, conservation organisations and other societal actors' (Ladle and Jepson, 2008: 111). This approach recognises actors (actants in ANT) that play roles which are equally as important as the biological factors that may be driving extinction directly. These authors emphasise that it is the process described by the noun 'extinction' and not the state described by the adjective 'extinct' that is of concern here. 'Species extinction is a powerful cultural term in many societies because it can resonate with feelings deep in the human psyche' (Ladle and Jepson, 2008: 114). They argue that once a species is identified as 'at risk of extinction it is subject to strong cultural forces that create the context for successful conservation or otherwise', in which the behaviour of conservationists and others plays an important part. Although not suggested by these authors, it is at this point that creative writers may become involved. An animal studies reading will need to recognise that the text in question may play a part in constructing a narrative around an extinction process and it is highly likely that it will be called in aid by conservationists hoping to improve public engagement with their species recovery work. These authors stress that extinction has multiple meanings, some of which have greater resonance beyond the discourse of ecology.

The authors identify six types of extinction (Ladle and Jepson, 2008: 112). What they call Linnaean extinction is where the species is not yet known to taxonomists, but is calculated to be becoming extinct while still unknown to science; Wallace extinction is where the species is known, but has not been documented for many years; Phoenix extinction is where it is lost in the wild, but genetic material is available in store or in closely related varieties; Ecological extinction is where the species is lost in the wild but lives on in captivity; Local extinction is where it is lost from a locality, but exists elsewhere; and True extinction is where it is known to be lost with no genetic material being preserved. They divide this last category into contemporary extinction, where a population has been known since the birth of the conservation movement in the middle of the nineteenth century, and historic extinction, where there is no authenticated live record. Of these categories, Linnaean extinction will lead to a general feeling of unease that is perhaps more relevant to the environmental humanities than to an animal studies reading, although there may be an exception in science fiction. It is the types of extinction that are most likely to lead to conservation action programmes, where humans might play a close part with the nonhuman species, that will attract creative writers, through captive breeding and release, habitat management (as in the heathland example discussed above), restoring lost species from genetic material, and translocation to where the species formally existed (beavers and red kites in the UK are examples). Lost species can also capture the creative imagination, but here we must imagine our kinship with species, some of which, such as the dinosaurs, died out before humans evolved. These ideas should be kept in mind in as we explore narratives about the extinction process.

Shifting baseline syndrome

Extinction is a topic that is very dependent on being aware that extinction is happening. That is not always obvious. In 1962 Rachel Carson warned in *Silent Spring* that hearing songbirds in the spring was at risk if we continued to use what she termed 'biocides', in particular DDT in agriculture. Her courage, in standing up to the heavy-handed attempts of the chemical industry to ban the book, raised public awareness of the risk and the need to monitor the abundance of species that might otherwise be lost. Both professional and amateur naturalists in Britain have been engaged in this task, particularly since the UN Convention on Biological Diversity placed an obligation on signatories to conduct regular reviews of biodiversity. The UK National Biodiversity Network is one such database that is freely available for specialists and also literary scholars, to check on the status of any particular species.

The multidisciplinary framework for literary animal studies places an obligation on literary scholars to acquaint themselves with the science. There is, however, a problem in that even among experienced naturalists, there is a tendency to regard the abundance of a species when they first meet it as the baseline for future population assessments. Even rapid extinction can happen over several human generations; older naturalists will have a different baseline to those just starting out. This phenomenon has been named 'shifting baseline syndrome' which 'describes a gradual change in the accepted norms for the condition of the natural environment due to lack of past information or lack of experience of past conditions' (Soga and Gaston, 2018: 222). The consequence of this syndrome is increased tolerance for progressive environmental degradation.

Literary scholars need to be aware of the possibility that the scientific data may be incomplete, but also when reading a literary work they have to be open to the possibility that the author was also working to a shifting baseline. Some literary authors were accomplished naturalists, so that if Coleridge said he saw a nightingale it would be trusted. Others might be drawing on literary tropes such as the myth of Philomela who was converted to a nightingale, and could perhaps find the bird in a place where there was no historic record. A reading a poem, by say Edward Thomas, from the beginning of the twentieth century must take account of the familiarity that readers of the time would have had with his use of imagery, while those reading the same poem in the twenty-first century may not make the same connections.

Stop and think

It is species that become extinct, although that may be caused by the destruction of their habitat, as in the lowland heath example discussed above. What has literary animal studies to offer in this existential threat to all living beings? Should this important topic be left to the wider environmental humanities that can make the connection between biodiversity loss and climate change? Firstly consider the commitment to posthumanism in literary animal studies. Is the loss of biodiversity only important insofar as it impoverishes human experience, or does it also matter to the species that are left behind? Just as we suffer from shifting baseline syndrome, so too do the individual animals in a species, as each generation shares the world with fewer individuals of its species. Is there any mileage in according subject status to a species, entitled to the same rights as an individual? What are the consequences for human–animal relations when an individual of the species becomes the focus of human attention on account of its rarity? There are no clear answers to some of these questions, but the topic is too important for students of literary animal studies to set it aside.

Reading extinction narratives

Emerging as a separate field of study, with close connection to both animal studies and the environmental humanities, 'extinction studies' has as its focus the cultural reaction to the loss of biodiversity and the extinction of species. Creative writers have been drawn to telling the stories of these extinctions and to the sometimes heroic efforts to reverse the loss. Where these narratives involve animals, there is a tendency to focus on species, rather than the loss of whole assemblages of multispecies complexes. These can be guilds, in a habitat, where several species that perform a similar role (such as pollinators) become extinct; the loss of a keystone species so that the ecosystem will collapse, and trophic collapse where extinction of top predators is the result of their prey becoming scarce, perhaps in turn when the food source of herbivores is facing its own extinction battle. Some conservationists defend their focus on the top trophic level by arguing that a healthy presence of a carnivore signifies the overall health of the ecosystem.

Extinction studies are at their most powerful when they adopt an interdisciplinary framework that calls on inputs from zoology, environmental ethics, anthropology, history and the humanities. Rose et al. take an even broader approach in biocultural responses to extinction from 'the wider frames of understanding and meaning making that exist beyond the academy' (Rose et al., 2017: 2). For these authors, there is 'no singular phenomenon of extinction; rather, extinction is experienced, resisted, measured, enunciated, performed, and narrated in a variety of ways to which we must attend' (Rose et al., 2017: 2–3). They do not treat extinction as an abstract concept, nor do they dwell overly long on humanity's responsibility for the decline in biodiversity. Opting for a story-telling approach, they aim to explore the fate of a particular species in a multispecies world, with the aim of exploring 'what extinction means, why it matters, and to whom' (Rose et al., 2017: 3). Introducing his monograph of extinction stories about birds, van Dooren set out his aim to use such stories to deepen the dialogue between the environmental humanities and animal studies, both 'thoroughly interdisciplinary fields where the humanities and social sciences are drawn into conversation with the natural sciences' (van Dooren, 2014: 13). The stories that these and other authors tell are therefore of interest to students of animal studies, as texts for analysis, and ways of understanding the connections between animal studies and the other disciplines that share an interest in biodiversity loss and extinction.

In her contribution to extinction stories, Rose takes us to Hawaii to explore the story of monk seals that are critically threatened. Her first contact is with an individual named KP2, or in Hawaiian *Ho'ailona,* an individual recently returned from participating in a physiology project in California. Her initial excitement was somewhat blunted as, this supposedly 'outgoing, human-oriented, playful seal' snoozed in front of her. Later she got the opportunity to see a wild seal hauled out on the beach. She questioned why this encounter was so thrilling. Her research was dedicated to 'communities that emerge in encounters with animals at the edge of extinction. They are contingent, episodic, and imbued with an ethical call' (Rose, 2017: 118). She concludes that the 'more [she] works with multispecies communities, the more [she] realize[s] that the big philosophical questions apply to all meaning-making creatures' (Rose et al., 2017: 140). By observing seals on the beach she was able to see 'multiple forms of meaning, expression, and creation' (Rose et al., 2017: 140).

In an afterword to the Rose et al. book, Despret considers the story of the North American passenger pigeon, which was once so numerous that it darkened the sky on its annual migrations, but has now been hunted to extinction. Although we remember the name of this species, we have forgotten the affect that its physical presence provoked (See also Jørgensen, 2019: 89–117). Now, this species is a signifier for how quickly a taken for granted species can disappear altogether, rather like the dodo, but in more recent memory. 'But what the world has lost is not what people mourn. // What the world has lost and what truly matters, is a part of what invents and maintains the world' (Despret, 2017: 219). Despret continues exploring this loss in a narrative that could be read as a prose poem. Her story shows how much human experience is impoverished when a species is lost. It raises the question, relevant in an animal studies reading, whether extinction matters more to the humans that mourn its loss, than to the individual birds, who lacked the population statistics to know that they were the last of their line.

For van Dooren it is the urban penguins that come ashore to breed in the mouth of Sydney Harbour in Australia, that spark his interest. The little penguins (*Eudyptula minor*) breed mostly on islands off the coast of Australia, but this now tiny mainland colony is considered to be an 'endangered population' (van Dooren, 2014: 64). Their access to their traditional breeding grounds is often blocked by the seawalls that the owners of sea shore properties build to protect them from erosion. Approaching this conflict between property owners, conservationists and the birds themselves, van Dooren broadens his attention from the stories that humans tell to construct places, to focus on nonhuman animals as 'generators of meaning' (van Dooren, 2014: 67). In this respect he draws on von Uexküll's concept of *umwelt* as the experience an animal has of the world it inhabits and its perceptual surrounds (van Dooren, 2014: 67). This concept, discussed in chapter 1 above, provides a way to bring the nonhuman animal's viewpoint into focus. It also provides a way to move beyond narratives that dwell for too long on how humans respond emotionally to extinction. For van Dooren, his interest is wider than the shoreline that provides the little penguins' nesting places:

> Specifically, I am interested in how these penguins 'story' these places, how breeding places are rendered historical and meaningful to penguins. In using the term 'story,' my claim is not that penguins know and 'do' places in the same way that people do, but simply that their relationship with place might be productively understood through this conceptual lens. (van Dooren, 2014: 68)

Although there are many pathways to extinction, van Dooren suggests that 'it is the loss of an important place that leads inexorably to their end' (van Dooren, 2014: 84–5). He suggests that if we were to become more sensitive to the place-making practices of nonhuman animals, it would open the way for 'more sustaining possibilities of life across species and generations (van Dooren, 2014: 85).

Another important narrative is the impact on the human imagination, of once familiar animals disappearing from the everyday experience (Miller, 2021: 605). Humans are now surrounded by a world of vanishing animals. John Berger saw this progressive absence of species as activating a compensatory mechanism that was in part responsible for the development of zoos (Miller, 2021: 605). Extinction has had a good deal of attention in the environmental humanities, but for Miller, because it 'self-evidently proceeds through animal death, it is an important theme for understanding the cultural representation of animals, which is to say animal studies in the common shorthand' (Miller, 2021: 605–6). Although the environmental humanities and animal studies each have their own focus, they clearly have overlapping concerns in extinction (Miller, 2021: 606).

Miller selects *Last Chance to See* for his analysis, which was conceived by science fiction novelist Douglas Adams and biologist Mark Carwadine, first as a radio series, then a book published in 1990. It has subsequently transferred to television with Stephen Fry joining Mark Carwardine. This progression from radio to television reinforces the point made by Ladle and Jepson above: once rarity and risk of extinction are declared, they set in motion strong cultural forces. 'Extinction narratives tend to operate through the "genre templates of elegy and tragedy"' (Miller, 2021: 607, citing Heise, 2016: 14). In contrast, *Last Chance to See* adopts a 'comic rather than elegiac mode' (Miller, 2021: 607). For Heise this is a counterpoint to familiar environmentalist tropes, where nature's beauty is linked to foreboding about its imminent destruction. Miller uses Heise's reading of this text to 'demonstrate the necessity of an animal-focused approach' and to explore how such an approach differs from an ecological perspective, particularly through 'divergent approaches to global capital' (Miller, 2021: 607).

The progression from radio, to book, to television 'highlights the process of commodification whereby the franchise's disappearing animals become established as a form of cultural capital' (Miller, 2021: 609). It is also significant that the authors' travels took place as international policy about biodiversity was taking form in preparation for the Rio Earth Summit in 1992, at which the CBD opened for signature. As Miller reports, critics, including Vandana Shiva, saw CBD as an initiative by the Global North 'to "globalise" the central management and ownership of biological diversity', reinforcing the point made by Braverman in chapter 8 that international conservation becomes a new way to deliver colonialism. Scarcity of animals becomes commodified through ecotourism. 'If (perhaps when) the global tiger population is reduced to a single wild specimen, it is hard to imagine that the beleaguered animal would not be pursued by travel writers and film crews determined on a final opportunity to translate its being into soaring prose or stunning cinematography' (Miller, 2021: 611).

While *Last Chance to See* is distinctive for its comic register, Miller draws attention to 'Adams's parting evocation of Mauritius at the end of their time there [which] encapsulates a mournful atmosphere that counterpoints the humour elsewhere'. In this last episode the image of roosting fruitbats 'is evidently gauged to be resonant, the sun setting, as it were, on another species; the bats flapping across "the darkening sky" operates metonymically as a sign of wider catastrophe' (Miller, 2021: 613). Miller cites Heise in claiming that species serve as a proxy for ecosystems and biodiversity. These known species that are at risk of extinction have attracted attention and must stand also for all the species, unknown to taxonomists (Ladle and Jepson's Linnaean extinction), that are becoming extinct without ever entering cultural discourse. For Miller, this text is important for focusing public and institutional attention on the extinction crisis and for exposing 'the tensions between critical perspectives' (Miller, 2021: 617). In particular he stresses the need to 'cultivate critical practices to remain anchored to the unapprehendable, or partially apprehendable, qualities of animal being, and the ethical demands they make of us' (Miller, 2021: 617). For Miller this is what literary animal studies is for.

Extinction in speculative fiction

The concept of the Anthropocene is now well established in the humanities, even though it has now been rejected by geologists as a new geological epoch, separate from the Holocene interglacial that we have been in for the last 11,700 years (Witze, 2024). For Heise, this concept can be the foundation of new imaginings: 'For pessimists the Anthropocene signals the enormous scope of negative human impacts on the environment; for optimists, it opens up the possibility of reimagining the nature of the future not as shaped by human beings' (Heise, 2016: 203). Because of the Anthropocene's emphasis on human agency it can stand in tension with those strands of posthumanism that emphasise the importance of nonhuman agents (Heise, 2016: 203). It does, however, offer scope for narratives based on science fiction or the wider genre of speculative fiction. In this context Heise discusses Alan Weisman's use of the trope of human extinction in his 2007 *The World Without Us,* which explores what would happen in natural technological and urban environments if humans were to disappear (Heise, 2016: 216). In some cases these fictions look far into the future, but some situate themselves in a modern world where some cataclysm has transformed everyday experience in mysterious ways.

One example of this form of speculative fiction, cited by Heise, is Jonathan Lethem's *Amnesia Moon* (1984), which is set in North America where everyone agrees that something has changed, but they are not sure what. This and other examples are what Heise calls the 'presentification of the future: it features a society that is barely distinguishable from the present but presents it as if it *were* speculative fiction' (Heise, 2016: 219, original emphasis). Heise contrasts two types of speculative fiction: one in which 'the present appears as the past of imaginative futures' and the other 'as an already incompletely realised future'. She suggests that the Anthropocene can be seen as the latter for its use of the same tropes as those that are held out for the future of other terraformed planets, in which the future shaping of ecosystems is in the hands of humans (Heise, 2016: 219).

In the long-term narrative of the Anthropocene, humans have been influencing their environment and the species they share it with, for the last ten thousand years, with epochal changes in the last two centuries. Heise contrasts how scientists are content to treat the human as a species as the actant in these changes, but this is much more difficult in the social sciences and the humanities, 'to whom historical, social, and cultural differences between communities stand out more sharply than they do to natural scientists' (Heise, 2016: 220).

Texts that move beyond questions of individual identity, to considering what the political order would look like if it took seriously the participation of its nonhuman citizens, are, suggests Heise, the most interesting. She selects as an example Margaret Atwood's MaddAddam trilogy, which includes encounters between the remnant population of *Homo sapiens,* the genetically engineered posthumans and the part-human genetically engineered pigs. This fiction challenges ideas of human exceptionalism in imagining other species that have different and perhaps superior capabilities and are not amenable to being managed by this much reduced human society. In Atwood's telling, the remaining humans hybridise with the genetically engineered posthumans, to form a community that can agree a peace treaty with the 'pigoons' (Heise, 2016: 228). Can these fictions teach us how to be open-minded when we consider our future relationship with other species? Heise suggests that these issues come to the forefront when we consider the animals that cohabit with us in our cities rather than those that can be corralled in the wilderness to be seen but not engaged with (Heise, 2016: 234).

Biodiversity in domesticated species

One of the weaknesses of biodiversity discourse is that it is confined to species that are considered to be wild, at the expense of those that were domesticated thousands of years ago. Feral populations of previously domesticated species are often selected for elimination, as for example, with feral pigeons that inhabit our towns, where they might have been classified as pests. Far from urban centres, steps may be taken to protect their wild 'genetically pure' cousins that inhabit remote sea cliffs, so that they cannot hybridise with feral birds. A challenge for literary animal studies is to escape from the dominant narratives deployed by governmental and non-governmental conservation organisations, which tend to cast domesticated species as a problem, where they compete with wild species for the use of resources, or alter the ecosystem so as to threaten the biodiversity of the natural environment. It is not just domesticated animals that threaten biodiversity – landscapes given over to intensive arable agriculture can be completely devoid of living animal species, wild or domesticated.

As literary animal studies draws on ideas about the welfare and rights of animals, there will be many aspects, particularly with intensive animal rearing, that have negative associations in critical readings of animal texts. Welfare standards can also be low in some breeds of dogs where the anatomy described in the breed standard is prone to painful health problems and early death. On the other hand, less intensive animal husbandry using 'naturalistic grazing' techniques can enhance the biodiversity of an area. Many of the species that are supported in such systems have coevolved with the introduction of agriculture over the last ten thousand years, or adapted to the new grazers as the Pleistocene species such as mammoth, bison and aurochs were hunted to extinction. It is no accident that rewilding is often predicated on finding a suitable grazer that will hold back the development of closed canopy woodland, to allow heathland to flourish, as discussed above, or to create open spaces where shrubs and flowers, and the animals that depend on them, can flourish. Some animals have exacting requirements: hazel dormice need trees to be close enough together to be able to move through the wood at canopy level, but with sufficient light getting through for hazel, bramble and mistletoe to grow in the shrub layer. The herbivores to create these conditions could be reintroduced: wild species, such as beavers or bison, varieties bred to resemble extinct animals, such as Heck cattle bred to resemble aurochs, or ancient breeds of domesticated animals that are known to support a biodiverse community.

Animal farming is under attack from many quarters: from nature conservationists for the reasons above, from environmentalists for the methane – a powerful greenhouse gas, belched out by ruminants – and from vegans, who hold that rearing animals for food is morally wrong. In these circumstances narratives about the genetic diversity that resides in domesticated herds can be overlooked, sometimes altogether, or when texts which do address this issue are not considered for a sympathetic animal studies reading. Haraway raised this issue in *When Species Meet*:

> Try as we might to distance ourselves, there is no way of living that is not also a way of someone, not just something, else dying differently. Vegans come as close as anyone and their work to avoid eating or wearing animal products would consign most domestic animals to the status of curated heritage collections or to just plain extermination as kinds and individuals. (Haraway, 2008: 80)

I would add a third way, that is, to release previously domesticated animals to live as wild. This solution was adopted in the 1930s when the last islanders left Hirta in the St Kilda archipelago off Scotland's north-west coast. The Marquess of Bute, the new owner of the islands, released a balanced flock of Soay sheep on the island of Hirta, a breed that would have been familiar to the Iron Age shepherds. His motivation was to preserve the short grass that supported the huge colony of breeding seabirds. Grazing grass to this height had been dependent on the departing islanders and the sheep they took with them. The Soay sheep live as wild, but are prone to periodic population crashes from starvation and parasite load. If these animals were not counted as wild, the current owner, the National Trust for Scotland, would face prosecution under animal welfare laws.

For many breeds that are no longer commercially viable, release to revert to the wild is not an option – most require intervention by humans, to shear their fleeces or to assist in birthing. For these breeds their preservation in heritage collections is already a reality. These commercial pressures were already being felt when Hardy wrote his rural novels. In his description of the Greenhill sheep fair, he lists the competing breeds: 'The great mass of sheep consisted of South Downs and the old Wessex horned breeds; the latter class Bathsheba's and Farmer Boldwoods's mainly belonged' (Hardy, 2000 [1874]: 265). Also at the fair were Oxfordshire, 'effeminate Leicesters', Cotswolds and 'a small flock of Exmoors' (Hardy, 2000 [1874]: 266). Each breed would have had its devotees, but the inclusion of Leicester sheep, whose breeding was revolutionising the improvement of breeds, is a foretaste of the pressure that there would be on the old breeds. The Dorset Horn, which is assumed to be the breed that Hardy had in mind, is now at risk and is already in Haraway's category of small flocks of heritage breeds. Hardy was writing at a time of social change that would bring to an end the rural society that managed the lowland heath and the dominance of the breeds that they used to maintain it. Before the breed started moving towards extinction, examples taken to the United States were used to breed a form where the ewes no longer had horns. These so-called Polled-Dorsets have returned to England, but are themselves now a threatened breed. To be able to breed new forms in this way, there must be variability in the gene pool of the breed. Darwin recognised that variability is the prerequisite for the evolution of new forms and the emergence of new species. Biodiversity is not just at breed level, but also within the breed. The small flocks in heritage collections will have less diversity than those breeds that are widely used, and thus have the genetic diversity to adapt to different environmental pressures. Breeds and species with low genetic diversity are on the pathway to extinction, even if that does not register in our cultural experience of these animals.

Most controversy has been attached to Haraway's use of the word 'extermination' as the fate of domesticated animals that are no longer required. Some people have taken this as an attack on veganism and in favour of eating animals, and of breeding companion animals. It is the possibility of extinction that should concern us in an animal studies reading. Is biodiversity only a concern for wild animals? Can we be relaxed about extinction for domesticated animals, while being very concerned about the same fate for wild species and subspecies? Have we considered what the effect will be on the ecosystem and the other animal species that have coevolved to live with domesticated species? Will wild herbivores come in to take their place – deer or geese for example? Will we then have to manage these wild herbivores by shooting them if they encroach on arable crops, overgraze an area or inhibit the development of forest? There is a risk that issues such as these are erased from the narrative in an animal studies reading that has adopted a particular political stance – though even resisting such narratives will inevitably be political.

Critics of Haraway see her work as providing cover for the exploitation of animals. Kuura contests that view as a simplistic reading of Haraway's writing on domesticated and companion animals. 'In addition to interpreting her argument as depoliticised, Haraway has been read as connecting politics, and in particular vegan politics, to dogmatism' (Kuura, 2023: 6). For Kuura a more nuanced reading is necessary: 'Haraway acknowledges that "vegetarianism, veganism, and opposition to sentient animal experimentation can be powerful feminist positions"; she does not merely agree that they would be the only feasible feminist positions' (Kuura, 2023: 7). The situation is complicated by there being no pure option that we could move towards. Some writers suggest that the way to solve this complexity is to withdraw altogether from human–animal relations, as the only way to avoid thinking that nonhuman animals exist for us. In contrast Kuura cites authors who stress that an animal rights theory should acknowledge that there are 'situations where nonhuman animals have close relations with people. For these authors, citizenship theory provides a framework for conceptualising these relations politically (Kuura, 2023: 8). The complexity of these issues precludes the development of a single theory that avoids hard choices. For Haraway, 'cosmopolitical questions arise when people respond to seriously different, felt and known, finite truths and must cohabit well without final peace' (Kuura, 2023: 12). This unsettledness, with the ever-present risk 'that any decision to act may foreclose other lives requires constant vigilance concerning power relations' (Kuura, 2023: 16).

Erasing domesticated animals from the discourse of extinction, or being indifferent to decisions that will eliminate gene lines that have coevolved alongside ourselves to construct the complex multispecies ecosystems that make up the inhabited landscape, is a dangerous oversimplification. While the elimination of sheepherders, as well as Native Americans, from a 'wilderness' national park in the United States may be feasible, in much of Europe wild animals, and humans with their domesticated species, have followed the retreating ice to establish an interdependent multispecies community of humans, with both domesticated and wild animals. That is not to deny the arguments of vegans or critical animal scholars, but to suggest that any decision may have unintended consequences. Haraway makes the case for these decisions to be subjected to examination from multiple viewpoints to arrive at a consensus that is in the interest of all the species that coexist in our shared space.

Stop and think

How can we work toward a posthuman reading of animal stories, when wild animals that seem to be at risk of extinction will attract all manner of governmental and non-governmental interventions? Literary animal studies, in its conversations between the humanities and the sciences, must take account of the political influences that commission and interpret the science, from the international treaty obligations of the CBD to the activism of naturalists on behalf of their loved species. We have seen in chapter 8 how nature conservation can be put in service of the colonial project. Resistance to colonialism seeks to let the subaltern speak; can we extend this to the animals whose stories we tell, and to the literary scholars who read them? Can we identify and resist human interest that is behind these stories? If so where do we stand with animals that are already entangled with us in a multispecies world? In that respect do the human societies that are critically dependent on this entanglement have any rights, or must they be dispersed, the humans to reserves or to cities, and the animals to heritage collections or to be exterminated? Thinking about these issues, it is evident that there are no simple answers and we have to learn to live with the conflicting entanglements in a multispecies world in which diversity and difference is to be welcomed. In such worlds humans are both actors and are also acted upon.

Extinction of cultural diversity

Just as knowledge about the distinctive breeds of sheep that populate Hardy's rural novels fades from everyday memory, so too do the local names that people have given the animals that live around them. Concerned for this cultural extinction, Robert Macfarlane sought to reintroduce these words to our culture in his 2017 book *The Lost Words*, illustrated by Jackie Morris. Taking as his starting point the vernacular names for species that are now disappearing from our culture, Macfarlane has written what he calls spells, rather than poems, to provoke thought about the species whose names are no longer used. Widely successful, this book, with its appeal to children, mitigates the risk that they will grow up detached from direct contact with wild creatures in a culture that has erased them from discourse.

For scientists the proliferation of vernacular names makes it difficult to know if two authors are speaking of the same species. Linnaeus provided the solution with his binomial Latin names in which the first denoted the genus and second the species within that genus. This gained rapid acceptance around the world, although the naming of species that already had vernacular names contributed to a colonising discourse that overwrites Indigenous culture. The British Ornithological Union (BOU), whose cofounder was Henry Baker Tristram discussed in chapter 8, is the authority for maintaining the British list of birds in collaboration with the International Ornithological Congress. The rationale for the BOU's initiative to standardise the English names on the list, rather than rely on the Latin names, is instructive:

> The British Ornithologist's Union (BOU) recognises the value of, and is keen to move towards, a standardised global avian taxonomy. As such we wish to adopt one of the current global taxonomies, and use this for all BOU activities, including the British List.
>
> From 1 January 2018 the BOU will adopt the International Ornithological Congress (IOC) World Bird List for all its taxonomic needs, including the British List. (British Ornithologists' Union, 2017)

For the British list they do, however, admit a number of 'vernacular' names that are the most familiar identifier for British birds by British birders. Just as Linnaeus spread scientific names across the rich local engagement with animals and plants, this list helps to reinforce the colonising programme as the spread of English helps drive out local languages and dialects, including the names and cultural meanings of species, in each distinct community. Edwin Morgan's concrete poem, 'The chaffinch map of Scotland', is composed entirely of regional names arranged so that the lines on the page make out a map of Scotland. The musicality of these names gives the poem its rhythm when read aloud.

The list does allow British birders to refer to the 'lapwing' rather than the international name 'northern lapwing', but this bird, which is now retreating from much of its former breeding area, has a very rich array of vernacular names. Once, the natives of Cumbria would look forward each spring to gathering 'tewit' eggs; those of Lincolnshire would welcome the return of the 'pyewipes' to the ploughed farmland each autumn. The books I read when young, variously referred to the 'lapwing' for its tumbling flight showing alternately white and dark, the green plover for the iridescent green sheen in sunlight, or the onomatopoeic 'peewit' for its evocative two-tone call. This richness is explored by Hannah Copley to provoke thinking about vanishing for this species and as metaphor for the gradual disappearance of a father into addiction.

In Copley's 2024 collection, *Lapwing,* which includes a long sequence interspersed with encounters with these birds, she both expresses the richness of the cultural discourse and naming of this much loved bird, and draws from this imagery metaphors for the deceit and vanishing of an addicted father. In the first poem in the sequence numbered 'I' she parades some of the alternative names for this bird: 'Otherwise known as peewit, otherwise known / as tew-it, otherwise known as Vanellus vanellus / of the family Charadriidae …' (Copley, 2024: 6). The phrase 'otherwise known as' recurs throughout the collection. In poem 'XIX' 'Lapwing / considers applying for keystone status / but without the paperwork / or proof of worth or impact beyond grief's / extended vector … what is there to write' (Copley, 2024: 44). The Lapwing depends on cows having grazed the meadow to provide the hollows to form its nest, it depends on dung and decaying vegetation that fuel the detritus pathway for the worms and larvae that it eats. It is not a keystone species in this ecosystem as others would fill the niche if it became extinct. From a human viewpoint, it is the rich cultural meaning of this bird that give us a feeling of loss were the present decline to progress towards extinction.

For Copley the visual effect of lapwings' looping flight provides the metaphor for loss in the fading memory of a loved one tumbling towards dementia:

> And she remembers his stories.
>   Lapwing, quenched,
> slowly tumbling
> from high singularity
> into the scrape of his thoughts. (Copley, 2024: 4)

In the 'V' sequence she suggests 'birds have their demons too' before developing the theme of avoidance in 'Peewit has his ways of flitting, / or feigning each intended cry' (Copley, 2024: 16). As we watch this decline, we document the retreat by saving voucher specimens. In

Ladle and Jepson's terminology of Phoenix extinction, this genetic reserve would keep open the potential for reintroduction. Copley ends her prose poem, 'SIGHTING: Shemya, Alaska 2006', with 'Archived as a study/skin and partial skeleton with two frozen genetic samples' (Copley, 2024: 32). In a sense Copley's collection is also an archive of cultural memories that might, if initiatives like Macfarlane's *Lost Words* thrives, lead to the emergence of a culture that will in turn arrest the decline of the lapwing before it tumbles to extinction.

It is species such as the lapwing or the water vole – which conservationists are at pains to remind us is 'Ratty' from *Wind in the Willows* – that get the most attention when they start to decline towards extinction. These are the species that have a cultural presence that commands our attention in extinction studies. Animals that are not sentient enough, are difficult to identify, live wholly underground, or have fleeting life cycles, are likely to be represented in Ladle and Jepson's category of Linnaean extinction. They will vanish without being known to science or having a cultural presence. It is as well to remember that these are also the species at risk of being passed over by animal studies of literary works. One exception is the new interest in probiotics, including all the nonhuman animals that are necessary to make a human individual, which if neglected will hasten the progression of the sixth extinction (Lorimer, 2020). The biodiversity of these creatures challenges human exceptionalism and calls into question what it means to be an individual. Without these commensal organisms we would not be able to function.

Further reading

Maclean, Norman (ed.) (2010) *Silent Summer: The State of Wildlife in Britain and Ireland*. Cambridge: Cambridge University Press.

Yeo, Sophie (2024) *Nature's Ghosts: The World we Lost and How to Bring it Back*. Manchester: Harper North.

References

Bennett, Julia (2017) 'Whose place is it anyway? An actor-network theory exploration of a conservation conflict', *Space and Culture* 21:2, pp. 159–69.

British Ornithologists' Union (2017) *Taxonomy and the British List*. https://bou.org.uk/british-list/taxonomy/ (accessed 7 July 2025).
Copley, Hannah (2024) *Lapwing*. Liverpool: Liverpool University Press
Despret, Vinciane (2017) 'Afterword: it is as an entire world that has disappeared' in Deborah B Rose, Thom van Dooren and Matthew Chrulew (eds) *Extinction Studies: Time, Death and Generations*. New York: Columbia University Press, pp. 217–22.
Haraway, Donna (2008) *When Species Meet*. Minneapolis: University of Minnesota Press.
Hardy, Thomas (2000 [1874]) *Far from the Madding Crowd*. Ware: Wordsworth Classics.
Heise, Ursula K. (2016) *Imagining Extinction: The Cultural Meanings of Endangered Species*. Chicago: Chicago University Press.
Jørgensen, Dolly (2019) *Recovery of Lost Species in the Modern Age: Histories of Longing and Belonging*. Cambridge, MA: MIT Press.
Kuura, Irni (2023) 'Fostering feminist politics of veganism: on the "political" in Donna Haraway's approach to food, eating and animals', *Redescriptions: Political Thought, Conceptual History and Feminist Theory* 26:1, pp. 4–20.
Ladle, Richard J. and Jepson, Paul (2008) 'Towards a biocultural theory of avoided extinction', *Conservation Letters* 37, pp. 111–18.
Leakey, Richard and Lewin, Roger (1996) *The Sixth Extinction: Biodiversity and its Survival*. London: Weidenfeld and Nicholson.
Lorimer, Jamie (2020) *The Probiotic Planet: Using Life to Manage Life*. Minneapolis, MN: University of Minnesota Press.
Macfarlane, Robert (2017) *The Lost Words*. London: Hamish Hamilton.
Miller, John (2021) 'Last chance to see: extinction in literary animal studies and environmental humanities' in Susan McHugh, Robert McKay and John Miller (eds) *The Palgrave Handbook of Animals and Literature*. London: Palgrave Macmillan, pp. 605–20.
Mitchell, Audra (2015) 'Beyond biodiversity and species: problematizing extinction', *Theory, Culture and Society* 33:5, pp. 23–42.
Rieppel, Oliver (2007) 'Species: kinds of individuals or individuals of a kind', *Cladistics* 23:4, pp. 373–84.
Rose, Deborah B. (2017) 'Monk seals at the edge: blessings in a time of peril' in Deborah B. Rose, Thom van Dooren and Matthew Chrulew (eds), *Extinction Studies: Time, Death and Generations*. New York: Columbia University Press, pp. 117–48.
Rose, Deborah B., van Dooren, Thom and Chrulew, Matthew (2017) *Extinction Studies: Time, Death and Generations*. New York: Columbia University Press.

Soga, Masashi and Gaston, Kevin J. (2018) 'Shifting baseline syndrome: causes, consequences, and implications', *Frontiers in Ecology and the Environment* 16:4, pp. 222–30.

van Dooren, Thom (2014) *Flight Ways: Life and Loss at the Edge of Extinction*. New York: Columbia University Press.

Conclusion

The turn to animals in the humanities took its inspiration from the extension of rights to human others from marginalised races, genders and classes. The reasonableness of the claim that nonhuman animals should have rights similar to those of all humans was predicated on prior work by ethologists, who had shown the range of their capabilities that falsified claims of human exceptionalism. It also depended on the philosophers who had challenged the dualism between human and nonhuman animals advanced by Descartes and Aquinas. Creative writers have a role in expanding our imaginative landscape to admit these often marginalised others. They can introduce new ways of seeing the natural world that do not depend on statistical analysis of data, or the sometimes narrow viewpoint of objective science.

Literary animal studies continues to draw on advances in the social sciences and philosophy, and on the scientists who find new ways to explode the myth that animals are machines, whose behaviour is determined only by their genetic makeup and the environmental pressures on their material bodies. It seems likely that this advance in knowledge will continue, and that a scholar of literary animal studies will need to be constantly open to new insights. The dynamic cross-disciplinary nature of literary animal studies is one of its attractions.

Literary animal studies reads the advances in thinking about agency and subjectivity of nonhuman animals, with and against the representation of animals in literary texts. It searches for insights in historic texts to assess the degree to which the authors were part of the move towards this changing way of narrating our nonhuman kin. We can see the emergence of sympathy and empathy towards animals in literary texts, around the time that ethical concern for their welfare was growing. Contemporary creative writers, schooled in current thinking about animals, will add another perspective. At a time when many species are being lost to extinction, and humans' own relationships with animals are changing, it is essential that the voices of nonhuman animals are listened to.

As we have seen, many strands of theory contribute to an animal studies reading. At times it will be necessary to consider the animal in the context of all the environmental and cross-species social relations that make up its *umwelt*. We also need to pay attention to differences in human societies, particularly for the way Indigenous people frame their own identity through their relationship with animals. Gender, neurotypical vs neurodivergent ways of thinking, race and class all play a part. For domesticated animals, town and country dwellers may have different ways of living with animals, based on the day-to-day familiarity and attendant duty of care.

How animals die is as important as how they live. Killing animals for meat is abhorrent to some literary animal studies scholars. Refusing meat satisfies part of our ethical responsibility to other species, but it also raises new ethical dilemmas. Domesticated herbivores have coevolved with humans over 11,000 years. Could we let them live out their lives as companion animals? Or should we deny them the chance to reproduce, until they become extinct? What would we then do about the wild herbivores – deer or greylag geese, for example – that move in to take their place? Culling the surplus, or introducing top predators are spoken of as solutions. Each of these questions raises new ethical dilemmas and questions about what the animals themselves want. Temple Grandin deployed empathy for animals facing slaughter for human consumption, to see the situation from the animals' viewpoint as means to reducing their stress and pain. Those species that came to domestication along the commensal pathway exercised agency: is that still a choice they would make even as they would end their life in the slaughterhouse? Literary animal studies is most powerful when approached from a broad perspective. That might draw on sister disciplines that inform the study.

Literary animal studies complements ecocriticism by allowing consideration of the subjectivity of the individual nonhuman animal. There will be many occasions where the two disciplines will be in conversation. But where ecocriticism is concerned with global environmental matters, such as climate change, we should heed Latour's warning that we cannot scale up local effects to explain the stability or otherwise of global systems. Further, we should be aware that western conservation models may well inform some strands of ecocriticism, and these need to be interrogated for their furtherance of colonial or capitalist agendas. While literary animal studies is underpinned by ethical considerations, critical animal studies is explicitly committed to action. If that action allows the animals agency through the coproduction of research, it may avoid taking a didactic standpoint that is not compatible with an open-minded research model. Given the pressing crisis of extinction, the strand of extinction studies may well stand alone, but it should be remembered that it is species that become extinct when more individuals die than survive to maturity. There are important differences between literary animal studies, with its focus on the individual, and extinction studies where it is on the species.

Similarly, vegan literary studies is relevant in allowing those who refuse meat into the conversation, but at the risk of focusing on the humans rather than on individual animals. One of the risks is that literary animal studies becomes fragmented into ever smaller areas of special interest. The discipline is at its best when it is attentive to the subjectivity and agency of the individual nonhuman animal, and when it deploys a wide array of ways to make meaning of that animal and its *umwelt*. Further, we have seen that challenges to what makes an individual animal have come from the understanding that all animals live communally with other organisms, not least in their guts. Just as the theory that informs literary animal studies advances, so too do the meanings we attach to animals change with advances in science and technology.

Currently extinct animals may soon make a reappearance as ways are found to bring them back to life from stored DNA. These de-extinctions raise ethical issues. Perhaps the most controversial thought is that we might be able to bring Neanderthals back from extinction. If it is acceptable to bring back aurochs, why not fellow hominids? That is at present seen as a step too far (Greely, 2013). There is, however, a place for speculative fiction to imagine a world in which *Homo sapiens* has to share the biosphere with another hominid. In which case the flow of ideas would be from literature to ethics and philosophy. Literature may have to imagine a life without most of the animals that we are familiar with, and without the 'environmental services' they provide to enable human existence. A world without pollinators seems too close for comfort, but we still lack the imagination to understand the consequences for ourselves and the other animals that depend on ripening fruits. Where science discourse has not captured the public imagination, there is an opening for creative writers to imagine such a world.

The advance of artificial intelligence (AI) may open up new lines of enquiry for literary animal studies. For many years the zebra finch has made a major contribution to biology and genetics studies (Griffith and Buchanan, 2010). There are now developments where AI can be used to recognise individual zebra finches (Barkham, 2020). In this case AI extends the capability of the human researcher to follow the fortunes of individuals, which would not otherwise be possible. A further development in AI is in machine learning for the interpretation of birdsong – again the zebra finch is used as an example – better to link behaviour to underlying neural processes (Koch, Marks and Roberts, 2024). The scope of AI for extending human capabilities is enormous; another intriguing possibility is its use to 'translate' whale communications. Will it soon be possible to listen in to their chatter, or even to enter into a conversation with another species (Sharma et al. 2024)? Will AI really tell us what another species is saying, or will it send us in a wrong direction by inventing discourse that is not there? Will a whale speak in prose, poetry or song, and how will that stir a creative response from our writers?

It would be understandable if scholars in literary animal studies were reluctant to engage with knowledge gained through AI, when the same tool is being directed at creative writing so that machine learning can be used to write 'literary texts'. The profligate use of data storage as AI is trained on the work of creative writers brings with it environmental challenges. How many animals must be displaced by the huge data centres, with their equally huge demands on energy and water? Is there space in these data centres to set them to work on biosemiotics, until now the subject studied by some ethologists?

The path ahead for literary animal studies will be strewn with such obstacles, but the opportunity to close the subject/object gap between human and nonhuman animals will make the effort worthwhile. It is perhaps appropriate to conclude by stressing that it is the belief that creative writing has something to add to our understanding of human–animal relations, that makes literary animal studies an important field of study. There will be a lot of work to do for philosophers, social scientists and literary scholars as AI takes hold, in parallel with a decline in biodiversity. Literary animal studies is important and essential work as we face this changing world.

References

Barkham, Patrick (2020) 'AI model developed to identify individual birds without tagging' *Guardian* 27 July.

Greely, Hank (2013) 'On not de-extincting *Homo neanderthalensis*' SLS Blogs 18 February. Stanford Law School.

Griffith, Simon C. and Buchanan, Katherine L. (2010) 'The zebra finch: the ultimate Australian supermodel', *Emu* 110:3, pp. v–xii.

Koch, Therese M. I., Marks, Ethan and Roberts, Todd F. (2024) 'AVN: a deep learning approach for the analysis of birdsong' posted as a preprint before peer review.

Sharma, Pratyusha et al. (2024) 'Contextual and combinatorial structure in sperm whale vocalisations' *Nature Communications* 15, article number: 3617.

Index

EU authorised representative for GPSR:
Easy Access System Europe, Mustamäe tee 50,
10621 Tallinn, Estonia
gpsr.requests@easproject.com

www.ingramcontent.com/pod-product-compliance
Lightning Source LLC
La Vergne TN
LVHW020724290926
849104LV00028B/315
* 9 7 8 1 8 0 7 0 7 2 2 8 5 *